IRISH LAW TEXTS

LAND LAW

by

Robert A. Pearce, B.C.L., M.A.
Lecturer in Law
University College, Cork

LONDON
SWEET & MAXWELL
1985

Published in 1965 by
Sweet & Maxwell Limited of
South Quay Plaza
183 Marsh Wall
London E14 9FT.
Computerset by PB Computer Typesetting,
Pickering, North Yorkshire
Reprinted in 1995 by the Alden Press, Oxford.

British Library Cataloguing in Publication Data
Pearce, Robert A.
Land law.—(Irish law texts)
1. Real property—Ireland
I. Title II. Series
344.15064'3 DK 217

ISBN 0–421–31200–9

Introduction

Both Irish jurisdictions have long suffered from the problems associated with the lack of a developed local legal literature. This lack of development has been particularly acute in the Republic of Ireland, where it is only in the last few years that any works at all have appeared in the main fields of law and where many gaps still remain. The combination of the small market for law books in the Republic and a considerable lag between the achievement of political independence and the emergence of a corpus of indigenous law deterred the production of legal literature. For many years law students and the legal profession made do with the older editions of English text-books or else did without. In Northern Ireland, the problems were never so acute since the local law generally kept pace with changes in Britain. Nevertheless, there are also significant differences between the available works on English law and procedure and the law taught and practised in that jurisdiction.

Over the last two decades a variety of factors has brought about change. In the first place there is a much greater output of local law both in legisation and through court decisions. The number of students in the universities and other third level colleges who are studying law has increased enormously. There has also been a proportionate increase in the numbers engaged in the full-time teaching of law with correspondingly a greater number of academic lawyers available to undertake research and writing. The size of the legal profession has doubled in both jurisdictions in the last decade.

One happy result of the new circumstances has been the coincidence of acute concern about the dearth of works devoted to Irish law and sufficient local demands to encourage authors to write and publishers to publish. It was in these circumstances that *Irish Law Texts* was conceived. The series aims to produce reasonably priced works on the main fields of Irish law to meet the needs of the broadest legal legal population.

Books in the series are concerned primarily with the law of the Republic of Ireland, which is the larger Irish jurisdiction and the one which has seen the greatest changes in legal principles and statute law from Britain. However, wherever possible, reference will be made to the law of Northern Ireland, particularly the decisions of the courts. *Irish Law Texts* therefore hopes to make a contribution to the needs of students and the professions in both parts of the island.

Kevin Boyle
Series Editor

Preface

In writing this book, I have had foremost in my mind those who are making their first acquaintance with land law. Land law is not a study of how land and houses are bought and sold. That is the concern of conveyancing. Instead, although the distinction is by no means clear-cut, land law is concerned with the theory governing the rights and interests which may exist in land. The abstraction of this theory can sometimes appear off-putting, but at the heart of land law there is only a limited number of concepts and once these have been mastered it requires no great effort to understand the detail. In this text I have set out those guiding principles and as much of the detail as will ordinarily be required by students and in practice. For those who wish to go further, a fuller discussion will usually be found in Professor J. C. W. Wylie's definitive works, *Irish Land Law* and *Irish Conveyancing Law*. I have also sought to relate the theory to practice. I have, for instance, included basic examples of the kinds of form used in the transfer of land (the names in which will be familiar to those acquainted with the *Irish R.M.* stories of Somerville and Ross). The systems of registration of deeds and registration of title have also been introduced wherever they are relevant.

In its scope, the book is intended to cover the syllabi of the majority of third level courses on land law. I have not included any account of planning and development law or of the modern protective legislation concerning landlord and tenant since, important though they are, they are rarely taught as an integral part of third level courses on land law. Nor, for the same reason, is there anything more than an introduction to equity and trusts, although in other respects the book is intended to meet the needs of students preparing for the examination in Real Property of the Incorporated Law Society of Ireland.

The book deals with the law both of the Republic of Ireland and of Northern Ireland. With the exception of the modern rules relating to succession to property on death, there is little difference between the two jurisdictions, and it has been possible to cover both in a single narrative, pointing out the differences where they occur. In neither jurisdiction has there been any comprehensive legislative reform of land law since the 1880s. It is not disputed that large areas of land law are overdue for reform. In Northern Ireland a survey published in 1971 recommended significant legislative change, and detailed proposals are now being investigated by the Land Law Working Group. The deliberations of this group are likely to lead to legislation within the next few years. There is little prospect of any similar reform in the Republic of Ireland in the foreseeable future.

I particularly wish to thank Herbert Wallace of the Queen's University, Belfast. He read through the entire book in typescript. I am indebted to him for his helpful comments, especially in relation to the law in Northern Ireland, but also more generally. I am grateful as well to Marcella Doyle and Valerie O'Connell for converting my manuscript into typescript with commendable speed and efficiency.

The law is stated as at January 1, 1985.

Robert A. Pearce
University College, Cork

Contents

Table of Cases

Table of Statutes

Irish Statutes

(a) *Statutes of the Parliament of the United Kingdom of Great Britain and Ireland*

(b) *Acts of the Oireachtas*

(c) *Statutes of the Parliament of Northern Ireland*

British Statutes

Constitution of Ireland (1937)

Part 1

Introduction

1. The Nature and Classification of Property

1. What is property?

"Property and law are born together, and die together. Before laws were made, there was no property; take away laws and property ceases." So said Jeremy Bentham in his *Theory of Legislation.* The law of property is concerned with the management of things, and land law with the management of land. Land is a scarce resource, and the law must regulate competing claims to its use and enjoyment. The way in which the law decides between these competing claims is very much influenced by the political ideology of the State. Ireland, North and South, is capitalist rather than communist and this is reflected in the rules concerning the use of land. Most land is in private ownership, some is in State ownership, and comparatively little is freely enjoyed by the public as a whole. Amongst the few examples of communal rights to enjoy land may be cited the public rights to the use of highways and navigable tidal waters. The study of land law is therefore essentially a study of private rights in land.

The purist might say that it is only where there are private rights that property exists. Property, he would say, does not denote the thing over which rights exist. It connotes instead the bundle of rights themselves which one person can enforce against others in relation to a thing. It is in this sense that Proudhon spoke of property as theft. The rights of the person we consider to be the owner of a thing are largely concerned with the right to control the use and destination of a thing, and hence the right to exclude others from its use. The word property is commonly used, however, to refer to the object of ownership, or even more generally, to anything of economic value. If a man by his will left all his "property" to his wife, that gift would include any sums of money he was owed by others as well as tangible things.

2. Property in intangibles

The fact that rights which have no tangible object are recognised as property means that the law of property is not concerned only with physical things. It is concerned also with abstract things. An author's copyright is for instance as much his property as a volume which is standing on his bookshelf. Of course the only way in which an author can enjoy his copyright is by asserting that right against others. He can permit a publisher to reproduce his work, and he can enjoin those who reproduce his work without permission. Rights in relation to material property are just as much concerned with relationships with others. The "owner" of a house who has mortgaged it to a building society will want to know what will happen if through personal misfortune he is no longer able to meet the mortgage repayments. May the building society, for instance, eject him from the house? Has he the power to sell the house himself?

Land law is concerned with intangible property too. The right to fish in a river can be enjoyed exclusively by someone who does not own the river or the river bank, and we would not consider a building society which has lent money to assist in buying a house as owning the house itself. A central feature of Irish land law is in fact that land as such is never owned. A person holds instead what is known as an estate in the land, which is an abstract right to the enjoyment of land for a period of time. The concept of estates has an historical origin and is explained in detail in Chapter 7. It is closely allied to the concept of tenure which is explained in Chapter 6.

3. The importance of possession

The holder of an estate in land has a right to the possession of land: that is, a right to occupy the land and to exclude others from it. Depending on the nature of the estate, the right can be immediate, or it may arise only at some future date. The position of a person with an estate entitling him to possession immediately and for ever—an estate known as the fee simple absolute in possession—is for all practical purposes indistinguishable from that of an outright owner, but Irish law is rarely concerned with the question of ownership. Disputes relating to the possession of land, for instance, are not concerned with who is the owner of the land. Instead, it is sufficient for the plaintiff to show that he has a better right to possession than the defendant. In many cases the plaintiff has only to show that he was in possession before being wrongly ejected by the defendant. It is never necessary for the plaintiff to establish that he has the best possible right to possession (*i.e.* that he is owner). There is therefore considerable truth in the common saying "possession is nine points of the law." It is true also in another sense, for the rights to bring an action in the tort of trespass for direct interference with land or in nuisance for an indirect interference are available, not to the owner, but to the person in possession: *Harper* v. *Charlesworth* (1825); *Marcroft Wagons Ltd.* v. *Smith* (1951) (trespass); *Newcastle-under-Lyme Corpn.* v. *Wolstanton Ltd.* (1947) (nuisance).

4. Possession as proof of ownership

It is the ordinary practice for a purchaser of land to investigate the vendor's title, that is, the basis upon which the vendor claims to be entitled to the property. Title is proved in one of two ways, depending upon whether ownership has been registered. Where ownership has not been registered, which is the position in relation to most land in urban areas, the vendor establishes his right to deal with the land by showing that he and those through whom he claims have possessed the land for a sufficiently long period to exclude any reasonable possibility of a better right. The period over which a vendor was contractually bound to give such proof was fixed by the common law at a minimum of 60 years, in the absence of contrary agreement. The period was reduced to 40 years by the Vendor and Purchaser Act 1874, s.1. The vendor produces the deeds or other instruments by which the land has been transferred in the past, and these must form an unbroken chain extending back for at least the appropriate period to a *good root of title*, which is a deed dealing with the whole interest in the land which is being transferred. As we shall see later, it is important that the purchaser (or his solicitor) examines these documents of title, or *title deeds*, for they should not only prove the vendor's right to sell, but they may also disclose the existence of the rights of others which the purchaser must respect (see "The doctrine of notice," p. 13 below). This method of proving title is backed up by a system of registration of deeds introduced by the Registration of Deeds Act 1707, the Act still in force in the Republic, but renewed by the Registration of Deeds Act (N.I.) 1970 for the North. Under this system, records (known as *memorials*) of deeds are kept at central registries in Dublin and Belfast respectively. The system acts as a guard against the fraudulent (or even innocent) suppression of deeds and also has implications for priorities. A deed, or other document, a memorial of which has been registered, takes priority over another deed which has not been registered (except that a person who has actual notice of a prior instrument cannot claim priority by virtue of registration: see p. 16). Registration of a memorial of a deed, however, in no way guarantees the validity of that deed.

5. Registration of ownership

The traditional method of proving ownership is inconvenient since the title deeds—and if the land or house has changed hands frequently, there could be a substantial number—must be properly examined on each transfer. A new system was introduced to Ireland by the Local Registration of Title Act 1891, and is now governed by the Registration of Title Act 1964, for the Republic and by the Land Registration Act (N.I.) 1970, for Northern Ireland. With this system, the ownership of the land is registered, and the title of the person registered as owner is guaranteed. On a transfer, the vendor proves his title by supplying a copy of the *folio*, the centrally-kept record containing the details of ownership and other matters. There is no need for the purchaser to enquire into previous transfers, (see *Guckian* v. *Brennan*, 1981) and with certain exceptions, the folio is conclusive since most dealings concerning the land have to be recorded on the register to be effective. Registration was compulsory for land bought out or vested in tenants under the Land Purchase Acts. These Acts applied to the vast majority of agricultural land in Ireland with the result that the ownership of most agricultural land is now registered under the 1964 and 1970 Acts. The extension of registration of title into urban areas has been exceedingly slow, so that for most urban land it is necessary to prove title by the old means of title deeds. It should be emphasised that although registration of deeds and registration of ownership (or title) are both systems of registration, they are mutually exclusive, and the system of registration of deeds will be gradually displaced as registration of title is extended.

6. The classification of property

Although land law has changed remarkably over the past seven centuries, some of the language of land law owes much to times long ago. The most basic of divisions of property in Irish law, into real property and personal property, can only be explained by reference to history. The ordinary remedy of the royal or common law courts (see Chapter 3) was the remedy of damages. In relation to land, however, the courts would order the return of the land itself. This court order would be enforced, if necessary, by the officers of the court. The court action, since it permitted the recovery of the thing (or Latin *res*) claimed was known as a real action, and hence the property so recoverable was called real property or *realty*. All other property, in respect of which there was only the personal action for damages, was known as personal property or *personalty*. Perhaps not surprisingly at a time when land and domestic animals were the chief forms of wealth, items of personal property were also known as *chattels* (from the word cattle).

The early possessory actions by which land could be specifically recovered were available only to freeholders, who, in the technical language of the time had *seisin* (pronounced seezin). A leasehold tenant did not have seisin and was able originally only to rely upon a personal action for damages against his landlord. A leasehold interest in land was therefore considered to be only a chattel, that is, personal property. By the fifteenth century, however, leasehold tenants were given an efficacious remedy for the specific recovery of possession—a remedy so useful that it was in fact used by freeholders to recover possession from wrongdoers. A new terminology was thus applied to leasehold interests in land. They were known as *chattels real* since they were interests of a "mongrel amphibious nature" in the words of Sir William Blackstone.

Property therefore falls into three classes—real property (consisting of freeholds); chattels real (consisting of leaseholds); and pure personalty (consisting of property other than land).

7. Realty and personalty in the modern law

The distinction between real property and personal property used to be important. Originally only personal property (which includes leaseholds) could be disposed of on death by will. Even when it was made possible for wills to dispose of real property, the distinction between real and personal property survived, since in the absence of a will, real property passed to the heir according to the ancient rules of descent, while personal property was divided more equally between the surviving next-of-kin. It was not until 1925 in England, 1955 in Northern Ireland, and 1965 in the Republic of Ireland that statutory rules were introduced assimilating the rules for the distribution of real and personal property on death. The result of this assimilation has been that in respect of deaths in Ireland since 1956 or 1967 (when the legislation came into force in the North and South respectively), the distinction between real and personal property has ceased to have any great significance, except in so far as those terms are expressly used by a testator in his will. For the passing of property on death, see Chapter 12.

Apart from express references to real or personal property, there are only a few relics remaining of the distinction. For instance an estate tail (see Chapter 7) can be created only in real property and not in personal property. Such relics are no credit to the law.

2. The Diversity of Rights in Land

1. The multiplicity of rights

One of the most striking aspects of land law is the very great diversity of rights which are recognised as capable of existing in relation to land. The common law, for instance, recognised the division of the ownership of land over time in a way which was never possible in relation to pure personal property until the intervention of equity (see Chapter 3). It is possible in land law also for a person to have legally enforceable rights over land belonging to another in a way which was never (until perhaps comparatively recently) possible over pure personal property. For instance, the right of one landowner to draw water from a well on his neighbour's land has no direct counterpart in relation to pure personal property.

The reasons for the recognition of more diverse rights in land than in personal property are not far to find, although they are becoming less obvious. Land differs significantly from most forms of personal property. It is permanent, particularly when compared with domestic animals, the paradigm chattels. Since land can exist for ever (or as near as makes no difference), it is far easier to envisage a predetermined succession of owners over time than it is with a domestic animal, where the prospect of future enjoyment is far more likely to be lost with the expiry of the beast. Of course the distinction is much less marked if the "land" consists of some prefabricated temporary structure with a limited design life, and where the chattel might be an extremely valuable work of art which has already survived several centuries and could be expected to survive for the same period again. Nevertheless, during the formative years of the law's development, land, as the principal form of wealth, was seen as having a permanence which could not be matched by any chattel. Similarly, so far as rights over the property of others is concerned, a multiplicity of rights in land is far more easily envisaged than in personal property.

2. The classification of interests

Interests in land can be assembled into two categories: those which confer a right to the land itself; and those which confer a right in the land of another. Like most legal classifications, these two categories are of uncertain extent, and it is not always clear into which category a particular interest should go. For instance, leasehold interests create a particular problem. At one end of the spectrum of leasehold interests, the tenant with a long lease of say 999 years, or with a leasehold fee farm grant giving him a right to the land for ever would certainly be considered to have a right to the land itself. At the other end of the spectrum, a tenant with a weekly tenancy would more likely be considered a person with only a right in the land of another, albeit his right is a right of possession. Similarly the right to take fish from a river, if owned independently from the river bank, could be considered a right in the land of the riparian owner, but it is also the profit of piscary (see Chapter 16) which is capable of ownership in its own right, and is itself considered to be "land" (see Chapter 4).

Assigning particular interests to the appropriate category is therefore to some extent arbitrary and is dictated by convenience as much as by logic. The arrangement which has been adopted in this book has been to deal in Part 2 with interests in land which would popularly be considered to confer a right to the land itself, and therefore amount to ownership, while rights in the land of another are dealt with in Part 4. Part 3 deals with the ways in which the ownership of land may be transferred.

3. A practical example

The variety of interests with which land law is concerned can be illustrated by means of an example. Let us take 1–7 Personalty Place, a single detached house and a short terrace of three houses: see Figure 2.1. Each of the terraced houses relies upon its neighbour or neighbours for support and therefore requires an easement of support (Chapter 16). The owner of number 3 may have a right of way through the yard of number 1 to give access to his own yard from Realty Road (Chapter 16). The occupier of number 1 may be a tenant paying rent (Chapter 11). Number 3 may be held in fee farm grant (Chapter 6) and have been given by will by the previous owner to his son (Chapter 12) subject to a right of residence in favour of his widow (Chapter 15). Number 5 may have been acquired on mortgage with the aid of a loan from a building society (Chapter 18), and the boundary fence between numbers 5 and 7 may have fallen down some years ago, and been re-erected in the wrong place (Chapter 13).

Number 7 may have been the subject of a marriage settlement under which it was given to Hugh for life, then to his wife for her life (if she survives him) and then to their children (Chapter 7). All of the houses may be subject to a covenant prohibiting their use for the purposes of trade or business (Chapter 17).

Figure 2.1:Numbers 1–7 Personalty Place

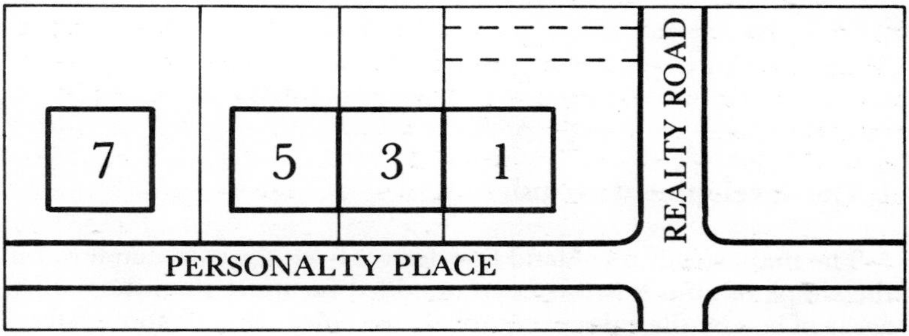

It may also be the case that Personalty Place is under the flight path of the local airport and overlies a coal seam (Chapter 5). A developer may have in mind acquiring part of the grounds of Number 7 to erect a block of flats (Chapters 4 and 10), but he will, of course, require planning permission (Chapter 5) and the building he erects might be likely to darken the greenhouse at Number 5, (Chapter 16).

That so many problems and issues would exist at the same time in so short a street is most unlikely, but the catalogue given here does not exhaust the possibilities. They are explored in the following parts of this book.

3. The Influence of Equity

1. The development of equity

The main structure of land law derives from the common law, but the shape of land law has been moulded far more than most other areas of law by the rules of equity. These rules are now administered in the same courts as the rules of common law, but this was not always so, and there are still occasions on which the rules of law (meaning common law) and the rules of equity can produce divergent results.

The rules of equity owe their origin to the notion that the King or Crown was the source of all justice. Justice, as it was administered in the common law courts, the first Royal Courts established, tended to be inflexible. In particular, the common law courts had a special form of procedure based on what is known as the writ system. In order for an action to be brought to court it was necessary for a writ to be issued specifying the nature of the claim and the facts upon which it was based. There was a different writ for each cause of action, and although it was possible for new writs to be created, the invention of new writs was restricted. There were many cases, therefore, in which a case might be without a remedy for the want of a suitable writ.

The disappointed litigant would sometimes petition the King, as the fount of all justice, for redress. These petitions were at first heard by the King in Council, but were later referred to the Chancellor. By the sixteenth century petitions were made directly to the Chancellor, who made the decrees in his own name. As petitions became more frequent, the Chancellor thus developed his own court, known as the Court of Chancery, independent of the common law courts. The Chancellors were originally clerics, but after the end of the seventeenth century, by which time the jurisdiction of the Chancellor had been established as an independent system of justice, only lawyers were appointed to the office. Ireland had its own Lord Chancellor, who like most royal office-holders, had an

English background and followed the practices and procedures of his counterpart in London.

The Chancellors did not adopt the strict procedural approach of the common law courts, but instead based their decisions upon what they considered to be just and equitable, and upon what they believed to be required in conscience. While in time the rules of equity, as they came to be called, became more settled, they remained more flexible than the rules of common law. Equity acknowledged rights which were not recognised at common law, and gave remedies which could not be obtained at common law. The Chancellor could, for instance, make a decree for the specific performance of a contract, or grant an injunction restraining a defendant from breaking a contract, while the common law courts were normally restricted to making an award of damages. A defendant who failed to observe a decree of the Chancellor was liable to imprisonment for contempt.

2. The use

One of the most important contributions made by equity in the development of land law is the use, and its modern-day counterpart, the trust. This is an arrangement under which a person holds property, not for his own benefit, but for the benefit of another. The usual way in which such an arrangement arises is where the owner of property transfers the property to T, directing T that the property is to be held for the benefit of B. At first this was done for temporary purposes, for instance where a knight going on a crusade wished to provide for his wife and children during his absence. Later, this form of arrangement was used to make permanent provision, as for the benefit of a religious order which was prohibited by its rules from the direct ownership of property. Arrangements of this kind were not recognised by the common law courts as imposing any enforceable legal obligations on the holder of the property who was, in their eyes, the properly constituted owner. The Chancellor, however, took the view that it would be inequitable for the legal owner (or feoffee to uses, as he was called) to ignore the terms under which he received the property. He was bound in conscience by them and would be obliged by a Court of Equity to observe them. The legal owner had therefore only the shell of ownership, since the right to enjoy the property lay in the beneficiary or *cestui que use* for whose benefit the feoffee to uses had been directed to hold the property.

At first the use, as it was originally called (from the Latin *ad opus*, meaning on behalf of), was enforced only against the feoffee to uses himself, but subsequently, by gradual steps, the use became enforceable against anyone who received the property except for a "bona fide purchaser of a legal estate for value without notice" (see p. 14 below).

Following its recognition in equity, the use became very popular as a vehicle for landholding. Through the use it was possible for some of the incidents of feudal tenure to be avoided. It was also possible for a person to create a use under which the name of *cestui que use* was to be declared by his will, although it was not until the Statute of Wills (Ireland) 1634, that a will directly disposing of land could be made.

3. The Statute of Uses (Ireland) 1634

Largely, it is thought, because of the effect which the popularity of uses had on feudal revenues, the English Statute of Uses was passed in 1535 with the apparent object of abolishing uses. The Statute was at first effective for this purpose, so that to restore the power to dispose of land upon death it was necessary to enact the Statute of Wills in 1540. The Statute of Uses operated by converting the equitable rights of the *cestui que use* or beneficiary into legal rights. It was soon found that the Statute could therefore be used as a new means of transferring land. By creating a use in favour of the person to whom it was intended to transfer the land, the transferee would, by virtue of the Statute, have his equitable right to the land converted (or executed) into a legal right. The use which was converted by the Statute of Uses into a legal right could be created by contracting to transfer the land and receiving the purchase price. Equity then treated the person paying as entitled to the land under an implied use. It did so by an application of the maxim of equity: "equity treats as done that which ought to be done." The form of transfer under which a use was created in this way and then converted into a legal right was known as a bargain and sale. There were other ways also in which the Statute of Uses could be exploited to enable land to be transferred without recourse to the cumbersome feudal method of feoffment with livery of seisin (see p. 102 below).

Nearly a century elapsed before the Irish equivalent, the Statute of Uses (Ireland) 1634, was enacted, together with the Statute of Wills, (Ireland) 1634. These Statutes were identical in operation to the English Statutes, but the effect of the Statute of Uses was just about to be substantially altered by judicial decision. In *Jane Tyrrel's Case* (1557) the common law judges decided that uses declared in a deed relating to land which had been transferred by way of bargain and sale were void for inconsistency since they attempted to create a "use upon a use." After some hesitation the courts of equity, by the second half of the seventeenth century, took the view that in such a case the second use should be recognised. Since the use was not recognised by the common law courts, the result was that the use, a century or so after its abolition in England, was brought back to life. As a matter of convenience in terminology, a use which is not converted by the Statute of Uses into a legal interest is called a trust, although the terms "use" and "trust" are, for legal purposes, synonymous.

4. Uses to which the Statute of Uses did not apply

Even before equity's recognition of the "use upon a use," there were uses to which the Statute of Uses did not apply. The Statute applied only where freehold land was given to the feoffee to uses, so that it did not apply to leasehold land. Neither did the Statute apply where the feoffee to uses had active duties to perform, such as selling the land. The Statute did not apply also where the feoffee to uses was a corporation and not a natural person.

5. The operation of uses and trusts

The use, and later, the trust, resulted in two kinds of ownership being recognised: legal ownership, *i.e.* ownership recognised by the common law courts, and equitable or beneficial ownership, *i.e.* ownership recognised by the courts of equity. The two could exist simultaneously. Where the same person was recognised as owner both at law (meaning common law) and in equity, he was described as the legal and beneficial owner. Figure 3.1 illustrates the relationship of legal and equitable ownership before the Statute of Uses where land was given to A to be held to the use of B. The effect of the Statute of Uses upon the arrangement is shown by Figure 3.2. The creation of a use upon a use is shown by Figure 3.3. Land is given to A to the use of B to the use of (or upon trust for) C. The use in favour of B is executed by the Statute of Uses to give him legal ownership, but equity compels him to treat C as the beneficial owner.

6. The doctrine of notice

Equity did not deny the title of the legal owner although it did oblige him to hold the property in accordance with the terms upon which he had received it. Where the legal owner parted with the property in a way which was inconsistent with the trust, the question arose of whether the recipient was bound by the trust. The same question arose where the owner of property affected by other equitable rights— such as the right to enforce against him a contract to sell the property—parted with it inconsistently with those rights. Legal rights, *i.e.* common law rights, were normally enforceable on

Figure 3.1: A holds to the use of B before the Statute of Uses

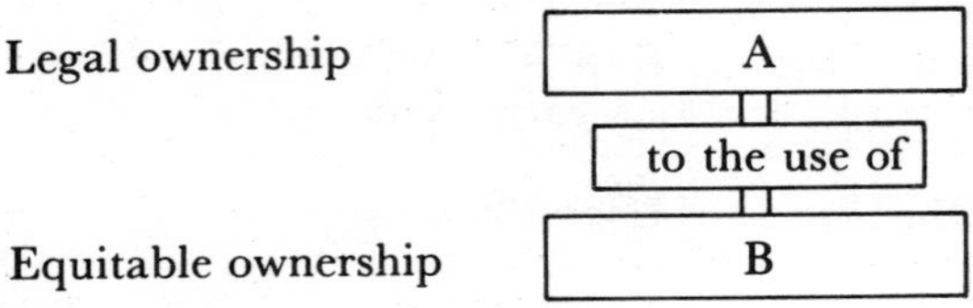

Figure 3.2: Land is given to A to the use of B after the Statute of Uses

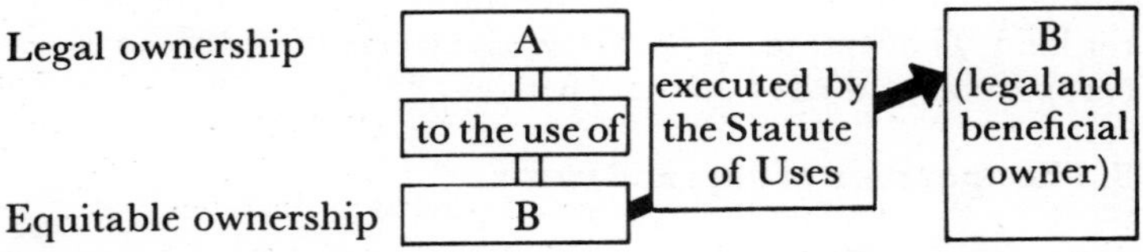

Figure 3.3: Land is given to A to the use of B upon trust for C after the recognition of the use upon a use

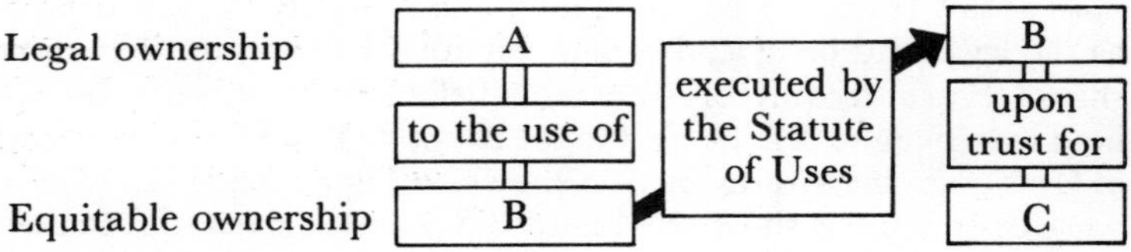

the basis that the first in time would prevail over rights subsequently created, and the same rule was applied between equitable rights. This was expressed in the maxim "where equities are equal the first in time prevails." A person taking a legal interest in property would, however, be entitled to take free of equitable rights if he could show that in relation to those rights he was a *bona fide purchaser of a legal estate for value without notice*. A shorthand description of such a person is "equity's darling." In the circumstances, equity felt that he was not bound in conscience by the equitable rights.

The elements which have to be satisfied by "equity's darling" may be taken in turn. (i) He must take in good faith (*bona fide*). This is related to the question of notice, but it would mean, for instance, that a purchaser under a collusive sale designed to defeat the equitable rights of others would not be protected (see *Midland Bank Trust Co. Ltd.* v. *Green* (1981). (ii) He must have acquired a legal interest in the property. As we have already noted, as between equitable interests, the first in time prevails. However a purchaser for value of an equitable interest will take free of a *mere equity* of which he has no notice. A mere equity is a non-proprietary equitable right, such as the right to rectify a conveyance or to have it set aside on the ground of undue influence. (iii) The purchaser must have given money or money's worth for the legal interest (or equitable interest, where he claims to take free of a mere equity), or be within what is called "the marriage consideration." A marriage which has not already taken place is treated as value given by either or both spouses and their issue for any gift or promise in consideration of that marriage. The word "purchaser" standing on its own would not imply that value had been given since the legal meaning of the word is wide enough to include anyone to whom property is transferred, including by way of gift. (iv) The last requirement is that the purchaser must have taken without notice. The forms of notice were recognised in the Conveyancing Act 1882, s.3. There are three types of notice. The first is *actual notice*: in other words, the purchaser in fact knows of the right in question. Hearing a vague and unspecified rumour does not amount to notice: *O'Connor* v. *McCarthy* (1982). The second is *constructive notice*. A purchaser is treated as if he knows those things which he would have discovered by the exercise of reasonable diligence. Were it otherwise, a purchaser would be able to turn a blind eye to matters which ought to put him upon enquiry. Among the usual and reasonable enquiries a purchaser is expected to make are examination of the title deeds or other documentary evidence of ownership and an inspection of the land. The physical state of the land may indicate a likelihood of an equitable right inconsistent with the interest which the vendor has agreed to sell (see *Hervey* v. *Smith*, 1856), and if there is an occupier on the land, the purchaser must enquire what those person's rights are (see *Hunt* v. *Luck*, 1901). A purchaser is bound by the rights of any occupant of the land of whom he made no enquiry. A purchaser may therefore have constructive notice of the rights of a tenant in occupation of the land sold, or of a deserted wife's right to an equitable interest in the family home by virtue of a contribution she has made to the purchase price (see *Northern Bank Ltd.* v. *Henry*, 1980). For the application of the doctrine of notice to the rights of occupiers where the vendor is himself in occupation, see Pearce "Joint Occupation and Doctrine of Notice" (1980) Ir.Jur.). A purchaser is not excused from notice of such matters as he would have discovered had he inspected the property on the ground simply that there was no time to make such an inspection (*Northern Bank Ltd.* v. *Henry*, above).

A purchaser who fails to inspect the title deeds and land acts at his own risk. In many cases of course a purchaser does not himself inspect the title documents to the property, but this eventuality is covered by the third type of notice, which is *imputed notice*. A purchaser has imputed to him the actual or constructive notice in relation to that specific transaction of any agent he employs, for instance a solicitor or estate agent.

7. Modern application of the doctrine of notice

The equitable doctrine of notice has to a large extent been supplanted by legislation. The system of registration of deeds, introduced by the Registration of Deeds Act 1707, replaces the doctrine of notice by a system of registration in regard to interests with a documentary origin in unregistered land. Even here, however, the equitable principle that a statute may not be used as an engine of fraud has meant that a person who has actual notice of prior interest cannot claim priority by virtue of registration (*Agra Bank Ltd.* v. *Barry* (1874); Registration of Deeds Act (N.I.) 1970 s.4(3). Where *title* to land has been registered, which is the case in regard to most agricultural land in Ireland, the special statutory rules in the Land Registration Act (N.I.) 1970 and the Registration of Title Act 1964, apply and the equitable doctrine of notice is excluded. But, by section 72(i)(*j*) of the 1964 Act (Sched. 5, Pt. 1, para. 15 to the 1970 Act in Northern Ireland), the rights of a person "in actual occupation" of the land are protected except where enquiry is made of him and he fails to disclose his rights. The doctrine in *Hunt* v. *Luck* (above) has thus been carried forward into registered land although in Northern Ireland the statutory provision does not apply to rights capable of substantive registration as burdens (under Sched. 6 to the 1970 Act).

There is one instance in which legislation has given the doctrine of notice a new lease of life. The Family Home Protection Act 1976, which prohibits a disposition of the family home without the consent of a spouse with no legal title, does not apply to conveyances to "a purchaser for full value" (s.3(3)). "Purchaser" is defined to mean a "...person who in good faith acquires an estate or interest in property" (s.3(6)). It has been held that this reference to "good faith" incorporates the doctrine of notice: *Somers* v. *W.* (1979). A purchaser will therefore not be considered to take in good faith if he has actual, constructive, or imputed notice that the property concerned is a family home (but see s.3(7) for a modification of the rule relating to imputed notice).

Part 2

Ownership and its Limits

4. The Subject Matter of Ownership

1. The land or the estate

As has already been pointed out (p. 3), although in ordinary usage a person might be described as owning land, he can be more accurately described as holding land for an estate in fee simple, or in fee farm grant, or as the case may be. Nevertheless, since a person entitled to such an estate in land normally has all the rights relating to the land, including the right to possession, there is little difference in substance between the two. Applying the notion of ownership to the estate rather than to the land itself does, however, have advantages in cases where more than one person might claim to be the owner of the land. Where a landlord with an unencumbered right to land for ever has granted a lease for 99 years to a tenant, who is to be described as the owner of the land? The tenant is entitled to possession of the land for the period of the lease, and can even exclude the landlord from the premises, except where the landlord has expressly been granted a right to enter for specific purposes. On the other hand (setting aside any statutory rights on the part of the tenant under protective legislation), the landlord will automatically become unencumbered owner on the expiry of the lease, and is in the meanwhile entitled to payment of the rent. Both landlord and tenant therefore may claim to be owners of the land. In terms of estates, however, the tenant has a leasehold estate for 99 years, carrying the immediate right to possession of the land itself, while the landlord has the freehold *reversion*, since the right to possession of the land reverts to him on the expiry of the lease. Both landlord and tenant therefore own an estate, but neither owns the land in the sense of being entitled outright.

The use of the concept of ownership in relation to the estate rather than to the land itself is confirmed by the system of registration of title referred to in Chapter 1. Separate registers are kept for entering ownership of freeholds and leaseholds.

Despite this, however, it is often convenient to refer to the "owner of land," for even though the description may lack precision, it is a useful shorthand, and will be used on occasion through this book.

2. Intangible land

One characteristic feature of real property was that on the death of an owner leaving no will it passed to the owner's heir: see Chapter 1. An alternative name for such property was an "hereditament," meaning property passing to an heir. Not only were freehold estates classified as hereditaments, but so also were various other interests which did not carry a right to possession of the land itself, such as easements, profits and rentcharges (see Chapter 16 and p. 36). Rights to possession of a field or building and so on were considered to be corporeal hereditaments while rights to intangible interests were considered to be incorporeal hereditaments. By the same process of substitution by association and by which the word "estate" can describe either a tract of land (as in "the Fota estate"), or the duration of a person's interest in land (as in "an estate in fee simple"), so also the word "land" may be used to describe both the solid part of the earth's surface, and also corporeal and incorporeal hereditaments, although the latter might more properly be considered as rights in or over land.

3. Identifying boundaries

Even though the property lawyer might insist that it is the estate which is owned rather than the land, it is important to define where one person's land ends and another begins. Land—apart from oceanic islands—is not self-contained in the way that cows and cars are. The boundaries of land are not always clearly defined. A fence or a hedge may divide the gardens of two houses in a street. Two fields may be divided by a wall. But even this kind of boundary may be imprecise. Which of the two neighbours has the fence, hedge or wall on his land? Or does the wall straddle the boundary so that half falls on the land of each neighbour? Is it even, perhaps, in the wrong place? The answer to such questions is frequently unclear, and disputes between neighbours over boundaries are not at all uncommon.

It is comparatively rare for accurate boundaries between neighbouring plots of land to be fixed by the original grants. When there is a dispute over a boundary, this is generally resolved by an examination of the title deeds transferring ownership of each plot. Physical features on the land which have served as boundaries—such as walls and hedges—can offer considerable assistance in the resolution of boundary disputes. They can clarify an uncertainty in any descriptions in the title deeds, and even if one owner has overstepped the limits of his territory as defined in his title deeds, he can acquire title by adverse possession for a period of at least twelve years (see Chapter 13). The same principles apply whether ownership of the land is registered or not. Even in relation to registered land, where the land to which each owner is entitled is clearly marked on a map kept by the Registrar, this, and any description of the lands in the register, is not normally conclusive as to the boundaries or extent of the land (Registration of Title Act 1964, s.85; Land Registration Act (N.I.) 1970, s.64(1)).

4. Land as space

The commonest way in which land is divided is in the horizontal plane, where one field, for instance, may be subdivided into a number of building plots. Land, however, should not be seen as an area, but as a space for it has a vertical as well as a horizontal dimension. The ordinary rule is that the owner of the surface owns the space above, as well as the space below. This is classically expressed in the latin phrase, "*cuius est solum eius est usque ad coelum et usque ad inferos*"—the owner of the soil owns up to the heavens and down to the depths. Applications of this maxim can be seen in *Kelsen* v. *Imperial Tobacco Co.* (1957), where the tenant of a single storey shop was held to be entitled to prevent (through the action of trespass) the erection from a neighbouring building of a sign which projected over the roof of his shop. In *Woolerton and Wilson Ltd.* v. *Richard Costain Ltd.* (1970) it was held to be a trespass where a crane used for the erection of a tower block was allowed to swing in the airspace over neighbouring land, although the operation of an injunction to prevent the continuance of the trespass was postponed to enable the tower block to be completed. It has since been held that the trial judge was wrong to postpone the operation of an injunction: see *Trenberth* v. *National Westminster Bank Ltd.* (1979).

The rights of the owner of the surface to the airspace above are not unlimited. Statutory rights to overfly private land are conferred by the Air Navigation and Transport Act 1936, s.55 in the Republic and by the United Kingdom Civil Aviation Act 1949, s.40 in Northern Ireland. At common law also it has now been established that a landowner's right to the airspace above his land extends only so far as necessary for reasonable use of the surface. This was in *Lord Bernstein of Leigh* v. *Skyviews & General Ltd.* (1977), where the plaintiff claimed that the defendants had trespassed on his land by flying over it to take aerial photographs. The judge rejected the claim observing that "I can find no support in authority for the view that a landowner's rights in the airspace above his property extend to an unlimited height."

As well as extending upwards, a landowner's rights also extend downwards. The owner of the surface was at common law entitled to all mines and minerals below the surface (except for gold and silver, to which the Crown was entitled: *Case of Mines*, 1567) although by the Constitution of Ireland, Art. 10 and enactments such as the Mineral Development Act 1979 and by statute in Northern Ireland, rights to coal, oil, gas and most other valuable minerals are now vested in the State. Subject to the statutory and common law exceptions, an intrusion beneath the surface of a man's land would be as much a trespass as an intrusion into the airspace above his land (see *Eardley* v. *Earl Granville* (1876); *Edwards* v. *Lees Administrators* (1936)). Here again, however, rights probably do not extend to an unlimited depth. It might not be a trespass to make use for heating of geothermic rock many thousands of feet below the surface. It is, however, very clearly a wrong to extract rock salt beneath the land of a neighbour by means of brine pumping, even from a considerable distance away, where the result is to undermine support for the neighbour's buildings: *Lotus* v. *British Soda* (1971).

Land comprises then, not only the surface, but also what lies on or above the surface, and what there is below. The upper floor of a building is as much land as the ground floor or the cellar. If the owner of land used as a gravel pit excavates and sells the gravel, the space which is left behind remains his land. It remains his land even if the space fills with water. Land is a space containing constituents which may change from time to time. It includes everything which finds its way naturally into the space, and can also include things added by man (see "Fixtures," below).

5. Dividing land vertically

As has already been pointed out, land is ordinarily divided horizontally. Division in the vertical plane is also, however, possible. Where a building is divided into apartments, the apartments can be let separately, or even sold outright as "flying freeholds." Quite what happens where the building is destroyed has not yet been resolved. In the case of a lease it is possible for the lease to be frustrated (see Chapter 11). In the case of a "flying freehold," it might well be that the owner of the flat would retain ownership of the airspace previously occupied by his part of the building, even though the building is no longer there. The purchase of a "flying freehold" or a "flying leasehold" involves other considerations too. The owner will want special rights of access and rights of support, rights which are capable of being granted as easements: see Chapter 16.

The sale of minerals (where these do not belong to the State or to the Crown) may also result in a vertical division of land. It is possible to sell simply the right to enter and remove the minerals (a right known as a profit á prendre: see Chapter 16). Alternatively, the strata themselves in which the minerals are found can be sold so that when the minerals have been removed the purchaser retains ownership of the vacant spaces.

Possible though the division of land into slabs is, it remains the exception. In one case, for instance, a farmer who had sold several acres of turf for use in making lawns stood to gain a tax advantage if he could show he had sold the freehold in the space occupied by the turf. As the consequence of this would have been that any crops planted by the farmer would have their roots in his land, with their leaves waving in his airspace, but with two inches of their stems trespassing in the "land" (airspace) owned by the purchaser of the turf, Megarry V.-C. considered that the farmer's claim verged on the ridiculous, and was a result which could have been achieved only by the very clearest of words, which had not been used in the case he had to decide: *Lowe* v. *J.W. Ashmore Ltd.* (1971). Similarly, in *Grigsby* v. *Melville* (1973), the owner of a pair of semi-detached houses sold one, but claimed to be entitled to continue to use the cellar beneath it, since the only access to it was from the house he had retained. In rejecting this claim, the judge at first instance, Brightman J., observed:

> "A purchaser does not expect to find the vendor continuing to live mole-like beneath his drawing-room floor. I would expect the conveyance of a house to include all that lies beneath its roof. I think that is how a conveyance should be interpreted unless there is a reason for construing it otherwise."

6. Fixtures

Some things incorporated into land clearly become part of the land. This is obviously true of things such as fertilisers and manures which when spread upon land lose their previous identity. It is true also of seeds which grow into plants. Other things, which have not lost their identity, do not become part of the land simply because they are found upon it. A car parked in a corporation car park does not become the corporation's. A book lent to a friend does not become his when he places it on his bookshelf.

In between these two extremes, however, it is more difficult to determine whether something is in law part of the land upon which it is found. English and Irish law do not accept the proposition that anything which may be removed from land without damage is not part of the land. There may be little difference between the pile of stones in a builder's yard, kept for resale, and very similar stones arranged as a field boundary in the form of a dry stone wall, yet the latter, removable without damage though they may be, are fixtures, *i.e.* part of the land, while the former are not. The reason is that the test to determine whether something is a fixture contains two elements. The first element is the degree of annexation. In other words, how securely is the article in question attached to the land? The more securely it is attached, the more likely it is to be considered part of the land. Thus permanent buildings of bricks and mortar on concrete foundations are almost certain to be fixtures while mobile buildings on wheels are not. This element is not however in itself conclusive for even things which are firmly fixed, such as in one case, *Leigh* v. *Taylor* (1902), a tapestry tacked to wooden battens nailed to a wall, may be held not to be fixtures, but to retain their character as chattels. Conversely, a statue held in position only by its own weight has been held a fixture where it formed an integral part of the architectural design of a stately home: *D'Eyncourt* v. *Gregory* (1866). This is because the second element of the test for fixtures—the purpose of annexation—is determinative. If a thing is attached to land for the purposes of making it a permanent improvement to the land, it will be a fixture. If it is attached simply for the purposes of use or display it will not be a fixture (see *Holland* v. *Hodgson* (1872); *Berkley* v. *Poulett* (1976). The purpose of annexation is determined objectively, having regard to all the relevant circumstances such as the nature of the article and its value, and the extent of the interest of the person who affixed it both in the alleged fixture (compare *Lyon & Co.* v. *London City and Midland Bank* (1903) and *Vaudeville Electric Cinema Ltd.* v. *Muriset* (1923)) and in the land (*Leigh* v. *Taylor*, above; *Spyer* v. *Phillipson* (1931)). The specific intention of an individual owner is not normally relevant. Something attached to land may become a fixture even though it did not previously belong to the landowner (*Lombard and Ulster Banking Ltd.* v. *Kennedy*, 1974) or may even have been stolen (*Gough* v. *Wood and Co.*, 1894).

7. The importance of fixtures

The question of whether something is a fixture can arise in a variety of contexts. One of the commoner is on a sale of land. The buyer of a house is clearly entitled to the building, its doors, windows, and so on. Equally clearly he is not entitled, unless they have been specifically sold to him, to articles of movable furniture. Is he though, entitled to the television aerial, floor coverings, curtain rails, light fittings and fitted electrical appliances in the kitchen? He is if they are fixtures. If they are not, they may be removed by the vendor. Since there is frequently room for differences of opinion—and the test for fixtures is not precise—it is always advisable at the time that the contract for sale is entered into to clarify which articles are included in the sale, and which apparent fixtures are excluded.

Disputes over fixtures can also arise in relation to mortgages, for on the default of the borrower the lender is entitled to sell the land, together with any fixtures, whether the fixtures were attached before or after the mortgage was made (see the *Vaudeville Electric Cinema* case, above. Mortgages are discussed in Chapter 18). Amongst other instances in which questions concerning fixtures have arisen are on the expiry of a limited interest in land, between landlord and tenant, and on the death of a landowner who leaves his real property to one person and his personal property to another.

8. Removal of fixtures

An unencumbered full owner of land may always remove fixtures since this is simply part of his rights of ownership. For others, where a thing is a fixture, then being part of the land, it may not ordinarily be removed without the consent of those entitled to the land. For instance, a tenant who erects buildings on land he holds from a landlord makes them part of the land, and he may not remove them either during the lease or at its end (subject to some exceptions dealt with later): *Elwes* v. *Maw* (1802); *R.* v. *Smith* (1974); Malicious Damage Act 1861, s.13. If the tenant obtains a new lease on the expiry of his existing lease, the new rent will be based upon the improved value of the land unless express (or statutory) provision has been made for the value of fixtures and improvements added by the tenant to be taken into account: *Ponsford* v. *H.M.S. Aerosols Ltd.* (1979). Similarly, since fixtures form part of land subject to a mortgage, they may not be removed by the mortgagor *i.e.* the borrower, without the agreement of the mortgagee, *i.e.* the lender (*Longbottom* v. *Berry*, 1869). Exceptionally, a person attaching a fixture may remove it without the consent of the others interested in the land, and even though he may not be entitled to the fee simple. This exception arises between landlord and tenant in the case of what are known as "tenant's fixtures." It became established at common law, although it was not always so, that a tenant could remove trade, ornamental and domestic fixtures which he had himself added to the property. He had to remove them either during the tenancy, or during such reasonable period thereafter as he remained in possession in his capacity as tenant (*Ex p. Brook*, 1878). Included in the category of tenants' trade fixtures have been held to be such things as machinery (*Lawton* v. *Lawton*, 1743) a market gardener's plants (*Wardell* v. *Usher*, 1841) and petrol pumps at a filling station (*Smith* v. *City Petroleum Co.*, 1940). Objects which have been held to be removable as ornamental and domestic fixtures have included ornamental wooden panelling (*Spyer* v. *Phillipson*, 1931) and kitchen ranges (*Darby* v. *Harris*, 1841). At common law, farmers were not permitted to remove agricultural fixtures, even if this caused no damage: *Elwes* v. *Maw* (1802). This was altered by section 3 of the Landlord and Tenant Act 1851, which permitted the removal of agricultural fixtures subject to certain conditions.

The common law exceptions were given statutory recognition and extended to agricultural fixtures by section 17 of Deasy's Act (the Landlord and Tenant Law Amendment Act, Ireland, 1860). This permits the removal by a tenant of fixtures "erected and affixed to the freehold by the tenant at his sole expense, for any purpose of trade, manufacture, or agriculture, or for ornament, or for the domestic convenience of the tenant in his occupation" of the premises, provided that the removal can be carried out without substantial damage to either the land or the fixture. The removal must take place during the tenancy, while the tenant is in possession, or within two months of the end of a lease which ends by an uncertain event and without the act or default of the tenant.

The common law, but not the statutory exception for "tenant's fixtures" (*i.e.* trade, ornamental and domestic fixtures) applies to another, very similar case. That is where land is subject to a settlement under which two or more people are entitled to the land in succession (see Chapter 7). Land may be given, for instance, to A for life, and then to B. In such a case, the personal representatives of A (the persons appointed to deal with his property on his death: see Chapter 12) may remove objects attached by A to the land for the purposes of trade, ornamentation or domestic use (*Lawton* v. *Lawton*, 1743).

5. Limits to the Ownership of Land

1. Ownership is not absolute dominium

Ownership cannot be seen as absolute dominium over the thing to which an owner is entitled. The law places limits upon the ways in which an owner may enjoy his property. Some of these limits arise because of the need to balance the competing claims of neighbours. If the owner of a semi-detached house were at liberty to play continuously loud music he would interfere with his neighbour's peace and tranquillity. Hence the general maxim of the tort of private nuisance —*sic utere tuo ut alienum non laedas*—so use your own property as not to injure another's. The owner of land is permitted to use his own land only in ways which do not unreasonably interfere with his neighbour's enjoyment. Similarly, every landowner is entitled to have his land supported in its natural state by the adjoining land and correlatively a landowner must not excavate his own land in a way which removes his neighbour's support: *Latimer* v. *Official Co-operative Society* (1885).

2. The criminal law and the law of tort

Other restrictions on the use of land arise not in favour of neighbours but in favour of the public at large. Just as the criminal law makes it an offence for the owner of a gun to use it as a murder weapon, so, in a similar way, it is a criminal offence to use a house as a brothel, or to use it as a place where prohibited drugs may be freely used. So also it is both a criminal offence and a tort to use land in a way which amounts to a public nuisance. Examples of public nuisances include quarrying and blasting operations causing dust and debris to fly over a wide neighbourhood (*Att.-Gen.* v. *P.Y.A. Quarries*, 1957) and organising a pop festival causing excessive noise and traffic congestion in the vicinity: *Att.-Gen. for Ontario* v. *Orange*

Productions Ltd. (1971). A landowner will also be liable for public nuisance where the state of his land is such as to endanger the safety of users of an adjoining public highway, for instance where premises on a highway are in dangerous disrepair (*Wringe* v. *Cohen* (1940); *McKenna* v. *Lewis* (1945)) or where a tree overhangs the highway at a height at which passing traffic may collide with it (*Lynch* v. *Dawson*, 1946).

The occupier of land may be liable in a species of negligence for injuries caused to visitors, including trespassers, by the state of the premises (Occupiers Liability Act (N.I.) 1957, *McNamara* v. *E.S.B.*, 1975), and liability in negligence for the state of the premises extends also to passers-by (*Gillen* v. *Fair*, 1955) and neighbours (*Leakey* v. *National Trust*, 1980). The view formerly taken that the owner of land would not normally be liable for injuries arising from his inaction, but that he would be liable only for injuries arising from positive acts (see *Giles* v. *Walker*, 1890) has now been discredited (see *Goldman* v. *Hargrave* (1967); *Leakey* v. *National Trust* (1980).

3. Planning law

Very clearly in the domain of public law is the statutory regulation of the development of land. A farmer may not use his land for housing, nor a dentist convert his house to a surgery, nor even, in some cases may a home owner change the colour of the exterior walls of his house, without planning permission first being obtained. Under the Planning (N.I.) Order 1972, as amended, and, for the Republic, the Local Government (Planning and Development) Act 1963, no development of land may take place without prior consent having been obtained from the appropriate planning authority. Development is widely defined to include most building operations, changes in the use of property, and changes in the external appearance of buildings, although there are certain exceptions for development within well-defined limits which can take place without planning permission. Measures which can be taken to ensure compliance with development control include the power to make orders to prevent use in breach of planning permission, extending even to an order that an offending structure, even if completed, should be demolished. In the Republic, development without planning permission is a criminal offence.

In most cases, planning permission may be refused without compensation (although the legislation does provide for compensation to be payable in certain cases). The planning laws, since they restrict a freedom which landowners previously had, might be seen as confiscatory, although the House of Lords in 1960 held that the need for planning permission did not amount to a taking of property without compensation (*O.D. Cars Ltd.* v. *Belfast Corporation*, 1960). Similarly, Kenny J. in *Central Dublin Development Association* v. *A.G.* (1969) held that the Republic's Local Government (Planning and Development) Act 1963 did not infringe Articles 43 and 40.3 of the Constitution. The ownership of land cannot therefore be seen as carrying an unqualified right to change the use of land, or to develop it.

4. Public rights and rights reserved to the State

As has already been pointed out in Chapter 4, both in Northern Ireland and in the Republic the rights to most valuable mineral and energy resources are vested in the State. The State is also entitled to treasure trove, that is, articles of gold and silver hidden or concealed upon land, where the owner is unknown (*Att.-Gen.* v. *Moore*, 1893). And, although a man's home may be his "castle," powers of entry (in many cases only in limited and specific circumstances) are conferred upon a wide range of public officials and officials of certain semi-state bodies (such as the electricity supply boards). Rights of the public are much more limited. The public may of course use lands dedicated for use as a public highway, but only for the purpose of passing and repassing. The owner of the soil retains a residual right so that he can, for instance, sue for trespass a person who loiters on a highway passing over his land to spy on racehorses being trained: *Hickman* v. *Maisey* (1900).

5. Protective legislation

A significant encroachment upon "absolute" ownership, limiting the rights of the owners of land has taken place with the legislation protective of tenants, legislation which has a comparatively modern origin. Under legislation originally introduced to deal temporarily with housing shortages following the First World War, the rents which could be charged for certain residential properties were artificially restricted, and the tenants were given security of tenure. These and similar restrictions were continued from time to time until it looked as though they would become a permanent feature of Irish land law. In a challenge to the rent restriction legislation in force in the Republic, *Blake* v. *Att.-Gen.* (1982), however, it was held that the Republic's rent restriction legislation was unconstitutional as an infringement of the property rights of the landlords. As a direct result, following some interim legislation, and a ruling of unconstitutionality on the first attempt at statutory change (*Re Article 26 and the Housing*

(Private Rented Dwellings) Bill 1981) new laws protective of tenants were introduced by the Housing (Private Rented Dwellings) Act 1982. This Act, as amended by the Housing (Private Rented Dwellings) Act 1983 provides for payment of rentals much closer to those obtainable in the open market, with provision for review by a newly created Rent Tribunal. It also reduces considerably the security of tenure given to tenants. Under the new legislation, only existing tenants and their spouses are given an indefinite right to security of tenure. There is a right for a member of a tenant's family to succeed to the tenancy, but in such a case the security of tenure will not extend more than 20 years (in a few cases 25 years) from the commencement of the Act, May 21, 1982. Rent allowances are payable under the Social Welfare (Rent Allowance) Regulations 1982 and 1983 in cases where there is likely to be substantial hardship arising from the increases in rent.

In Northern Ireland the rent restriction laws have been substantially reshaped by the Rent (N.I.) Order 1978, but the essence is still that rents are artificially controlled, and tenants given security of tenure. The security of tenure continues through two transmissions from an existing tenant to a member of his family.

6. Continuation of tenancies and leasehold enlargement

In addition to the protective legislation in favour of residential tenants, there is also legislation both North and South giving existing tenants rights against their landlords to require the grant of a new tenancy or enabling them to acquire the landlord's interest in the property: see Landlord and Tenant (Amendment) Act 1980; Landlord and Tenant (Ground Rents) (No. 2) Act 1978; Business Tenancies Act (N.I.) 1964; Leasehold (Enlargement and Extension) Act (N.I.) 1971.

7. Restrictions on sale and letting

The Land Purchase Acts of the nineteenth and early twentieth centuries were designed not only to achieve what Irish judges have described as a "peasant proprietorship" (see *Foley* v. *Irish Land Commission*, 1952) in which the majority of farmers have the freehold in the land they farm, but also to rationalise landholdings in the "congested districts," mainly along the western seaboard. As part of the land purchase scheme, therefore, land subject to a land purchase annuity may not be let, sublet or subdivided without the consent of the Land Commission in the Republic, or of the Northern Ireland Department of Finance. In the Republic, restrictions continue in respect of agricultural land even after the annuity has been paid off: Land Act 1965, s.12.

8. Other restrictions

The restrictions outlined above are by no means the only restrictions on the ownership of land. A landowner may be liable for the payment of rates on land in his occupation, and may also be liable in the Republic for the residential property tax introduced by the Finance Act 1983. The land is also liable to compulsory purchase; will have to be licensed if it is used for certain purposes such as the sale of alcoholic liquors; and will have to comply with public health and sometimes fire regulations. If land is sold as a dwelling in the Republic, then it may not be made the subject of a new ground rent: Landlord and Tenant (Ground Rents) Act 1978. A similar prohibition has been proposed for Northern Ireland. The list of restrictions could be continued.

9. The new property

The notion of ownership as a "bundle of rights" has already been referred to (see Chapter 1). The extent of those rights has been progressively reduced since the nineteenth century when Challis, in his textbook on the *Law of Real Property* was able to declare of the fee simple estate that it

> "confers, and since the beginning of legal history it has always conferred, the lawful right to exercise over, upon, and in respect, to the land, every act of ownership which can enter into the imagination, including the right to commit unlimited waste."

Many of the changes which have taken place since 1885, when Challis wrote, have effected a redistribution of rights. The redistribution has in most cases operated towards the State, but in the area of the law of landlord and tenant, the protective legislation has operated to reallocate certain rights from one private individual, the landlord, to another, the tenant. In this respect it could be claimed that a "new property" is being created in favour of tenants, their rights deriving primarily from their status. Even in the Republic, where the Constitution gives special protection to the institution of private ownership (Art. 43), it is recognised that the State may regulate these rights in accordance with the principles of social justice and for the common good (Art. 43.2). Thus it is that the constitutionality of public regulation of land use has been upheld. On the other hand, the rent restrictions legislation which "restricted the property rights of one group of citizens for the benefit of another group" was held to be unconstitutional because

> "This is done without compensation and without regard to the financial capacity or the financial needs of either group, in legislation which provides no limitation on the period of restriction, gives no opportunity for review and allows no modification of the operation of the restriction. It is, therefore, both unfair and arbitrary. These provisions constitute an unjust attack on the property rights of landlords of controlled dwellings and are, therefore, contrary to the provisions of Article 40.3.2 of the Constitution" (*Blake* v. *Att.-Gen.*, 1982).

The legislation in question was adjudged to be unconsitutional not simply because it deprived landlords indefinitely of the right to occupy the land. A regime could be contemplated in which a lawful occupier always has the right to remain indefinitely. The legislation was unconstitutional because it changed the pre-existing regime in a way which was unfair and arbitrary in that it did not apply to all landlords and tenants, but only to some, and those to whom it applied were chosen without relation to any socially defensible criterion.

6. Fragmentation of Ownership Through Tenure

1. The Norman Conquest

The foundations of modern Irish land law date back to the Norman invasion of the twelfth century. As William the Conqueror had in England a century before, in 1066, the King claimed Ireland by right of conquest. The Norman conquest of Ireland was not achieved as speedily as it had been in England, but the consequences for landholding were the same. By virtue of conquest the land became the King's. Of course the King could not enjoy all the land directly himself. Instead, he granted the land to certain of his subjects to be held from him in return for homage, fealty and services. The land was granted to these subjects as a reward for assisting the King in his conquest or for submitting to him without battle. The landholders were called tenants, a word derived from the Latin *tenere*, to hold, and the conditions on which they held the land constituted their *tenure*. The tenants of the King, or *tenants in chief*, themselves made subgrants of the land to others and so on until eventually the land was held by the possessor or *tenant in demesne*. This resulted in a pyramidal structure of landholding with the King at its apex (see Figure 6.1 below). The process of granting land in return for services, so creating a new rung in the pyramid, was known as *subinfeudation*.

2. Reservation of services

An essential feature of the feudal system was the reservation of services. At the time the feudal structure originated agriculture was the principal industry and land the greatest form of wealth. Services were reserved in the same way as a landlord would now seek rent from a tenant. The services could be of almost infinite variety. The King

Figure 6.1: The feudal pyramid

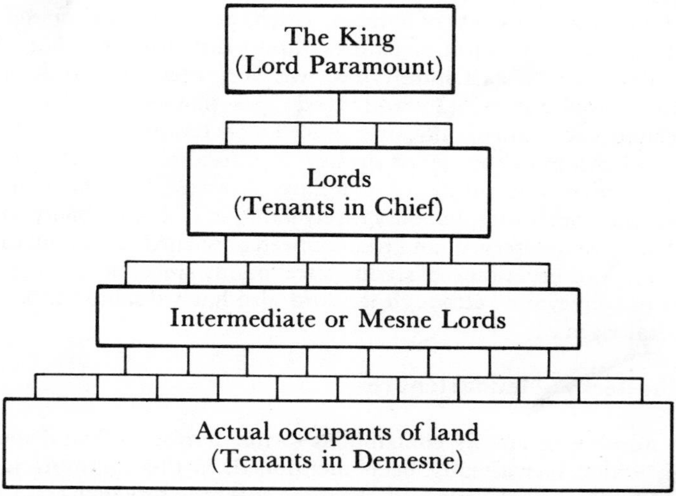

might require the provision of armed horsemen to serve him for a certain number of days each year. Mesne lords might grant land to tenants in demesne in return for agricultural or trade services. Other services were possible. Sir Edward Coke in his Commentary on Littleton's *Tenures* at page 86a gives the example of an obligation to act as a hangman or executioner. Another example given in Thomas Blount's *Fragmenta Antiquitatis* is that of Rolland, a tenant of lands in Suffolk who was obliged on Christmas Day "to make a leap, a whistle and a fart *coram domino rege*."

Although a few of the ancient tenurial services remain as historical curiosities (see Simpson, *An Introduction to the History of The Law Law*, p. 9), the vast majority have disappeared. Most were commuted into fixed money payments which with the ravages of centuries of inflation ceased in most cases to be worth collecting. A very few feudal landholdings subject to a perpetual money rent survive in Ireland and are known today as holdings in fee farm, although most fee farm grants have a different origin (see below).

Apart from the rendering of services, the feudal system had other features. As has already been observed, a tenant owed his landlord fealty and homage, and there were also spasmodic liabilities called *incidents*. A lord, for instance, was frequently entitled to a *relief*, or money payment of one year's value of the land, when a tenant died and a descendent succeeded to the land. In the event of a tenant dying without an heir, the land would pass by *escheat propter defectum sanguinis* to the feudal lord.

The very wide variety of tenures, which the ancient writers such as Littleton, in an account of tenures (first printed in or about 1481) classified into at least nine types, was very much reduced by the Tenures Abolition Act (Ireland) 1662. This, like its English counterpart some two years previously, reduced most tenures to a single type, free and common socage, or *freehold*. It also abolished many of the more burdensome incidents of tenure. *Copyhold*, a form of tenure which was sometimes, but only rarely found in Ireland (chiefly within the Pale) was preserved, and has not been abolished in Ireland to this day. The preservation is of significance mainly since there is a special form of conveyance although the lord also has valuable timber and mineral rights.

3. The decay of feudal tenure

A number of factors contributed to the demise of feudal tenure. One, which has already been mentioned, is the commutation of services into money payments. As these ceased to be worth collecting, so the mesne lords to whom they were due became untraceable and some of the intermediate links in the feudal chain between tenant in demesne and Crown disappeared.

A second factor in the decay of feudal tenure was the prohibition of subinfeudation. A tenant wishing to alienate land could do so either by substituting the transferee for himself as the tenant of his lord, a process known as *substitution*, or he could *subinfeudate* by granting the land to another to be held from him as mesne lord in return for services. The attractions of subinfeudation for a tenant were obvious. Not only would he receive a capital sum on the grant of the land; he would continue to receive an income in the form of services, usually a rent. For a lord, subinfeudation was less attractive. If a tenant in demesne subinfeudated for a rent of £1 per year, then it would be upon this annual sum that the value of incidents such as relief would be calculated rather than upon the gross annual value of the land.

A first attempt at regulation was made by the Great Charter of 1217 which prohibited tenants from alienating their lands unless they retained sufficient to meet any services they owed to their lord. A more significant step was taken by the Statute Quia Emptores Terrarum 1290, which enunciated the principle of free alienation without the consent of the lord, but prohibited alienation by way of subinfeudation. This prohibition on the creation of new tenurial relationships could have resulted in the gradual disappearance of all mesne tenants, as it did in England. It did not do so in Scotland since the Statute Quia Emptores did not apply there. Nor did it have this effect in Ireland because in the Crown forfeitures and resettlements of the seventeenth century it was common for the Crown grants to contain a dispensation ("*non obstante Quia Emptores*") permitting subinfeudation by the tenant in chief. Although there may have been doubts about the King's power to give such dispensations (see the Bill of Rights 1689) the validity of fee farm grants created under them has not been questioned in modern times, and many are in any case supported by public or private Act of Parliament (but see *Re Holliday*, 1922).

4. The effect of tenure

The effect of the concept of tenure is that more than one right exists in relation to the same land at the same time. The tenant in demesne had a *tenement* consisting of the right to the possession of land in return for whatever feudal service he owed. The lord had a *seignory* consisting of the right to receive the services and any incidents due, and these services and incidents issued out of the land. Where no mesne lord could be found, then the land was deemed to be held directly from the Crown. The Crown could thus claim to be ultimately entitled to all land, and hence the somewhat misleading dictum that "English [and therefore also Irish] land law still retains its original basis, that all land in England [Ireland] is owned by the Crown" (Megarry and Wade, *The Law of Real Property*, (5th ed., 1984, p. 12). In the Republic the State has replaced the Crown. The dictum is misleading because the concept of tenure underlines the difficulty of speaking of the "ownership" of land.

The most recent incident of feudal tenure to disappear is escheat, the right of a lord to take the land of a tenant who died without heirs and without nominating a successor to the land in his will. Escheat was abolished in Northern Ireland with effect from January 1, 1956 by the Administration of Estates Act (N.I.) 1955, s.1(5). Instead of escheat, the Crown takes land without an owner as *bona vacantia* in the same way as all other property (s.16). In the Republic escheat was abolished by section 11(3) of the Succession Act 1965, with effect from January 1, 1967. Instead, the State now takes ownerless property as ultimate intestate successor (s.73(1)).

The abolition of escheat has meant that the feudal concept of tenure has been deprived of virtually all its significance, except in those rare cases where feudal rent service is still due.

5. Leasehold tenure

Even though the common law was not generally applicable throughout Ireland until the seventeenth century, the concept of tenure was well established by the twelfth century. For reasons upon which historians have yet to agree, a *termor*, that is, a person taking land for a fixed term of years, was not treated in the same way as a freehold tenant. If he was ejected from the land, he was not originally permitted by the Royal Courts to recover the land directly from the wrongdoer. Instead, the termor had only a remedy against the person who had let the land to him. The *term of years* or *lease* was therefore treated as if it created only personal rights and not rights in land. By the fifteenth century, however, when it was decided that the lessee had a right to specific recovery of land against anyone who ejected him, the lease indubitably became an interest in land. It was, nevertheless, a right in land which had been excluded from the feudal system of landholding.

The relationship between a landlord and a tenant for years, although not a form of feudal tenure, nevertheless is a type of tenure. The tenant *holds* the land from the landlord; he normally pays a rent described as *rent-service*; and (except in Northern Ireland where it has been abolished), the landlord has the right of distress (see "Rent-charges", below) and often a right to forfeit a lease for breach of condition. A tenant desiring to alienate his right to the land may do so either by *assignment* (where the transferee is substituted for the tenant) or by *sublease* (where, as in subinfeudation, the transferee holds from the tenant). The grant of subleases was not prohibited by the Statute Quia Emptores 1290.

The lease was probably originally a device for parting temporarily with possession of land. If a lease was granted for a short time it enabled the proprietor to enjoy an income while preserving the capital intact. At a time when land was the only real form of investment, leases performed an important economic role: see Cheshire and Burn's *Modern Law of Real Property* (13th ed., 1982), p. 36. Where a lease was granted for an extended period, then it provided a way of alienating land subject to the reservation of a rent, notwithstanding the prohibition of subinfeudation by the Statute Quia Emptores.

6. Rentcharges

It was possible (and still is) to charge a rent upon land without creating any relationship of tenure. The rent could be payable in perpetuity or for any of the other periods recognised at common law (see Chapter 7). Since there was no element of tenure, the creditor was not entitled to any of the tenurial incidents, nor was he entitled to exercise the tenurial right of distress (*i.e.* the right to seize goods upon the land to enforce payment of rent). A rent, payable independently of tenure, and where there is no right of distress, was known as a *rent seck*. It was, however, possible, at the time of creating a rent, for a right to distrain to be given expressly. In such a case the rent is known as a *rentcharge* since the land is charged by the power of distress. By statute in 1712, the Distress for Rent Act (Ireland), and by the Landlord and Tenant Act (Ireland) 1741, rents seck were converted into rent-charges since these statutes gave the owners of rents the same power of distraint as landlords. This was confirmed by the Conveyancing Act 1881 which also gave the owners of rents a right to take possession of land to enforce payment of arrears.

By means of alienating land subject to a rentcharge it was possible, as with a lease, to avoid the Statute Quia Emptores. The conveyance of land subject to rentcharges has in fact been a common method of sale in parts of Britain, notably in Manchester and Bristol, but it has not been common in Ireland.

7. Types of fee farm grant

The expression "fee farm grant" may properly be applicable only to a certain kind of feudal tenure (see Simpson, *Introduction to the History of Land Law*, p. 73), but in Ireland it has come to be a useful description for any landholding subject to a perpetual rent. Such landholdings can arise in a variety of ways:

(i) *Feudal fee farm grants*. These are fee farm grants where the perpetual rent is a rent service payable by virtue of feudal tenure (see Sections 2 and 3 above).

(ii) *Grants subject to a perpetual rentcharge*. This type of holding is explained in Section 6 above.

(iii) *Deasy's Act grants*. At common law a lease could only be created for a fixed period of time, usually a period of years, and hence the alternative name for a lease, the *term of years*. This common law rule, however, was altered by the Landlord and Tenant Law Amendment Act Ireland 1860 which is commonly referred to as Deasy's Act. Section 3 of the Act provides:

> "The relationship of landlord and tenant shall be deemed to be founded on the express or implied contract of the parties, and not upon tenure or service, and a reversion shall not be necessary to such relation, which shall be deemed to subsist in all cases in which there shall be an agreement by one party to hold land from or under another in consideration of any rent."

As this section has been interpreted, it permits the creation of a lease at a rent which will last in perpetuity. There is no need for the landlord to retain a reversion, namely the right to possession of the land on the expiry of the lease. Such a reversion was essential under the law before the Act, and still is in England. Section 3 does, however, contain a contradiction. On the one hand it denies that the relationship of landlord and tenant is founded upon tenure or service. On the other hand it acknowledges that the tenant holds the land "from or under" a landlord in consideration of a rent. Since the rent is in the nature of a service (as opposed to a rent seck or a rentcharge) and the substance of tenure is that one person holds from another, it is submitted that the relationship of landlord and tenant can only be described as a tenurial relationship—leasehold tenure—although not, admittedly, a relationship of feudal tenure.

(iv) *Leasehold conversion grants.* A popular form of lease in the eighteenth century was one which although granted for a short initial period such as 21 years, contained a provision giving the tenant an option to renew the lease for a further period again with an option to renew. In this way the lease would be perpetually renewable. These leases were popular because certain bodies, such as the Church of Ireland and Trinity College, Dublin, were prohibited by statute (Ecclesiastical Lands Acts (Ireland) 1634 and 1795) from granting leases with duration of more than 21 or 40 years depending upon whether the land was rural or urban. For reasons which are not at all clear it also became common for leases for lives renewable for ever to be created. Under these the tenant held the land for the duration of the lives of three named people who could be quite unconnected with the land. The lease would come to an end when all three persons died, but the tenant had an option to have new lives substituted so that once again, through renewals, the lease could continue for ever. With both the perpetually renewable term of years and the perpetually renewable lease for lives the landlord benefited by the payment of a fine (a lump sum) by the tenant in return for the renewal.

With leases for lives renewable for ever it was often the case that a tenant might omit to obtain a renewal of the lives by having new names substituted in good time. Where this resulted in expiry of the lease, the landlord was nominally entitled to recover possession. The view of the courts from at least the early eighteenth century, however, was that as the intention had been to create a perpetual lease, the tenant could call, even belatedly, for a renewal upon making restitution to the landlord for the delay by paying any arrears of renewal fines. This practice was confirmed by the Tenantry Act (Ireland) 1779. This Act required a court to permit a renewal notwithstanding a delay on the part of the tenant provided that the tenant was not guilty of fraud, that he adequately compensated the landlord, and that he had not failed within a reasonable time to pay any renewal fines properly demanded by the landlord. A number of perpetually renewable leases survive in urban areas of Northern Ireland, although in the Republic they have now all been converted into fee farm grants or holdings in fee simple free of rent.

The first Acts permitting the conversion of perpetually renewable leases into fee farm grants applied to the whole of Ireland. By several statutes, Public and Private, such as the Church Temporalities (Ireland) Acts 1833 to 1860 and the Trinity College, Dublin, Leasing and Perpetuity Act 1851, certain categories of tenant under perpetually renewable leases were given a right to enlarge their interests into fee farm grants. A generally applicable right to convert a perpetually renewable lease into a fee farm grant was conferred on tenants by the Renewable Leasehold Conversion Act 1849. This permitted tenants of existing renewable leases to obtain a conversion into a fee farm grant at a simple rent with the value of the fines previously payable on renewal conflated into the annual rent. The Act also prevented the creation of any further perpetually renewable leases by providing that any such lease purported to be created after the commencement of the Act was to operate as a fee farm grant.

It seems that few tenants availed of the option to convert their holdings to a fee farm grant, but most such holdings in rural areas would in any case have been bought out under the Land Purchase Acts, as also would any holdings converted into fee farm grants. A radical measure relating to any remaining perpetually renewable leases in the Republic was contained in the Landlord and Tenant (Amendment) Act 1980. By section 74 any unconverted perpetually renewable leases for lives are automatically converted into holdings in fee simple free of rent. Since these holdings are free of rent they are not fee farm grants, although in other respects they have the characteristics of leasehold conversion grants.

8. Recovery of fee farm rents

Fee farm grants give rise to a number of special problems. Two of these relate to rent. There is first the problem of how the payment of rent can be enforced, and secondly the problem of whether a tenant can redeem the rent. It is worth dealing with those problems here. Some other problems concerning fee farm grants are discussed elsewhere. Chapters 10 and 11 deal with the way in which fee farm grants may be created and transferred, and Chapter 17 discusses the enforceability of covenants (*i.e.* undertakings relating to the use of land).

So far as concerns the recovery of rent, it is of little consequence to which category a fee farm grant belongs. Three remedies are available. The first is an action for debt, which is available in all cases and can ultimately be enforced by imprisonment for contempt. The second is the right of distress, explained above (p. 37), and which is available in feudal and leasehold fee farm by virtue of the relationship of tenure, and as been extended to the owners of rentcharges by statute. Distress has now been abolished in Northern Ireland. The final remedy is that of forfeiture or ejectment. Where the fee farm grant creates a relationship of landlord and tenant, the landlord has the ordinary leasehold remedy of ejectment for non-payment of rent: see Chapter 11. Where the fee farm grant is a feudal or rentcharge grant, then there can be a right of forfeiture, but only if this is expressly reserved by the grantor, or in the case of a feudal grant if the payment of rent is made a condition of the grant. A right of forfeiture may also be reserved on the grant of a leasehold fee farm grant in the same way. As the right of forfeiture was considered in equity to be simply a security for the payment of rent, equitable relief against forfeiture may be granted where any arrears of rent and costs are made good.

9. Redemption of fee farm grants

A tenant in fee farm wishing to obtain an unencumbered fee simple may always do so by private voluntary compact. There are also a number of statutes conferring further rights than this, and many fee farm grants were converted into unencumbered holdings under the Land Purchase Acts. Modern statutes in force conferring a right of enlargement on tenants are the Leasehold (Enlargement and Extension) Act (N.I.) 1971, and in the Republic, the (Landlord and Tenant (Ground Rents) (No. 2) Act 1978 (although there is some doubt as to whether this Act applies to tenants in fee farm as well as tenants under long leases).

7 The Division of Ownership Over Time

A. General

1. The temporal element of ownership

Land is not a perishable commodity. Especially when viewed as space, with components which may be changed from time to time, it has a perpetual duration. Even if a house in a town may not be expected to remain standing for more than another century or so, the land it occupies will remain long after the building is demolished. Besides this, using land to produce an income does not in most cases materially prejudice its capital value. Such things as turf, sand and gravel can only be extracted once over, but the use of land for farming or for residential purposes neither destroys the land nor reduces its future worth.

This permanance of land has enabled the creation of interests in land which are of limited duration. The common law never recognised the creation of limited interests in pure personal property. Only through the interposition of a trust could interests of a limited duration be created in chattels; apart from this an interest in chattels for a limited time could be enforced only as a matter of contract.

2. Successive enjoyment

The creation of interests in land of limited duration brings in the notion of the division of ownership over time. Since land has a perpetual existence, if A is given a right to that land for his lifetime, it must follow that someone else will be entitled to the land upon A's death.

There is always, of course, an element of succession. If E is entitled to land for ever, he cannot enjoy the land after his death, for he cannot take it with him. The land will be enjoyed by the person E nominates in his will. The beneficiary under the will, however, or the next-of-kin if he dies intestate (*i.e.* without a will) have a claim to the land only through E. E could disappoint them by choosing another beneficiary in his will, or by selling or giving away the land in his lifetime. The essence of a right to land for ever or in perpetuity is not that the owner may enjoy the land personally for ever, but that he has the right to control the destination of the property on his death.

The difference where A is given land only for his lifetime is that he has no control over the destination of the property on his death. The land must go to someone on A's death. But that person is not chosen by A. Suppose that E is entitled to land (Greenacre) for ever, and chooses during his lifetime to give Greenacre to A for A's life. On A's death the land will revert to E, or if E by this time is dead, to whoever is entitled under his will or under the intestacy rules.

3. Present rights and future enjoyment

In the example given above, where E gives land to A for life, A has a present right to present enjoyment. He is entitled to the enjoyment of Greenacre during his own life. It is possible to place a value upon that right. It is not equal to the open market price which the right to Greenacre for ever would realise upon a sale. Instead, the value of A's right requires an actuarial calculation based on two main factors; the income value of the land and A's life expectancy. If Greenacre were producing an income of £1,000 per year and A could be expected to live for about 15 years, the value of his right would be about £7,400, ignoring inflation and taxation but assuming an interest rate on investments of 10 per cent. This is because if A were to invest £7,400 at 10 per cent. compound interest, he would be able to withdraw £1,000 each year for 15 years, at the end of which period his capital would be completely exhausted.

If the open market value of Greenacre is £10,000 and A's right is worth £7,400, we can value E's right to the property on A's death at £2,600. E has no right to the enjoyment of Greenacre during A's life, but on A's death he will be entitled to the whole income of £1,000 per year, and to the capital value of Greenacre of £10,000. £10,000 in 15 years time, though, is not worth £10,000 now. It is worth only the sum which, if invested now, would at compound interest accumulate to £10,000 by the end of that period. It will be found that £2,600 at 10 per cent. compound interest will do just that. So E's right to Greenacre is worth £2,600 now. That is the present value of E's right to future enjoyment. Since it is certain that A will die, it is certain that E will eventually become the full owner of Greenacre. That gives him a present right to future enjoyment. It can be bought, sold and disposed of by will.

4. Estates in land

The ownership of land consists of a number of elements. We have already seen that land is to be considered as space. The concept of *tenure* explains *how* one is entitled to that space. The duration of an interest in land is explained by the concept of *estates*. A person who has an estate in land has a right to land on certain terms for a period of time. At its best that period will be indefinite so that the estate gives a right to the land in perpetuity. On the other hand, a person may be entitled to land only for his own lifetime, or for a set number of years. There is an almost infinite variety of periods for which land can be held. This variety is based, however, upon only a handful of standard estates which can be modified by just three basic devices.

The standard estates fall into two groups, the estates of *freehold*, and the estates of *leasehold*. These estates are so called because historically they correspond with freehold and leasehold tenure. As we shall see, however, it is now possible to have a combination of freehold estate and leasehold tenure, a possibility which has enabled the creation of certain kinds of fee farm grant (see pp. 37–39). The estates of freehold are the fee simple, the life estate and the fee tail. They are explained below. The estates of leasehold are the term of years, the periodic tenancy and the tenancy at will. They are also explained below, but further discussion of leasehold interests will be found in Chapter 11. As will be seen in Chapter 16, the concept of estates is also used in relation to easements and profits.

B. The Freehold Estates

5. The fee simple

The fee simple is the most ample estate in land known to Irish law. It is a right to land in perpetuity which can be disposed of by will or by alienation *inter vivos*, and which failing either form of disposition, will pass to the holder's intestate successor. With the abolition of escheat (see p. 35) there is no longer any way in which a fee simple may come to an end. Prior to this, the fee simple came to an end if the holder died leaving no successor, and the right to the land passed to the feudal lord. The relationship between a lord and his tenant was, indeed, originally personal, and lasted only for the lifetime of the tenant. It very early became the practice, however, for the tenancy to be passed from father to son, and in the course of time this practice matured into a legal right. By degrees, partly through statute, and partly through judicial decision, the inheritability and alienability of the fee simple became established. Full recognition to the principle of alienability was given by the Statute of Quia Emptores 1290 which decreed that

> "from henceforth it shall be lawful for every freeman to sell at his own pleasure his lands and tenements, or part of them."

The principle has also been recognised judicially in a long line of cases invalidating conditions unduly restricting alienation (see p. 57).

Like all other estates, the fee simple may be modified in one of the ways described later. A fee simple which is not so modified is known as a fee simple absolute, and a *fee simple absolute in possession*, which is an unmodified fee simple conferring an immediate right to possession, is the nearest estate to full ownership of land. One writer, indeed, has said that "the term 'fee simple' is merely a 'dignified' and, therefore, deceptive nomenclature for ownership" (Kahn-Freund in his introduction to Renner, *The Institutions of Private Law and their Social Functions*).

There is always a fee simple estate in land, out of which estates of lesser duration may be carved. There can sometimes be more than one fee simple estate, either because of a division of legal and equitable rights in the land, or because of the effect of tenure.

6. Reversions and remainders

When a limited interest (such as a life estate) has been carved out of a fee simple, the fee simple still remains, as a present right to future enjoyment on the expiry of the limited interest. The fee simple is not in possession, for the holder of the limited interest has the right to possession. Instead it is designated a *fee simple in remainder* or a *fee simple in reversion*. It is in remainder if it has been disposed of at the time the limited interest was created, for what remains of the fee simple has been given away. It is in reversion if the fee simple was retained when the limited interest was created, for the land reverts to the tenant in fee simple on the expiry of the limited interest. It retains the designation of a reversion even if the tenant in fee simple subsequently disposes of it. Someone entitled to a reversion is known as a *reversioner*, and a person entitled to a remainder as a *remainderman*.

7. The life estate

The smallest estate of freehold is the life estate, a right in the land which lasts for a single lifetime only. In the usual case a person will hold a life estate for his own lifetime, but the duration of the estate may be governed by the lifetime of another person, in which case the estate is known as a life estate *pur autre vie*.

Since the duration of a life estate is defined by a personal equation (*e.g.* "the life of A") it might be thought that a life estate confers a purely personal right which is incapable of alienation. It became established, however, that the holder of a life estate did have a power of alienation, although because of the principle *nemo dat quod non habet* (no one may give what he does not have), he could not alter the duration of the estate by means of a transfer. If, for instance, land had been given to A for his life, A could transfer to B. B would, though, have an estate limited to the duration of A's life. This is one way in which an estate *pur autre vie* can arise. It can also arise by an express grant, as where land is given "to X for the life of Y." The person upon whose life the duration of a life estate is based is known as the *cestui que vie*. More than one *cestui que vie* can be named in a grant, so that land can be given, for instance, "to T for the lives of P, Q and R." This form of estate was the basis of the lease for lives renewable for ever which was once very common in Ireland (see p. 38).

A life estate *pur autre vie* does not come to an end on the death of the owner if the *cestui que vie* is still living. Special rules of descent, known as the rules of *occupancy* formerly governed entitlement to the interest on the death of a tenant *pur autre vie*, but these rules have now been abolished by the Administration of Estates Act (N.I.) 1955, s.1(3) and the Succession Act 1965, s.11(1). The ordinary rules of succession now apply (see Chapter 12).

8. Waste

The rights of a life tenant are more restricted than those of the holder of a fee simple since a balance has to be drawn between the holder of the life estate who has only a limited right to present enjoyment, and the reversioners or remaindermen who have the right to future enjoyment. Some of these restrictions are found in the rules of *waste*.

Somewhat misleadingly, waste is any act resulting in a change to the land, even if that change is an improvement. The reversioner or remainderman would, however, be unlikely to obtain the ordinary remedies of injunction or damages for improvements or *ameliorating waste* since no damage has been caused and the injunction being an equitable remedy, it lies within the discretion of the court to refuse it where the owner of a future interest is not prejudiced: *Doherty* v. *Allman* (1878).

It will often be a question of dispute whether a change amounts to an improvement. Where it amounts to a disimprovement, the holder of a future interest will normally be able to intervene. The life tenant may, for instance, have committed what is described as *voluntary waste*.

This is an injury to the land caused by a positive act, such as the demolition of a building. Taking timber from land not being used as a timber estate also amounted to waste at common law, although a life tenant was entitled to *estovers*, being the wood required for household fuel and repairs, and for agricultural purposes. The common law rules relating to timber (which in most areas comprised only oak, ash and elm at least 20 years old) have been significantly modified by statute (see Wylie, *Irish Land Law*, pp. 215–216). A tenant for life could be held liable in damages for voluntary waste, made liable to account for any profits made, or restrained by injunction from committing the waste. He would be so liable unless on the grant of his life estate he was exempted from liability for voluntary waste by an express statement such as, that the grant was made "without impeachment of waste." Even a tenant made *unimpeachable of waste* in this way would not be permitted to commit acts of wanton destruction. In *Vane* v. *Lord Barnard* (1716), Lord Barnard was the life tenant of Raby Castle in County Durham, and his son was entitled to an estate in the Castle on his death. Following a difference between the two of them, Lord Barnard directed his servants to strip the castle of all its lead, iron, glass, doors and boards. Notwithstanding that he had been made unimpeachable of waste, the court granted a mandatory injunction requiring him to restore these articles to the property. Wanton acts of this kind are called *equitable waste*, and it would require the very clearest words to exempt a life tenant from liability for such waste.

While a life tenant will, in the absence of an express exemption, be liable for voluntary waste, he will not be liable for *permissive waste*, that is, injuries caused by inaction, such as through failure to repair a building, unless an express obligation has been imposed upon him on the grant of his estate.

9. Settled Land Acts

At common law, as already explained above, a life tenant can deal only with his own estate, and this rule applied to such matters as the grant of leases and the raising of money by mortgage as well as to outright sales. The common law position has been very substantially affected by the Settled Land Acts, which are considered in Chapter 14. These Acts confer on a life tenant very extensive powers of dealing with the land including powers of sale and leasing.

10. The fee tail

The last of the three estates of freehold is the fee tail. This is a right in land which is limited to a person and his descendants. It passes from the original holder, the tenant in tail, by the ancient heirship rules to descendants of the original holder only. The descent of a fee tail is the only case where the ancient rules of inheritance survive the Succession Act 1965 and the Administration of Estates Act (N.I.) 1955. It was called a fee tail since, though it was inheritable (hence a *fee*), the inheritance was cut down (*cf.* the French *taillé*) to direct lineal descendants. This estate was not recognised at common law, and is the creation of the Statute De Donis Conditionalibus 1285. It is an unusual estate in that it was originally treated as if it were a series of successive life interests so that although it would continue for as long as descendants of the donee survived, neither the donee nor his descendants could alienate more than a right to the land during their own lifetime. This restriction upon alienation was a direct effect of the Statute De Donis.

11. Barring an entail

It was not until the fifteenth century that, with the connivance of the courts, a method of alienation, thereby "*barring the entail*" was invented. Through a fictitious court action or compromise approved by court, a tenant in tail was enabled to transfer to a purchaser an estate, called a *base fee*, with a duration as long as the fee tail would have continued; if the tenant in tail was in possession, or if he had the consent of the person in possession, he could go further, and confer a fee simple upon the purchaser, depriving the reversioners or remaindermen of their interest in the land. These fictitious court proceedings, known as fines and recoveries, became purely formal conveyancing devices. They were abolished by the Fines and Recoveries (Ireland) Act 1834. This introduced instead a new conveyancing device, the *disentailing assurance*. This grand title describes a conveyance which purports to transfer the fee simple in the land (which of course the tenant in tail does not have). By a statutory sleight of hand this conveyance operates magically to confer upon the purchaser an estate in the land which the tenant in tail never had. In order to be effectual to give the purchaser a fee simple, however, two conditions must be satisfied. The first is that if the tenant in tail is not in possession, the consent of the "*protector* of the settlement" must be obtained. The protector is the person (if any) in possession under a prior freehold estate, or a special protector appointed in the grant of the fee tail. If the consent of the protector is required, but is not obtained, the effect of a disentailing assurance will be to confer on the grantee only a base fee. The effect is thus much the same as it was before the Act when entails were barred by means of a fine or recovery.

12. General and special fees tail

The fee tail could (and still can) be modified in two special ways. The estate is known as a fee tail general where it is given to one person and that person's descendants. Where it is modified it is known as a fee tail special. One form of fee tail special is where the descent is confined to the issue of two people already married, or capable of marrying. Another form of the fee tail special is where the descent is confined only to male heirs (*i.e.* males able to trace an unbroken line of descent through males). This is known as a fee tail male. It is in theory possible to create a fee tail female with (probably) corresponding rules, but of this Challis (in *The Law of Real Property*, p. 287) has observed that

> "No motive can be imagined which would be likely to induce anyone to limit a fee tail to heirs female, though nothing is more common than the limitation of a fee tail to heirs male. The former kind of limitation was probably suggested by the latter; and it probably exists only in the logical imagination of text writers."

13. The base fee

As explained above, a base fee is the estate resulting from a fee tail which has not been completely barred owing to a failure to obtain the consent of the protector of the settlement. It is in essence an alienable fee tail. It lasts only as long as the original fee tail out of which it was created would have continued, but it can be converted into a fee simple in three ways. The first is by the holder of the base fee acquiring the fee simple from the reversioner or remainderman, in which event the base fee is enlarged by the Fines and Recoveries (Ireland) Act 1834 into a fee simple as if the consent of the protector had been obtained to a disentailing assurance. This statutory provision means that the holder of the base fee takes a fee simple which is not subject to any restrictions applying to the fee simple remainder or reversion.

The second way of enlarging a base fee is by the execution of a fresh disentailing assurance with the consent of the protector, or after the protectorship has ended. This fresh disentailing assurance must be executed by the person who would have been tenant in tail had the fee tail not been partially barred, even though he may have ceased to have any interest in the land. The holder of the base fee does not himself have a power of enlargement by this means.

The final way in which a holder of a base fee may enlarge his estate into a fee simple is by continuing in possession for 12 years following the end of the protectorship, for by the Statute of Limitations 1957, s.19 and the Statute of Limitations (N.I.) 1958, s.23, this is deemed to be adverse possession. The holder of the base fee is thereby enabled to acquire a fee simple by limitation. The person entitled to the fee simple reversion or remainder is only able to enforce his right if the base fee ends within this 12 year period by the original tenant in tail and all his descendants dying.

14. Rights of a tenant in tail

Like a life tenant, a tenant in tail has only a limited estate in the land. He is not, however, subject to liability for waste, so that the restriction on alienation is the main factor distinguishing him from a tenant in fee simple. Even this restriction, as we have seen, may be overcome by a disentailing assurance, and a tenant in tail wishing to enlarge his own interest into a fee simple may do so by a disentailing assurance conveying the property to another person to the use of himself in fee simple. This use would be executed by the Statute of Uses (Ireland) 1634. An entail can only be barred, however, during the lifetime of the tenant in tail. There is not in Ireland (although there is in England) any power to bar an entail by will. There are also some exceptional cases where an entail may not be barred. In England, a few settled estates, such as the Blenheim Estate owned by the Duke of Marlborough, are subject to express statutory prohibition on disentailment, but no such statutory restrictions are believed to apply in Ireland. A tenant in tail "after possibility of issue extinct" is also unable to bar his entitled interest. This kind of tenant in tail is very rare indeed: such a tenant can only exist where the descent of a fee tail special is confined to the issue of a man and a woman, and one of the two has died before any children are born, so that there is no longer any possibility of issue.

15. Abolition of the fee tail

The fee tail was in not infrequent use up until the turn of this century. Amongst the landed gentry it was seen as a way of keeping land within the family, and the fee tail was a central element of the *strict settlement* (see Chapter 14). The utility of the fee tail in the twentieth century has, however, been very much reduced by the impact of capital taxation, and it would be extremely uncommon for a landowner to seek to entail his property. It is seriously open to question whether the archaic machinery of the law governing entails can justifiably be preserved for such rare cases in a modern system of land law. In the English property legislation of 1925, assimilation between real and personal property was achieved by making personal property entailable. Is it not time in Ireland to assimilate the law of real and personal property in this respect by abolishing the fee tail? This has been proposed for Northern Ireland by the Land Law Working Group.

16. A diagrammatic representation of freehold estates

It is possible to represent estates diagramatically. The fee simple can be shown as a ribbon which has a beginning but which has no end. It has a beginning because we can commence our look at the fee simple at any date, such as the date upon which, in the example in Figure 7.1 below, E acquired the fee simple. The ribbon has no end since the fee simple continues for ever, and time is represented by the horizontal dimension. The vertical axis represents the extent of a person's rights. The point at the bottom represents the right to possession, the top the residual rights. On E's sale of the fee simple to F in 1980, the transfer is shown as a transfer of E's rights to F: since the abolition of subinfeudation, F is substituted for E for all purposes of title following the date of the sale.

Figure 7.1: The fee simple

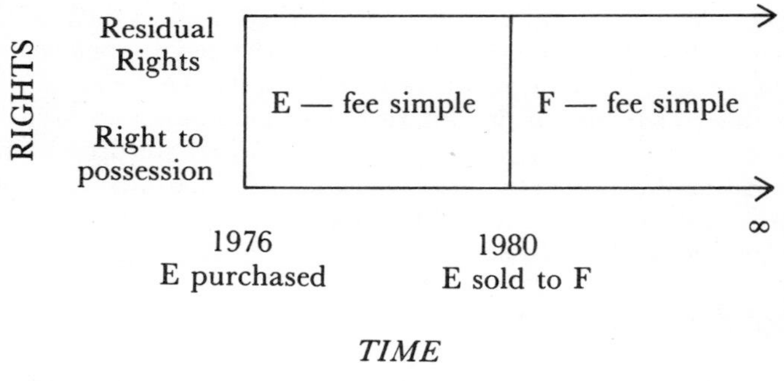

Estates of a shorter duration than the fee simple can be represented as "carved out" of the fee simple. In Figure 7.2 E owns a fee simple subject to a life estate which he created in favour of L in 1979. L has the right to possession, but he does not have such extensive rights as a person with the fee simple. He is subject, for instance, to the rules of waste. E has no immediate right to possession from 1979 until L's death, but he retains rights in the land (such as the right to prevent waste), and the right to possession will revert to him on L's death, which we know will occur before the end of time.

Figure 7.2: E has a fee simple subject to L's life estate

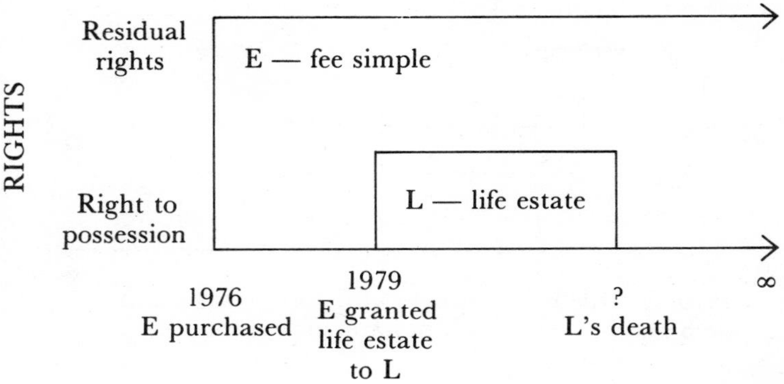

Figure 7.3 shows a more complicated arrangement. Here E in 1980 granted a life estate to L and a fee tail to F. The assumption is made that L will die before F and all his descendants. In this event L has a right in possession, but on his death F (or one of his descendants) will take possession by virtue of the fee tail remainder. The fee simple has still not been fully disposed of, so E retains a fee simple reversion.

Figure 7.3: E has the fee simple, and grants a life estate to L and a fee tail to F

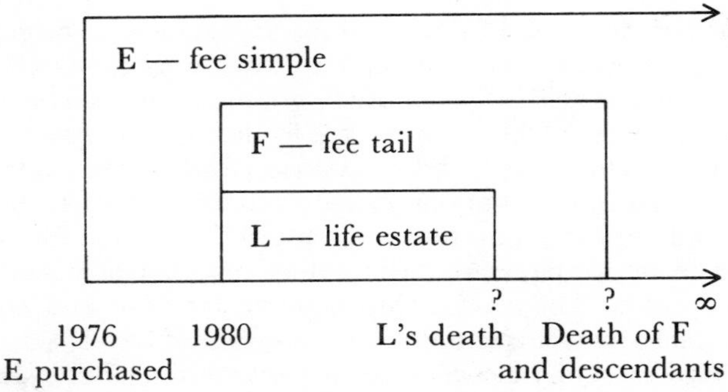

It is, of course, possible that F might die without descendants, or that he and all his descendants might die during L's lifetime. In this event he and his descendants will never take possession. This possibility is shown by Figure 7.4.

Figure 7.4: E has the fee simple, and grants a life estate to L and a fee tail to F

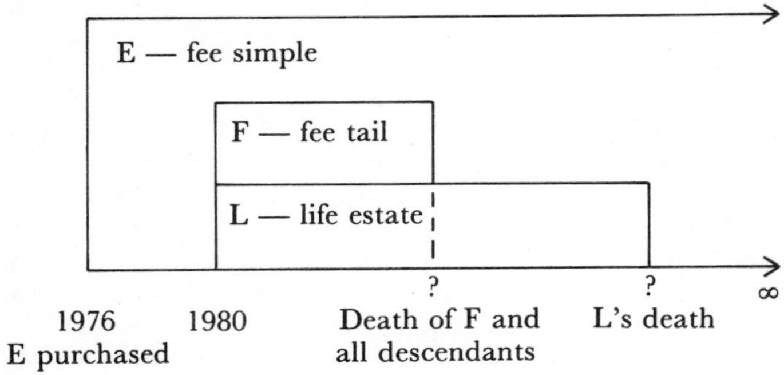

Even though they never in fact take possession, this is something which can be discovered only in the light of actual events, and until F and his descendants die, they have the next best right to possession after L. In all of these examples, the law's treatment of a vested right to possession in the future as a present right to future enjoyment is shown by E and F having continuing rights even though their right to possession is deferred.

C. The Leasehold Estates

17. Leasehold estates

Only the fee simple, the fee tail and the life estate were originally recognised as estates by the common law. They were the estates for which land could be held in free tenure (free and common socage), the only significant form of tenure under the feudal system to survive to the present day. They were therefore estates of freehold. As explained in Chapter 6, leases were not recognised at common law as creating estates in land until about the fifteenth century. Before that they were considered to be simple contracts creating only personal and not proprietary rights. The relationship between landlord and tenant remains essentially contractual—see Deasy's Act 1860, s.3—but leases are now recognised as creating distinct estates. That is, leases are rights to the possession of land for a time which exist as rights in the land itself, and not merely as rights enforceable only where there is privity of contract. Leasehold estates are generally classified into three kinds: the tenancy at will, the periodic tenancy, and the term of years.

Hello!!

18. Tenancy at will

The tenancy at will is in a sense not an estate at all. It exists where there is an intention to create a relationship of landlord and tenant, but where the parties have made no agreement express or implied about the duration of the relationship: *Bellew* v. *Bellew* (1983). The tenancy (subject to any statutory restrictions) can be determined without any minimum period of notice by either party at any time (*i.e.* at their will). Since, therefore, it confers no right to the land for a period of time it may be denied that it is an estate. A tenancy at will is the relationship of leasehold tenure without any estate.

Even though a tenancy at will may originally have begun without any express agreement as to duration, if rent is paid and accepted on a periodic basis, then a periodic tenancy will arise by implication, unless, as will only exceptionally be the case, the parties expressly agreed only to create a tenancy at will: *Manfield and Sons Ltd.* v. *Botchin* (1970). In most cases temporary arrangements for the use of land are created by way of licence rather than by tenancy at will. The existence of a tenancy at will is not to be inferred from the simple fact that the owner of land has allowed another person to take possession: *Cobb* v. *Lane* (1952).

19. Periodic tenancy

A periodic tenancy is a lease where the relationship of landlord and tenant continues for a succession of fixed periods, such as from year to year, from month to month or from week to week, until such time as it is determined by the appropriate period of notice by either party. A periodic tenancy may either be created expressly, or be implied from the payment and receipt of rent on a periodic basis. The notice required to determine a periodic tenancy is normally a whole period (a week or a month, or as the case may be) except in the case of a tenancy from year to year, where half a year's notice is usually sufficient. A longer or shorter period of notice may be expressly agreed to, although the right to determine a periodic tenancy by notice may not be entirely excluded: see *Bream's Property Investment Co. Ltd.* v. *Stroulger* (1948). There are also some statutory provisions which apply to certain kinds of periodic tenancy. Under the Housing (Private Rented Dwellings) Act 1982, s.10, for instance, a protected tenant wishing to give up possession must give his landlord not less than one month's notice in writing, and in Northern Ireland, under article 62 of the Rent (N.I.) Order 1978, at least four weeks notice must be given to determine a tenancy of a dwelling-house. Except by special agreement a tenancy cannot be brought to an end by notice except at the expiry of a full period, although a number of cases suggest that a weekly tenancy may be determined by at least one week's notice expiring on any day of the week: *e.g. Skelly* v. *Thompson* (1911) *contra Queen's Club Gardens Estates Ltd.* v. *Bignell* (1924). An agricultural or pastoral tenancy requires a full year's notice, but this notice may expire on any gale day (*i.e.* day on which rent is due): Notice to Quit (Ireland) Act 1876 s.1.

20. Term of years

A term of years is a lease which continues for a fixed period specified at the outset. The period may be comparatively short (perhaps a weekend, for the letting of a holiday cottage) or it may be comparatively long, as of 99 years for a residential lease, or even 999 years or more. The *Guinness Book of Records* states that the longest known lease concerns part of the cattle market in Dublin which was leased by John Jameson to Dublin City Corporation for 100,000 years from January 1863. A lease for a term of years comes to an end automatically at the end of the fixed period unless the lease expressly contains a provision conferring a right to a renewal, or permitting the premature termination of the lease by notice. For perpetually renewable leases see Chapter 6.

A tenant who remains in possession of the land (holds over) on the expiry of a lease for a fixed term without the consent of the landlord, but before the landlord seeks to recover possession, is known as a *tenant at sufferance*. A tenant at sufferance is not liable for rent as such, but is liable to a claim for "use and occupation." For the possibility of a tenant at sufferance acquiring a title against his landlord by adverse possession see Chapter 13.

21. Diagrammatic representation of leasehold estates

Figure 7.5: E has a fee simple and in 1980 grants a lease to T for 15 years

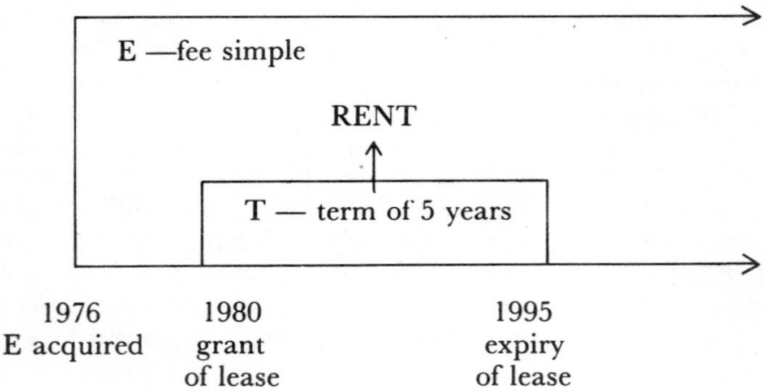

Leasehold estates can be represented diagrammatically in the same way as freehold estates: the major distinction is that since a term of years has a certain duration, it is possible to predict in advance the date of its determination. Thus in Figure 7.5, we can show that where E, the owner of the fee simple, has granted a lease to T for 15 years commencing in 1980, T's leasehold interest will expire in 1995. The residue of the fee simple remaining after the grant of a lease is always known as the reversion. Successive leases can be granted. Two methods are possible. One is to grant the second lease to commence on the expiry of the first. This is known as a reversionary lease. In the example above this would mean that E, having granted a lease to T expiring in 1995, could grant a lease to V commencing in 1995. The other method is that E may grant V a second lease which runs concurrently with the first, that is, a lease which commences at some date between 1980 and 1985. This is known as a lease of the reversion. The effect of such a lease is to make V the landlord of T, and as such, entitled to collect the rent during the currency of T's lease, and when T's lease expires, V will be entitled to take possession: see Figure 7.6.

Figure 7.6: E grants a fifteen year lease to T from 1980 and a twenty year lease to V from 1982

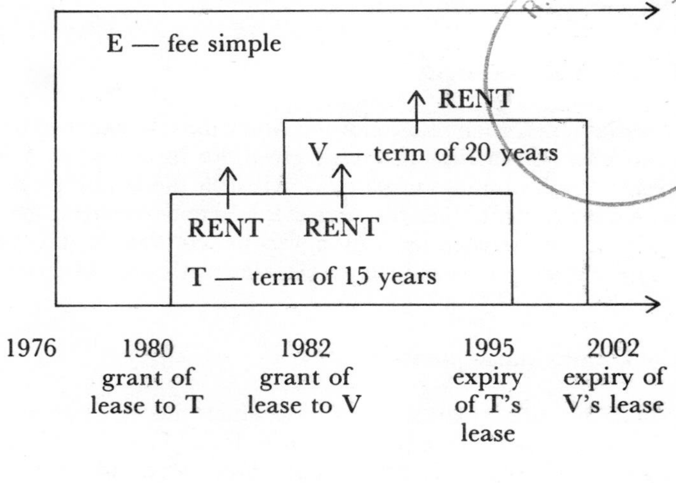

D. Compound and Modified Estates

22. Compound estates

It is possible for leasehold and freehold estates to be combined to produce a compound estate. Only the life estate will normally be compounded in this way (but see *Twaddle* v. *Murphy*, 1881). Three permutations are possible. First, the freehold and leasehold elements of the estate may be made consecutive, as where land is given to A for the life of B plus a further period of 21 years. Second, the two periods may run jointly, as where land is given to A for 21 years or for the life of B, whichever shall first expire. Third, the periods may be concurrent, as where land is given to A for the life of B or for 21 years, whichever shall be the longer. Compound interests are now uncommon, but they were sometimes used in the eighteenth and nineteenth centuries in the grant of leases, for when the right to vote was confined to freeholders, a lease for lives and years was considered a freehold so long as the *cestui que vie* was still alive.

23. Modified estates

The three main freehold estates and the term of years can be modified by way of conditions precedent and subsequent or by making the estates determinable. These three devices, when coupled with the basic estates, enable the creation of an almost infinite variety of estates.

24. Conditions precedent

A condition precedent is a condition which must be satisfied before an interest in land arises. If land is given, for instance "to A if he marries," A will obtain an assured interest in the land only if and when he marries. Until then his interest is said to be *contingent*, for if he dies without marrying, he will never be entitled to the land. Contingent interests are subject to certain restrictions discussed in Chapter 8.

25. Conditions subsequent

A condition subsequent is a condition which cuts short an interest which would otherwise have continued for a longer period. An example would be a gift of land "to A provided that he does not marry Y." At common law an estate *defeasible by condition subsequent* does not come to an end automatically on the condition being broken or taking place. Instead it continued until the grantor determined the estate by re-entry upon the land, either physically, or by way of action. Where a conditional interest of this kind is created by way of a use or trust, however, the occurrence of the event automatically operates to shift the beneficial interest from one beneficiary to another.

26. Determinable interests

A determinable interest is an interest which continues only until a certain event occurs. An example would be a gift "to A until he marries." On A's marriage, by the very definition of the interest conveyed, his right to the property automatically ceases. He does not have a longer interest which is liable to be defeated. He has an interest which is defined to continue only so long as a state of affairs continues. Such an interest is sometimes called an interest determinable by limitation.

27. Conditions and determining events distinguished

The distinction between a determining event and a condition subsequent is very narrow. It has been described by Lord Porter M.R. as "little short of disgraceful to our jurisprudence": *Re King's Trust* (1892); see also *Re Sharp's Settlement Trusts* (1973). To a certain extent the distinction is a matter of words, for depending upon the terminology, the same event may operate either as a condition, or as a determining event. The words "until," "during," "whilst" or "so long as" all connote a determinable interest. Expressions such as "on condition that," "provided that," or "but if" would create a condition subsequent. Some important consequences flow from the distinction, however. The mode of termination is one. Another concerns the interest retained by the grantor. On the grant of a fee simple defeasible by condition subsequent the grantor retains a *right of entry* for condition broken, which while it could not be disposed of at common law, was made devisable by the Wills Act 1837, s.3 and alienable *inter vivos* by the Real Property Act 1845, s.6. The remaining right of the grantor of a determinable fee simple, termed a *possibility of reverter,* probably remains subject to the common law rule that it cannot be disposed of *inter vivos* , although it will pass under the ordinary intestacy rules on the death of the grantor and the case of *Pemberton* v. *Barnes* (1899) suggests that it may be disposed of by will.

A more important distinction between conditions and determining events relates to their validity. Conditions have been treated more stringently by the courts than determining events. A condition totally or substantially restricting alienation is void, whereas a gift of property *until* alienation is valid: *Byrne* v. *Byrne* (1953); *Brandon* v. *Robinson* (1811). Similarly conditions in total restraint of marriage are void, while a gift *until* marriage is valid: *Duddy* v. *Gresham* (1878). In relation to other rules of public policy, conditions have been less leniently treated than determining events. A reason may be that if a condition is void, the estate to which it was attached is made absolute, as if the condition had been struck out with a blue pencil. Where a determining event is void for uncertainty or as against public policy, the whole interest fails.

E. Rules Governing Estates

28. Rules governing estates

It has already been observed that there are some restrictions on the creation of contingent interests (see p. 56). These restrictions are discussed in the next chapter. Apart from these restrictions, there is virtually no limit to the variety of estates in land which are capable of creation.

It is possible, however, to identify a number of rules concerning estates. The primary rule is that land having a perpetual existence, there will always be a fee simple, although lesser (or *particular*) estates may be created out of this fee simple. A second, subsidiary rule is that estates are ranked according to the order in which the holders of the estates are entitled to possession. The fee tail does not automatically prevail over a life estate. If land is given to A for life, and then to B in fee tail, B is not entitled to possession until A dies. The third rule flows from this. One person's estate may expire before he is ever entitled to possession. If in the example just given, B's fee tail is expectant on A's life estate, the fee tail will never vest in possession (*i.e.* never give anyone a right to possession) if B and all his descendants, if any, die during A's lifetime.

A fourth rule is that estates may be created out of estates less than the fee simple, but subject to any powers under the Settled Land Acts (see Chapter 14), the maximum duration of such an estate will be the duration of the estate from which it was carved. Thus, again in the example above, if A, who has a life estate, conveys a life estate to B, B will have a right in the land which will last for his own lifetime, or the lifetime of A, whichever is the shorter. Similarly, if A had granted T a lease for 1,000 years, that lease would automatically end on A's death.

A further point which should be noted is that there can be more than one fee simple extant in relation to the same land. In the case of a fee farm grant, the possessor of the land has a perpetual right to possession, or a fee simple in the land. That land is held, however, subject to an obligation to pay a perpetual rent. The person entitled to the rent has a fee simple estate in the rent, which is itself treated as land for certain purposes. More than one fee simple may exist also where there is a trust of land, for the concept of estates applies both to legal interests in land and to equitable interests in land. The position of a squatter in wrongful possession of land also is that he has a fee simple, although there is also a rightful fee simple proprietor with better title. Although the squatter can be evicted by the rightful owner, so far as anyone else is concerned, he has a right to the land for ever (see Chapter 13).

29. An algebra of estates

Taking the fee simple as a right to the possession of land for ever, with a power to alienate that right, conferring on the purchaser a power of alienation, Professor Bernard Rudden has devised a notation in which estates can be represented by formulae. The fee simple absolute in possession, for instance, is shown by the formula

$$a\infty(p\infty)$$

where	a	=	power to alienate
and	p	=	right to possession
and	∞	=	infinity and eternity

A life estate given to A, who has a life expectancy shown by 1, is shown by the formula

$$a\infty(p1)$$

and it follows that a fee simple expectant on this life estate is shown by the formula

$$a\infty(p\infty-1)$$

The notation can be extended to cover leases and other interests in land. For those who are comfortable with the use of formulae, this algebraic notation shows at once the symmetry of the doctrine of estates and the simplicity of its structure beneath an apparently complex appearance. For further reading on the algebra of estates, see Lawson and Rudden, *The Law of Property* (2nd ed.) pp. 88–95 and Rudden, "Notes Towards a Grammar of Property" [1980] Conv. 325.

8 Future Interests

A. General

1. Future Interests

We have already seen how the doctrine of estates enables the creation of rights in land in which enjoyment of possession is deferred until some date in the future. An interest in land conferring a right to possession only at some future date is said to be a *future interest*. It may well be a present interest in the sense that it is a present right to future enjoyment (see p. 42), but the expression future interest is a convenient shorthand.

2. Vested and contingent interests

Interests in land may be either *vested* or *contingent;* and vested interests may be either *vested in possession* or *vested in interest.*

An interest in land is vested where the person entitled to the interest can be indentified by name and there are no outstanding conditions to be satisfied before he is entitled to possession, save the expiry of any prior interests in the land. An interest vested in possession is one under which a person is immediately entitled to possession. An immediate right to possession must by definition be vested in possession. An estate vested in interest is one where, although the person taking is identified, and there are no conditions to satisfy, some other person has a prior right to possession. Thus if land is given to A for life, with remainder to B in fee simple, both A and B have vested interests. A's life estate is vested in possession. B's remainder is vested in interest.

A contingent interest is an interest which is given to a person who cannot be identified by name, or who must satisfy some outstanding condition, or both. For instance, a gift "to the eldest child of A living at his death" creates a contingent interest since until A dies the identity of his eldest surviving son cannot be ascertained. Similarly, a gift "to B, if he qualifies as a solicitor" is contingent unless B is already a solicitor, since he must satisfy that condition. In both the examples above it may be that the gift will fail, in the first case because A may have no children, or because they all die before him, and in the second case because B may never have the fortune to become a solicitor.

3. Vested interests liable to be divested

In the case of doubt as to whether a gift is vested or contingent, the interpretation which is preferred is the one under which the gift is vested. It is also possible for a gift to be vested, but to be liable to being divested (*e.g.* subject to defeasance by condition subsequent). A gift, for instance "to A, but if he dies under the age of 35, to B," would be construed as giving A an immediate interest, vested in possession, but liable to be taken from him (divested) in favour of B should A die before the age of 35.

4. Alienability of contingent interests

At common law it was held that a right in property could be transferred only if it was a present right. If it had no present existence, it was incapable of transfer. Contingent interests were viewed as only possibilities of entitlement to property (since the condition might not be satisfied) and hence were inalienable. By the Wills Act 1837, s.3, re-enacted in Succession Act 1965, s.76, contingent interests could be disposed of by will, and by the Real Property Act 1845, s.6 they could be disposed of by deed. A mere *expectancy,* however, cannot be assigned. An expectancy is a mere expectation of a possible benefit, not based upon any operative disposition. An example would be the expectation of a grandchild, the only surviving relation of his grandfather, to receive his grandfather's property on death. This expectation could be defeated at any time if the grandfather made a will leaving the property to others.

5. Reversions and remainders

The distinction between reversions and remainders has already been alluded to (see p. 44). A reversion is the residue retained by the grantor out of his own fee simple or other estate when he parts with less than his whole estate. A reversion is, in other words, what is left over of a larger estate after the expiry of a lesser estate derived out of it. The lesser estate, if taking effect in possession, is known as a *particular estate* since it consists of part only of the larger estate. Thus, in a gift by E, a person entitled to a fee simple, of a life estate to A, A's life estate is a particular estate, but since it does not dispose of the entirety of the fee simple, E has a fee simple reversion. Reversions need no express creation, for they arise by operation of law, and they are always vested in interest.

A remainder is an estate expressed to commence after the determination of a particular estate created by the same disposition. Thus if E gives land "to A for life, and subject thereto, to B in fee simple," B's fee simple is a remainder. A remainder cannot arise by operation of law, and must be expressly created.

A remainder and a reversion may both arise from the same disposition. If E, who has a fee simple, makes a grant "to A for life, then to B for life," but makes no grant of the fee simple, A takes a life estate in possession, B a life estate in remainder, and E has a fee simple reversion.

Remainders, unlike reversions, may be either vested or contingent.

B. The Common Law Remainder Rules

6. Contingent remainders

The common law's recognition of contingent remainders was slow. At first, mediaeval lawyers' predisposition for presentiating future interests (*i.e.* treating them as present rights to future enjoyment) meant that contingent interests were not recognised at all because of the difficulty (even impossibility) of saying who was entitled to a contingent remainder. When, finally, by the mid-fifteenth century contingent remainders were accepted as valid at common law, they were accepted only under rules which ensured that there would always be a person entitled to seisin (that is a person entitled to a freehold estate in possession: see p. 6), for as it was said; "the common law abhors an abeyance of seisin." This applied equally to both vested and contingent remainders. There are four main rules governing the validity of remainders, two of which are concerned with the continuity of seisin. Such is the inertia in the law of property that with one exception these rules continue to apply to legal remainders, although such remainders are now very rare indeed. The rules do not apply to gifts arising under trusts or under conveyances which employ the Statute of Uses (see p. 66) nor to gifts by will (see *Matthew Manning's Case* (1609); *Porter* v. *Bradley* (1789); and see Section 13 below).

7. Remainder must be supported by particular estate

The first common law remainder rule was that a conveyance had to confer an immediate right to seisin. It could not create a future interest unless there was an immediate particular freehold estate carrying seisin in the meantime. This rule could be expressed in the terms "a remainder must be supported by a particular estate of freehold." A conveyance "to A for life, remainder to B in fee simple" would satisfy this rule, but a conveyance "to B in fee simple upon the death of A," being an attempt to convey an estate only on A's death, with no supporting estate in the meantime, would be void. A purported conveyance, taking effect only upon the death of the grantor, while void *as a conveyance* under the common law remainder rules, could sometimes be treated as a will: *In the Goods of Slevin* (1938) *cf. In the Goods of Halpin* (1874).

Since leasehold estates were not considered to carry seisin, at common law an estate could not be granted to take effect on the determination of a term of years. A grant "to A for 21 years, remainder to B in fee simple" was void as to the purported grant to B just as if the grant had been simply "to B in fee simple 21 years from this date."

8. Remainder must vest in possession on expiry of particular estate

The first common law remainder rule was concerned with an abeyance of seisin at the time of a grant. The second rule insists that there should be no interval in which no one is entitled to seisin between the ending of one estate and the commencement of the next. If it was certain from the outset that an abeyance of seisin would occur before a remainder vested in possession, the remainder would be void. For instance, in a grant "to A for life, remainder to such children of his as shall attain the age of 21 years after his death," the remainder is automatically void since by the terms of the grant, no child can take an interest vested in possession on the death of A.

In other cases, it may not be possible to tell with certainty from the outset whether there will be an abeyance of seisin. For instance, in a grant "to A for life, remainder to his first son to attain the age of 21 years," no abeyance of seisin would occur if a child of A reached 21 before A's death. There would be an abeyance if A died before any son became 21. In a case of this kind it was permitted to "wait and see" what happened, and to decide upon the validity of the grant in the light of actual events.

The "wait and see" rule has now been abolished (see Section 16 below).

9. Remainder may not defeat particular estate

It was a rule of the common law that the right of entry to determine an estate defeasible by condition subsequent (see p. 56) could be exercised only by the grantor. Thus in a conveyance "to A for life, but if B shall marry, then to B in fee simple immediately," the right of entry to determine A's life estate could be exercised only by the grantor. If he did re-enter the fee simple reverted to the grantor, and B's remainder was defeated. But if the grantor did not exercise his right of entry, A's life estate would continue, and on its natural termination, B would be entitled in remainder. The remainder was not, therefore, void, but it could not take effect by cutting short a prior freehold estate.

This rule did not apply to a particular estate determinable by limitation (see p. 57) so that the gift above could have been fully effective had it been worded "to A for life or until B marries, then to B in fee simple."

10. A remainder after a fee simple is void

Again, at common law, a remainder could not be created to take effect after a fee simple. By making a grant in fee simple, the grantor exhausted the entirety of his estate, so that there was nothing out of which a remainder could be created. The same rule applied even in the cases of fees simple determinable by limitation and defeasible by condition subsequent. The right retained by the grantor after creating a determinable fee simple (see p. 57) was just a *possibility of reverter,* and after creating a fee simple defeasible by condition subsequent, he retained only a *right of entry* for condition broken. These rights could, like contingent interests, be disposed of by will or deed following the Wills Act 1837 and the Real Property Act 1845, but they could not be given to some person other than the grantor at the moment of their creation.

11. Destruction of contingent remainders

Contingent remainders had a precarious existence at common law, and a number of ways were invented to enable them to be artifically destroyed by the person entitled to the particular estate, sometimes in collusion with any vested remaindermen. A conveyancing device involving a trust was frequently used to prevent artificial destruction, and artificial destruction of contingent remainders was finally abolished by three statutes, the Real Property Limitation Act 1833, the Real Property Act 1845 and the Contingent Remainders Act 1877.

C. Future Interests in Equity

12. Shifting and springing interests in equity

Equity did not follow the common law by requiring compliance with the legal remainder rules. Seisin was a common law concept of no concern in equity for wherever equitable estates existed, they did so under a use so that there would always be someone entitled at common law who had seisin. This freed equity to allow the creation of two kinds of interest which the common law prohibited: shifting interests and springing interests.

A *shifting interest* is one in which, on the occurrence of some event, beneficial entitlement shifts from one person to another. An example would be a conveyance "to X in fee simple to the use of A in fee simple, but if B marries, to the use of B in fee simple." Had this been drawn as a common law conveyance it would be invalid for two reasons: for containing a remainder after a fee simple, and for containing a remainder which is to take effect by cutting short the prior estate. In equity, however, it is valid. X would hold the legal estate as feoffee to uses for the benefit of A or B in the way directed. Since the uses declared are directions to X as to how the property is to be held by him, there is no need for X or B to "enter" upon A's estate in order to determine it should B marry.

A *springing interest* is an estate which "springs up" in the future, without any express beneficial interest being declared in the meanwhile. This kind of interest is void at common law by reason of having no particular estate to support it (see Section 7, above) but once again the interposition of a use enables the creation of the interest in equity. Thus gifts "to X in fee simple to the use in fee simple of any wife whom A may marry" (a person as yet unidentified), or "to Y in fee simple to the use of A for life and five years from his death, to his children in fee simple" would confer valid equitable interests upon A's wife and children respectively, once they could be identified. Equity overcame the difficulty of identifying who was entitled to the beneficial interest in the property during the intervals when no beneficiary had been expressly named by the device of the resulting use (see p. 109): in the absence of any expressly declared use, the beneficial interest resulted or returned to the grantor.

13. Restrictions on equitable interests

The common law remainder rules did not apply to future interests created under a use, nor do they apply to their modern equivalent, future interests created under a trust. Similarly, gifts by will now take effect in equity only and so are not governed by the legal remainder rules (see Sections 6 to 9, above) although previously, under the rule in *Purefoy* v. *Rogers* some gifts by will were treated as creating legal contingent remainders (see Section 16, below). Such interests are, however, subject to the modern rule against perpetuities, which is discussed below.

D. Legal Executory Interests

14. The effect of the Statute of Uses

The effect of the Statute of Uses (Ireland) 1634 upon the creation of future interests was most important. Under the Statute, equitable interests in freehold land subsisting under a use were converted into the equivalent legal estates or interests (see p. 12). It was held that the execution of uses (*i.e.* their completion by conversion into legal interests) enabled the creation of legal interests which would not have been valid if they had to comply with the legal remainder rules. Legal interests created by means of a use executed by the Statute of Uses are known as *legal executory interests.*

15. Words required for creation of legal executory interests

It is essential for the creation of a legal executory interest *inter vivos* that a conveyance should contain words imposing a use for without this, the Statute of Uses cannot apply. in the case of gifts by will, a more liberal attitude was adopted following the Statute. Even if the words "to the use of" were not employed, a gift by will which would not have been valid under the common law remainder rules would be given effect to as an executory interest.

Under modern succession legislation, wills no longer operate to confer legal interests in real property in the beneficiaries named immediately upon the death of the person making a will. Instead, the property passes to the personal representatives of the deceased to discharge his liabilities and then pass on any surplus to the beneficiaries. As a result the interests of beneficiaries under a will are now equitable interests only. They are not governed by any of the rules relating to legal remainders or legal executory interests, but they are subject to the rule against perpetuities (below). Even when the personal representatives complete a gift by will by a transfer of the legal estate to the beneficiaries it has been held that this does not alter the original equitable character of the gift so as to import the legal remainder or legal executory interest rules: *Re Freme* (1891).

16. The Rule in Purefoy v. Rogers

Under a somewhat arbitrary rule known as the rule in *Purefoy* v. *Rogers* (1671), legal executory interests were required to comply with the common law remainder rules unless the result of this would be to make them void *ab initio*. The rule did not therefore affect the validity of legal executory interests which would have been valid legal remainders, nor those which would inevitably fail as legal remainders. But the rule did affect legal executory interests which as legal remainders would have been governed by the "wait and see" rule, (see Section 8, above). By requiring these interests to comply with the legal remainder rules, the gift over would be void if, in the events which occurred, it did not vest in possession on the expiry of the particular estate. Thus a gift by will or in a conveyance to uses "to A for life, with remainder to his first child to attain the age of 21 years" was valid under the rule in *Purefoy* v. *Rogers* only if a child reached the age of 21 within A's lifetime.

Apart from some doubts arising from its wording, section 1 of the Contingent Remainders Act 1877 effectively abolished the rule in *Purefoy* v. *Rogers* by validating contingent remainders to which the "wait and see" rule applied. The method of operation of the section is to turn contingent remainders invalidated by the "wait and see" rule into executory interests; the effect is thus to reverse the process of conversion required by the rule in *Purefoy* v. *Rogers*. The remainder would only be saved if it was valid as an executory interest, and so it would have to comply with the rule against perpetuities. Furthermore the Act did not affect the rules that remainders could not be created after a fee simple, without a particular estate, or to take effect by defeating the particular estate.

E. Rules Against Remoteness

17. Restrictions on the creation of future interests

A recurrent preoccupation of the law has been the quest to balance the desire of individuals to determine the future destination of their property and the principle of public policy that property should be freely alienable. The application of the rule of public policy can be seen in the common law's initial rejection of contingent remainders and in the rejection of fetters on alienation imposed by way of conditions subsequent (see p. 57). Other rules have, from time to time, been designed to guard against dispositions of property tying that property up for too long into the future.

Some of these rules have been short-lived. The most important to survive to this day is the modern rule against perpetuities, but one other rule, the rule in *Whitby* v. *Mitchell*, requires mention.

18. The rule in Whitby v. Mitchell

The rule in *Whitby* v. *Mitchell* (1890) appears to have been devised to prevent the creation of unbarrable entails by means of a series of successive life interests. The rule invalidated remainders given to the issue of an unborn person where the unborn person himself took an estate by the same disposition. A concise statement of the rule is:

> "If an interest in realty is given to an unborn person, any remainder to his issue is void, together with all subsequent limitation."

Thus in a gift "to A for life, remainder to A's first born son for life, remainder to that son's first born son for life, remainder to B in fee simple," the remainders to A's son's son and to B would be void if at the time of the gift A had no son.

The rule applied only to real property. It certainly applied to legal remainders, but it is unclear whether it applied to legal executory interests or to future interests in equity. Although never directly applied in Ireland, the rule probably applied here (see *Peyton* v. *Lambert*, 1858), but it has now been abolished as regards Northern Ireland by the Perpetuities Act (N.I.) 1966, s.15.

In the case of gifts by will, remainders void under the rule in *Whitby* v. *Mitchell* could be saved by an application *cy-près* (that is, as closely as possible). The cy-près doctrine had only a very limited application. If the will created a gift to an unborn person for life, with remainder to his children successively in tail, or to his issue by means of a perpetual series of life estates, the court could give effect to a testator's intention by treating the gift as a gift to the unborn child in tail. The cy-près rule has probably not survived in the Republic of Ireland since the rule introduced by section 95 of the Succession Act 1965 that a fee tail can be created in a will only by the use of strict technical language: see p. 135.

F. The Rule Against Perpetuities

19. Origin of the rule

When equity permitted the creation of future interests which did not comply with the legal remainder rules, there was a real possibility that gifts could have been made under which entitlement to the property could remain uncertain for many years. To prevent this, the judges introduced rules to limit the time within which contingent gifts must become vested. This ensured that the entire interest in the property would be alienable by agreement between the beneficiaries at the end of this period at the latest, for while an interest remains contingent, it may not be possible to identify the beneficiary. The period chosen for the rule against perpetuities was one taken by analogy from the strict settlement, the form of common law gift used to keep land within the family. In the strict settlement land was given to a living person for life, with remainder in tail to his unborn children. The maximum period for which a strict settlement could tie up the land was a generation plus 21 years, for on the death of the life tenant, the child entitled to the estate tail would be able to alienate the fee simple by means of a disentailing assurance once he had reached the age of majority. The perpetuity period therefore became a life in being plus a further period of 21 years.

20. Development of the rule against perpetuities

The rule against perpetuities had a slow development, and it was not until the early nineteenth century that it became settled. The common law rule continues to apply in the Republic of Ireland, but important statutory changes made by the Perpetuities Act (N.I.) 1966 apply in Northern Ireland. These are dealt with in Part G of this chapter.

The rule against perpetuities applies to all forms of future interest, subject to some specific exceptions, and with some doubt as to whether it applies to legal contingent remainders. The balance of judicial opinion in Ireland seems to be that contingent remainders, being governed by their own rules of earlier origin, do not need to comply with the rule against perpetuities: *Attorney-General* v. *Cummins* (1906); *Walsh* v. *Wightman* (1927); *Cole* v. *Sewell* (1843); but *cf. Re Ashforth* (1905).

21. Statement of the rule

The rule against perpetuities, as it developed, became a rule of remorseless application with a force approaching that of a statutory provision. A short statement of the rule, often taken as authoritative, is Gray's (from J.C. Gray, *The Rule Against Perpetuities,* one of the leading texts):

> "No interest is good unless it must vest, if at all, not later than twenty-one years after some life in being at the creation of the interest."

Megarry and Wade, *The Law of Real Property,* contains a fuller statement in two propositions:

"(i) Any future interest in any property, real or personal, is void from the outset if it may possibly vest after the perpetuity period has expired.
(ii) The perpetuity period consists of any life or lives in being together with a further period of 21 years and any period of gestation."

22. Rule concerned with vesting

The rule is not concerned with when interests will take effect in possession, but with when they vest in interest. If a gift must vest in interest within the perpetuity period, then it is valid, even if vesting in possession may not occur until after the expiry of the period. The difference between vesting in interest and vesting in possession was explained in Section 2, above. For convenience the word "vesting" in this part of the chapter refers only to vesting in interest.

One special feature of the rule against perpetuities is that in the case of class gifts (*i.e.* gifts to a group), the size of the share of each individual within the class must be known before the gift can be treated as vested. For instance a gift "to the children of A" where A is still alive does not vest until A dies, for only then can it be known how many children A has.

23. Possibilities, not probabilities

An interest is valid only if it must vest, if at all, within the perpetuity period. Any possibility that the interest might vest outside the perpetuity period will make it void, even if in all probability it will vest within the perpetuity period. For instance, if a person establishes a trust "for the next sailor to sail singlehanded around the world," the trust declared will be void for though it is probable that the condition will be satisfied within a few years, it is possible, within the terms of the trust, for that event to occur for the next time only after two or more generations have passed. It is not, at common law, permitted to "wait and see" what actually happens, for even if a contingency is in fact satisfied within the perpetuity period, the interest is invalid if the contingency could have been satisfied outside that period. In making predictions for this purpose, only facts known at the time when a settlement takes effect may be taken into account. In the case of a gift by will, the relevant date is the death of the testator, in a disposition *inter vivos,* the date of the settlement or other disposition. No account may be taken even of events known to have occurred by the time a question involving the rule against perpetuities arises if these events happened after the will or other disposition took effect. For instance in *Re Wood* (1894), the "magic gravel pit" case, a testator made a gift by will to such of his issue living when his gravel pits, then in the course of being worked out, were exhausted. This gift was held void, as the gift remained contingent until the beneficiaries could be ascertained when the pits were exhausted, and the gift did not confine that possibility of vesting to within the perpetuity period. It was irrelevant that the pits were likely to be worked out in five or six years, and it would have made no difference if this had happened by the date of the trial.

24. Failure of gifts

The rule against perpetuities is not concerned with the likelihood of a contingency being satisfied, but with the time within which it is capable of being satisfied. Even if perfectly valid under the rule against perpetuities, a gift may fail either because the contingency is never satisfied so that it never vests, or because the interest expires before it takes effect in possession. Some examples may be used to show this. The gift by will of Blackacre "to A for life, then to B for life, then to C in fee simple" is entirely valid, even if it happens that A is aged 25 and B aged 75 so that it is most unlikely that B's vested life estate will ever take effect in possession. Again, a gift "to X if he becomes President of Ireland" is valid, for no matter how unlikely it may be that X will become President of the Republic of Ireland he must do so, if at all, within a life in being, namely his own life.

25. Lives in being

A central element of the rule is the concept of lives in being. A gift is valid only if it is so drafted that it must vest, if at all, within lives in being plus 21 years. To qualify as a life in being a person must be alive at the time a disposition takes effect, and to be relevant to the operation of the rule against perpetuities, the duration of his life must govern vesting. He need not himself be a beneficiary. It is sometimes said that lives in being must be expressly or impliedly mentioned in the grant, but this is unhelpful. Anyone's life may be used. A good test was formulated by B.M. Sparks ((1955) U.Fla.L.Rev. 470):

> "The proper question to ask is: Can I point to some person or persons now living and say that this interest will by the very terms of its creation be vested in an identified individual within twenty-one years after that person dies?"

Such a person may be called a measuring life in being. The application of this test can be shown by some examples. Take first a gift "to A if he qualifies as a solicitor." A will be a measuring life in being since he can only qualify as a solicitor in his own life. On the other hand, take a gift "to the first child of A to land on the moon," where A is still alive. A cannot be a measuring life in being since a child of his could land on the moon more than 21 years after his death. Nor will any children he already has be measuring lives in being since they all might die and an afterborn child could land on the moon more than 21 years later. A's children would be measuring lives in being if A were dead when the gift was made, since the contingency is one which must, by the terms of the gift, be satisfied within their own lives.

Finally, in a gift "to the first man to set foot on Mars" there is no measuring life in being because it can be said of no one that his lifetime governs the date within which the contingency must be satisfied.

26. Saving clauses

A gift which would otherwise be void for perpetuity can be saved by the contingency being expressly limited to occur within the perpetuity period by a saving clause. For instance, a gift to the first man to land on Mars could be saved from perpetuity if it had been phrased "to the first man who, during the life of X, shall land on Mars." The gift can now vest only during the perpetuity period (here, the life of X), if it vests at all. Of course, if no man lands on Mars during X's life, the gift will fail for want of a beneficiary.

An extreme form of saving clause is the "royal lives clause" requiring vesting to take place within the lives of living members of the royal family. Such a clause might take the form "Provided that no gift shall take effect unless it shall have vested before the expiration of 21 years from the day of the death of the last survivor of all the lineal descendants of his late Britannic Majesty George V who shall be living at the time of my death": *Re Villar* (1929); *Re Leverhulme* (*No. 2*) (1943). Care must be taken, however, not to make the class of measuring lives in being so wide as to be administratively unworkable. A period defined as "21 years from the death of the last survivor of all persons who shall be living at my death" (*Re Moore,* 1901) was held void for uncertainty.

27. No lives in being

Where there are no measuring lives in being, the perpetuity period is just 21 years. This period was derived from the duration of an infant's minority, but it was held in *Cadell* v. *Palmer* (1833) that the period was applicable even without reference to any actual minority.

A life in being must be human. As Meredith J. said in *Re Kelly* (1932) in relation to a gift for the maintenance of the dogs of the testator;

> " 'Lives' means human lives. It was suggested that the last of the dogs could in fact not outlive the testator by more than 21 years. I know nothing of that. The court does not enter into the question of a dog's expectation of life. In point of fact neighbours' dogs and cats are unpleasantly long-lived. . . . There can be no doubt that 'lives' means lives of human beings, not of animals or trees in California."

In *Re Kelly* the gift for the maintenance of the testator's dogs was upheld for the 21 years following the death of the testator, provided any of the dogs lived so long. However a gift to take effect on the death of the last surviving dog was held void for remoteness. See also *Re Dean* (1889).

28. Periods of gestation

The perpetuity period may be extended by actual periods of gestation: that is the period between conception and birth. Such a period can be added to the perpetuity period at three points: at its commencement, for a person conceived but not yet born (said to be *en ventre sa mère*) may be treated as a life in being; at the end of a life in being, for the perpetuity period may be extended to allow a child *en ventre sa mère* at that date to reach the age of 21 years; and at the end of he perpetuity period, for here again a child *en ventre sa mère* is treated as alive. In each case the period of gestation may be added only if it actually occurs and the unborn conceptus is subsequently born alive. It is possible to construct an exceptional case involving three periods of gestation. Upon a gift by will "to such of my descendants as shall be living when my first grandchild attains the age of 21 years," the testator may die leaving a son born posthumously who in turn dies leaving his wife enceinte of the testator's first grandchild, and when that grandchild reaches 21, a descendant of the testator may then be *en ventre sa mère*.

29. Some unlikely possibilities

The remorseless application of the rule against perpetuities produces some results which would be comical were it not that they thwart the reasonable provisions of a person for family or friends. The gifts are not attempts against the public welfare by the predatory rich with long-term designs pressing against the limits of the rule against perpetuities, and their failure almost invariably arises through the ineptitude, ignorance or oversight of the legal advisor to whom a person has entrusted his affairs. Moreover, the result of invalidating a gift under the rule against perpetuities is often that the person "whom the testator clearly wished to restrict to a limited participation in his estate quitted the fray laden with the testator's money bags" (see Leach (1952) 68 L.Q.R. 35).

One of the unlikely possibilities is that of the fertile octogenerian. For instance, if a gift is made "to the first child of Mrs. X to marry" this is void under the rule against perpetuities since the first child of Mrs. X to marry may be a child born after the date of the gift (and therefore is not a life in being) and who survives Mrs. X and all brothers and sisters by over 21 years before the celebration of the marriage. It is the possibility of Mrs. X having children after the date of the gift that is the cause of the invalidity in this case. It might be thought that if Mrs. X is past the age of childbearing the gift would be valid. According to the English cases this is not so. They hold that (for the purpose of the rule against perpetuities) a woman is deemed capable of bearing children at any age: *Jee* v. *Audley* (1787); *Ward* v. *Van der Loeff* (1924). In *Exham* v. *Beamish* (1939) Gavan Duffy J. rejected this notion as inapplicable in the Republic of Ireland on the ground that it was repugnant to common sense, and did not survive the Constitution of 1937.

The converse of the fertile octogenarian is the precocious toddler. *Re Gaite's Will Trusts* (1949) involved a testamentary gift to such of Mrs. Gaite's grandchildren "as shall be living at my death or born within five years therefrom who shall attain the age of 21 years or being female marry under that age." Mrs. Gaite was then living. The perpetuity period could have been exceeded if, but only if, within the five years following the death of the testatrix, Mrs. Gaite gave birth to a child, and she and all her children and grandchildren already born died, leaving the afterborn child in turn to give birth to a grandchild of Mrs. Gaite, again still within the five year period. This grandchild could then survive to reach the age of 21 more than 21 years from the death of all potential measuring lives in being. This unlikely possibility would have made the gift void had the judge not ruled that since the parent of the grandchild could *ex hypothesi* only be aged under five, the grandchild would be illegitimate, and so not within the terms of the gift as English law then stood.

A third unlikely possibility, and an examination favourite, is the unborn widows trap. Take a gift "to A for life, then to any husband she may marry for his life, then to such of A's children as shall be living at the death of the survivor of A and any such husband." The disposition splits into three parts. A takes a vested life estate. This is valid. Any husband of A takes a life estate which must vest, at the latest, on the death of A, and so this is valid. The gift to the children is contingent upon them surviving both A and her husband, and will not vest until both A and any husband die. On a pessimistic prognosis (but one which is nevertheless possible) A may marry a man who was unborn at the date of the gift and so cannot be a life in being. If he survives her by more than 21 years, vesting would occur outside the perpetuity period. The result is that the gift to the children is void.

30. Wait and see

As a general rule, any possibility of vesting taking place outside the perpetuity period makes a gift void. It is not permissible to wait to see what happens. By way of exception, where a gift may vest upon either of two (or more) contingencies which are expressed to be alternatives, and one contingency is too remote, but the other is not, it is permissible to wait and see which contingency occurs. If the contingency which is not too remote occurs, the gift is valid. Thus in a gift by will "to such of my issue as shall be living on the decease of my last surviving child or on the decease of the last surviving spouse of any of my children as the case may be whichever shall last happen" there are two expressed alternative contingencies. If a child is the last survivor, the first branch applies, and the gift is valid. But if a spouse is the last survivor, the gift is void, for the second branch falls foul of the unborn widow's trap: *Re Curryer's Will Trust* (1938). "Wait and see" only applies where the alternatives appear expressly.

31. Class gifts

A class gift is a gift to a group. The essence is that the size of the group is not predetermined, but will vary according to the number who match the description. Thus gifts "to such of my issue who shall be living five years from my death", or "to the children of A" are class gifts. A gift of "£500 to each of my children" would not be a class gift, but a separate gift of £500 to each child, for the size of this share is unchanged by the number of children.

As has already been explained, for the purpose of the rule against perpetuities, a class gift is not treated as vested until the size of the class, and therefore the shares of its members, is known. If there is any chance of a person qualifying as a member of the class outside the perpetuity period, this invalidates the whole class gift. A gift "to such of A's children, born or hereafter to be born as shall attain 25 years of age" is accordingly void if A still lives. He may have children born after the date of the gift who reach the age of 25 only more than 21 years from his death (and his life is the only potential measuring life in being).

A single class gift cannot be severed so that members who qualify within the perpetuity period take, and those who do not so qualify do not take. The operation of the presumption in favour of vesting, however, means that a gift can sometimes be treated not as a single class gift void for perpetuity, but as a class gift vesting within the perpetuity period with a separate proviso void for perpetuity. An example is a gift "to all the children of A, provided that if any child of A dies under 21 leaving children who attain 21 such children are to take their parent's share." If A is alive, the proviso in favour of the grandchildren is void since they will not necessarily reach 21 years within lives in being. But since the proviso operates by divesting a gift to children which is vested on their birth, its invalidity does not affect the size of the shares of the children. The gift would accordingly operate simply as "to all the children of A." Had the gift been differently worded, as "to all the children of A *to attain 21,* provided that if any child of A dies under the age of 21 leaving children who attain 21 such children shall take the share which their parent would have taken had he attained 21," the invalidity of the proviso would invalidate the whole gift since the size of the children's shares is affected by whether grandchildren qualify. The whole gift is a single compound gift which cannot be divided into two parts: *Re Hooper's Settlement Trusts* (1948).

Some class gifts may be saved from invalidity by a rule of convenience known as the rule in *Andrews* v. *Partington* (1791). This is a rule of construction which emerged to allow the administrators of a gift to make a distribution to the members of a numerically uncertain class as soon as one member qualifies. Under the rule, a numerically uncertain class closes when the first member becomes entitled to claim his share, unless a contrary intention is disclosed in the gift. Thus in a gift "to such of A's children as shall qualify as solicitors," once any child of A qualifies as a solicitor, the class closes. Only children then born will share if they become solicitors. For instance, if there are four children, the first child to qualify will take a quarter share. If some of the other children qualify, they also will take a share, but if they die without becoming solicitors, the shares of the qualified children are augmented. Subsequently born children cannot take. The rule was not originally designed with the rule against perpetuities in mind, but it may have the incidental effect of saving a gift from being void for perpetuity: *Re Poe* (1942). Normally a gift "to the children of A who qualify as solicitors" would be void were A still living, but if he already has a child who is a solicitor at the date of the gift, the class is closed by the rule in *Andrews* v. *Partington* and will not be void for perpetuity on the ground that an afterborn child may join the class.

32. Gifts subsequent to a void gift

Unlike the effect of the rule in *Whitby* v. *Mitchell* the effect of a gift being void for perpetuity is not necessarily to invalidate all subsequent gifts. There are three possibilities. A subsequent vested gift remains valid. For instance in a gift "to A for life, remainder for life to A's first son to marry, remainder to B in fee simple," the gift to A's first son to marry is void if A is still alive and no son of his is already married, but this does not invalidate B's vested fee simple.

The second case is of a contingent but independent subsequent gift. The subsequent gift then stands on its own. If, for instance, in the above gift the remainder to B had been made contingent upon B marrying, this remainder would stand as valid on its own (or as void if the contingency had been too remote).

The third possibility is that the subsequent gift is not only contingent but also dependent upon the prior void gift, that is, so worded that it is contingent upon the natural failure of the prior gift. The subsequent gift then falls with the prior gift if the latter is void for perpetuity: *Re Ramadge's Settlement* (1919). An example would be a gift "to A for life, remainder to A's first son to marry, but failing any such son, to B in fee simple," where A is alive and childless. B's fee simple is void for perpetuity being contingent and dependent upon the gift to A's first son to marry.

A flow chart showing the effect of a void gift upon subsequent gifts is shown in Figure 8.1.

33. Powers of appointment

A power of appointment is the power of a person (the donee) who is not the owner of property to direct the destination of that property by selecting (or appointing) persons (the *appointees*) who are to be beneficially entitled. If an appointment may be made in favour of anyone the power is termed a *general power* of appointment; if the exercise of the power is restricted to a limited class, the power is a *special power*. For the purposes of the rule against perpetuities, the distinction between general and special powers is different. A power under which the donee may appoint the property to himself without the consent of any other person is a general power. All other powers are special. The reason for this is that a person with a general power

Figure 8.1: Validity of gift subsequent to void gift

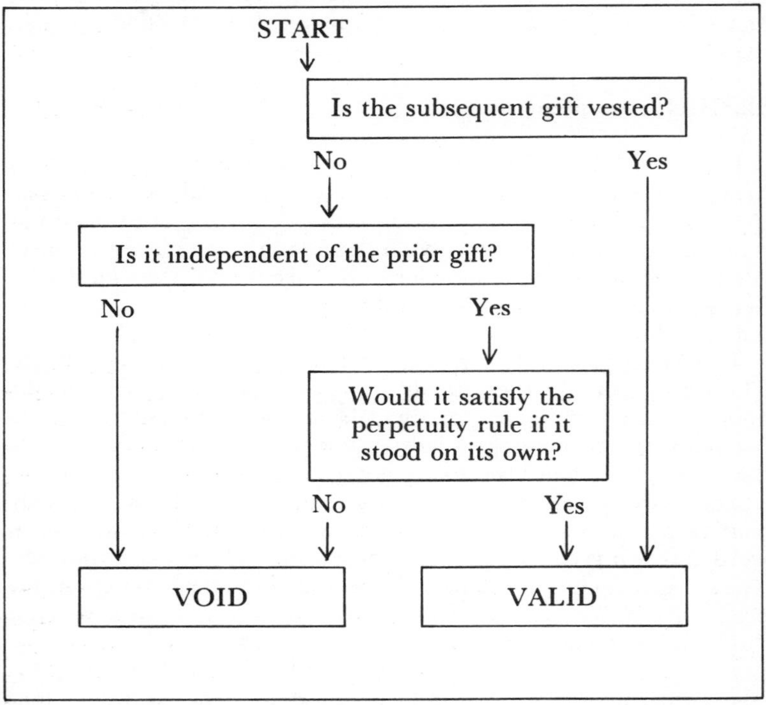

may "by a stroke of the pen" appoint the property to himself, and make himself the owner. General powers are accordingly treated as tantamount to ownership for the purpose of the rule against perpetuities. The power is valid provided that it must first become exercisable within the perpetuity period, even though it might possibly be exercised outside the period, and may in fact be exercised outside that period: *Re Fane* (1913). An exercise of the power is treated as if it were a disposition by an absolute owner, and the rule against perpetuities is applied to the interests made under the power as if the exercise of the power had been an original gift. Special powers of appointment are treated differently. A special power is void if there is any possibility that it could ever be exercised outside the perpetuity period dating from the instrument creating the power: *Re Abbott* (1893); *Re De Sommery* (1912). Furthermore, upon the exercise of a special power, the appointment relates back to the original gift creating the power. The original gift and the appointment are read together as one, and the perpetuity rule is applied as if the appointment had been made in the original gift, except that account may be taken of any facts and circumstances known at the date of the appointment: *D'Abbadie* v. *Bizoin* (1871); *Re Hallinan's Trusts* (1904). For example, if property were given "to A for life, remainder to such of his children as A may by deed or will appoint," and by his will A makes an appointment to such of his children as shall attain the age of 35 years, the exercise of the power will be valid if on A's death his youngest child is 15, for the maximum possible postponement of vesting is 20 years from A's death, and A was a life in being at the time of the original gift.

34. Determinable and conditional gifts

It has been held in both parts of Ireland that the possibility of reverter arising on the determination of a determinable fee simple is not subject to the rule against perpetuities: *Attorney-General* v. *Cummins* (1906); *Walsh* v. *Wightman* (1927). The determinable interest is also valid, and it makes no difference when the determining limitation may operate. The same principles apply to determinable interests in equity and to the resulting trust arising on the determination of the interest: *Re Cooper's Conveyance Trusts* (1956); *Re Chardon* (1928).

In regard to interests which are defeasible by condition subsequent, the effect of the rule against perpetuities depends upon whether the interest is legal or equitable. The rule against perpetuities does not apply to a common law right of entry for condition broken (*Walsh* v. *Wightman,* 1927), but such a right of entry cannot originally be made exercisable by anyone other than the grantor, although it can subsequently be assigned. Conditions subsequent in equity, however, are subject to the rule against perpetuities, with the result that if the condition may occur at too remote a date in the future, the interest upon which the condition is grafted becomes absolute.

35. Contracts, grants and options

Contracts are not subject to the rule against perpetuities since the rule applies only to contingent proprietary interests and not to personal rights. Where a contract creates proprietary rights (as for instance a contract for the sale of land), any proprietary rights arising outside the perpetuity period will be void, but without prejudice to the enforceability of the contract between the original parties: *South Eastern Ry.* v. *Associated Portland Cement Manufacturers (1900) Ltd.* (1910).

36. Exceptions from the perpetuity rule

A number of future interests are recognised as valid without needing to comply with the rule against perpetuities. This includes conditions or rights of forfeiture in leases and also covenants for the renewal of a lease contained in the lease itself (*Re Tyrrell's Estate* (1907); *Re Garde Browne,* (1911)); rights contained in mortgages (*Knightsbridge Estates Trust Ltd.* v. *Byrne,* 1939); provisions transferring the benefit of a gift from one charity to another (*Re Tyler,* 1891); limitations taking effect immediately upon the determination of an entailed interest (*Nicholls* v. *Sheffield,* 1787)); and rights of survivorship in a joint tenancy (*Re Roberts,* 1881).

G. Statutory Changes in Northern Ireland

37. The rule against perpetuities in Northern Ireland

The common law rule against perpetuities continues to apply in the Republic of Ireland without any statutory changes of substance. In Northern Ireland the rule has been substantially modified by the Perpetuities Act (N.I.) 1966. This Act significantly mitigates some of the rigours of the common law rule. It introduces a general concept of "wait and see" and abolishes some of the absurd possibilities such as the precocious toddler and the fertile octogenerian. The Act applies, with certain exceptions, to instruments taking effect in Northern Ireland after March 24, 1966.

38. "Wait and see"

Where a disposition is void under the common law rule against perpetuities, the 1966 Act provides, by section 3, that

> "the disposition shall be treated, until such time, if any, as it becomes established that the vesting must occur, if at all, after the end of the perpetuity period, as if the disposition were not subject to the rule against perpetuities. . . . "

The effect of this provision is that the rule against perpetuities in Northern Ireland no longer strikes down gifts on account of the *possibility* that vesting might occur outside the perpetuity period. A gift is void only if it is certain that vesting (if the gift vests at all) must occur outside the period. It is permitted under the Act to "wait and see" until that becomes certain.

39. The waiting period

Where the statutory "wait and see" rule applies, the duration of the waiting period is governed by measuring lives listed in section 3 of the 1966 Act. It is permitted to wait for these lives (if any) plus a further period of 21 years. The measuring lives listed are essentially the lives of the person by whom an *inter vivos* disposition was made, the lives of any beneficiaries or potential beneficiaries, their parents or grandparents or spouses, and the lives of any beneficiaries with prior interests under the disposition, their parents or grandparents. The list is divided into six groups with one group further divided into five subgroups. Where the number of persons satisfying the description in one of the resulting 10 categories is such as to render it impracticable to ascertain the date of death of the survivor, that category is to be disregarded.

To qualify as a measuring life, a person listed must be an individual in being and ascertainable at the commencement of the perpetuity period. The spouse of a beneficiary may be a measuring life even if not ascertainable until some later date. Each successive gift in a disposition is to be treated separately for the purposes of computing the waiting period.

40. The "unborn spouse trap"

The 1966 Act has a saving provision for surviving spouse (unborn widow) conditions (see the discussion in Section 29, above). By section 5 of the Act, subject to the "wait and see" provisions, where an unborn spouse still survives at the end of the waiting period, in order to save the limitation from perpetuity, the disposition is to be treated as if it had specified the end of the waiting period as the date for vesting instead of the date of the death of the surviving spouse.

41. Age reduction

Section 4 of the 1966 Act contains provisions where, in order to validate a gift, an excessive age requirement may be reduced. The common law rule is first applied. If under this, a disposition is void, the "wait and see" rules apply. If these fail to save the gift because the limitation specifies the attainment by a person of an age exceeding 21 years, but the gift would not have been void if the specified age had been 21 years, then the age may be reduced so far as is necessary to save the gift.

The section permits the retention of differential ages where separate age qualifications are contained in a gift.

42. Class reduction

Further saving provisions in the 1966 Act apply to class gifts. Once again, the common law and statutory "wait and see" rules apply. If the class gift is still void, then any potential members of the class whose inclusion is what infringes the perpetuity rule may be excluded by section 4. This class reduction provision applies after any excessive ages have been reduced, and may be combined with the age reduction provisions.

43. Ulterior and dependent gifts

Section 6 of the 1966 Act abolishes the common law rule about the failure of ulterior and dependent gifts. The validity of such a gift must be judged as if it stood on its own.

44. Determinable and conditional interests

By section 13 of the 1966 Act, determinable and conditional interests may only be brought to an end by the occurrence of the determining event or by a breach of condition if this happens within the perpetuity period. If the event or breach of condition has not by then taken place, the determinable or conditional interest becomes absolute, and any gift over is defeated.

45. Legal contingent remainders

Legal contingent remainders are, by section 14 of the 1966 Act, made subject to the rule against perpetuities.

46. Powers

The 1966 Act extends to powers. Where the Act applies, a special power is no longer void merely because it might be exercised outside the perpetuity period. It is only void under the "wait and see" rules if and so far as it is not in fact fully exercised within the period. The "wait and see" provisions apply both to the conferring and to the exercise of powers, and both donee and objects of the power may qualify as potential statutory measuring lives.

The Act clarifies the categorisation of powers as general or special, and exempts from the rule against perpetuities the administrative powers of trustees.

47. Contracts and options

Under section 11 of the 1966 Act, a contract which creates an interest in property (such as a contract for the sale of land) is void even between the original parties if it is void for remoteness as against a third party. An option to acquire for value any interest in land is made subject, by section 10, to a perpetuity period of 21 years only. By the same section, however, the perpetuity rule does not apply to an option to purchase the superior freehold or leasehold reversion on a lease if the option is exercisable only by the lessee or his successors in title not later than one year after the end of the lease.

48. Alternative fixed perpetuity period

As an alternative to a perpetuity period measured by lives in being, the 1966 Act, s.1, permits the express designation of a perpetuity period of a fixed number of years not exceeding 80. The period of years must be specified to be the perpetuity period. Where such a period is specified, the "wait and see" provisions apply for this period, if necessary. The fixed perpetuity period can be a convenient substitute for a "royal lives clause."

49. Presumptions of parenthood

The absurd common law rule that a person is conclusively presumed capable of childbearing at any age is abolished by the 1966 Act. By section 2 males under 14 years and females under 12 years or over 55 years are now presumed to be incapable of childbearing, although these presumptions can be rebutted by evidence.

H. The Rule Against Accumulations

50. Accumulations

An accumulation occurs where the income from investments is not paid out, but is saved and added to the capital of a fund. The validity of directions to accumate income was considered in the celebrated case of *Thellusson* v. *Woodward* (1799); on appeal (1805). Peter Thellusson directed that his residuary estate of £600,000 was to be accumulated for as long as any living son, grandson or great-grandson of his survived, and was then to be distributed between his issue. It was calculated that the accumulated fund could by that date amount to more than £30 million and even to £100 million and the income from the fund would be greater than the civil list. The accumulation was held valid, but caused such a stir that legislation restricting future accumulations was passed in England in 1800. Peter Thellusson's last surviving grandson died in 1856, but by that time the fund had been greatly depleted by mismanagement and the costs of litigation.

The English legislation of 1800 did not apply to Ireland. The common law rule, that a direction for accumulation is valid provided that it does not exceed the perpetuity period remained in force: *Longfield* v. *Bantry* (1885). One modification applying to Ireland was introduced by the Accumulations Act 1892. This provided, subject to some conditions, that accumulations of income for the purchase of land may not be made for longer than the minorities of any persons who would, if of full age, have been entitled to the income if there were no accumulation.

9 Co-Ownership

1. What is co-ownership?

The law recognises many ways in which rights in property may be simultaneously enjoyed by a number of different people. Leasehold tenure permits a landlord to enjoy an income from land while the tenant has possession and the right to profits. The doctrine of estates enables a life tenant and a remainderman both to claim existing rights of ownership. The term co-ownership, however, is used to describe the position where two or more people are simultaneously entitled to possession of property. This kind of ownership is extremely common. Very often, for instance, a husband and wife will together acquire the family home, and have it transferred into both their names. They are both then entitled to possession of the whole of the house. The wife cannot say to the husband that he may not enter the kitchen, nor the husband to the wife that she may not use the bathroom. If they could, then they would not have concurrent rights to the same land. The house would be divided into two separate landholdings.

Similarly, if a farmer leaves his farm to his four children, in the absence of any contrary agreement between the children, no child can identify a particular meadow or field as his. Each of the children may use the whole of the farm without a trespass. If the farm were divided, there would not be any co-ownership. There would instead be *several* or separate ownership of each divided part.

Co-ownership is not restricted to land. The family car may be owned concurrently by husband and wife, and so may the household furniture. Co-ownership is also possible between strangers and not just between relatives, although, except in some special circumstances, strangers would be less likely to want to share the right to possession.

2. Alternatives to co-ownership

The essence of co-ownership is that the co-owners are concurrently entitled to possession of the same juridical unit of property. But there are ways other than co-ownership in which a very similar result can be achieved. Where a number of people associate to buy a property, then instead of making the purchase directly, in which case they will hold as co-owners, they may form a company to make the purchase. The company will be a legal person holding the property as a sole owner. The interests of the subscribers to the purchase will be represented in their shareholdings.

A variant which is common in the United Kingdom may be used to provide residential accommodation. A registered non-profit friendly society constructs a housing development, and then grants leases of the dwelling units to members of the society under agreements which confer on the tenants a share in the capital value of the development varying according to the length of their occupation and any increase or decrease in the value of the development over this period. This kind of housing provision has been called co-ownership housing since the occupiers are both landlords (collectively, through the housing society) and tenants (as individuals) and there is an element of profit-sharing.

Another variant is used in some "timeshare" developments. A promoter establishes a company which acquires and develops a vacation complex. That company then grants leases conferring on the tenants a right to occupy a particular holiday unit for a certain week each year for a set number of years. It has been established that leases of this kind for discontinuous periods are valid: *Smallwood* v. *Sheppards* (1895). The tenants simultaneously enter into a maintenance agreement which ensures the upkeep of the units. Sometimes licences instead of leases will be used (see Chapter 15).

3. Types of co-ownership

The examples given in the last section are not examples of co-ownership or concurrent ownership since there is no simultaneous sharing of possession. There are only four ways in which Irish Law has recognised that proprietors may have concurrent rights of possession. These are joint tenancy, tenancy in common, coparceny and tenancy by the entireties. The first two types are by far the most important. Tenancy by the entireties is now defunct and coparceny is extremely rare.

4. The right of survivorship

Joint tenancy and tenancy in common are the two forms of co-ownership which predominate in the modern law. In both of them, two or more co-owners share the possession of land, or the rental income from it, if it has been let, and if the land is sold, they will share the purchase price. The main distinction between the two types of co-ownership is what happens on death. There are two alternatives. One is that on the death of one co-owner, the survivors automatically share the whole of the land. This is what happens in a joint tenancy. The alternative is that the interest of the deceased co-owner passes according to his will or on intestacy. This is what happens in a tenancy in common, or tenancy in undivided shares, as it is sometimes called. The use of the word "tenancy" has nothing to do with leases. It is used to show the ownership of an interest in land in the same way as one may speak of a "tenant in fee simple" in reference to an owner of the freehold. The different ways in which property devolves on the death of a co-owner can be represented diagrammatically. In Figure 9.1 a circle is used to indicate the bundle of rights which together constitute ownership. With the joint tenancy there is no division, even notional, of ownership. With a tenancy in common the ownership is divided into notional shares, rather like the shares in a company, although in neither type of co-ownership is the land divided.

The way in which on the death of one joint tenant the others take his place is known as the *right of survivorship* or the *jus accrescendi*.

5. The four unities

For a joint tenancy to exist, the "four unities" must be present. These four unities are:

(i) *Unity of possession.* This is common to all co-ownership. It means that the land (or other property) must not have been divided. Each co-owner must be entitled to the whole of the land.

(ii) *Unity of interest.* All the co-owners must hold the same interest in land. For instance, they must both be entitled to the fee simple or for life. There cannot be a joint tenancy when the interests of the co-owners are of different duration.

(iii) *Unity of title.* Joint tenants must all derive their title from the same document (*e.g.* will or conveyance) or act (such as the taking of adverse possession).

Figure 9.1: The devolution of co-ownership property on death

a. While D is alive

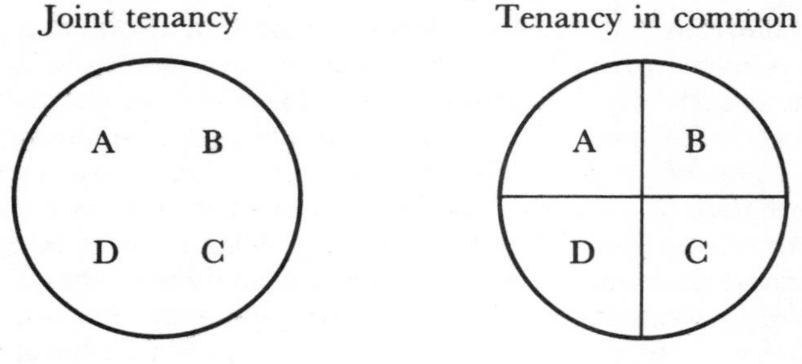

b. On D's death

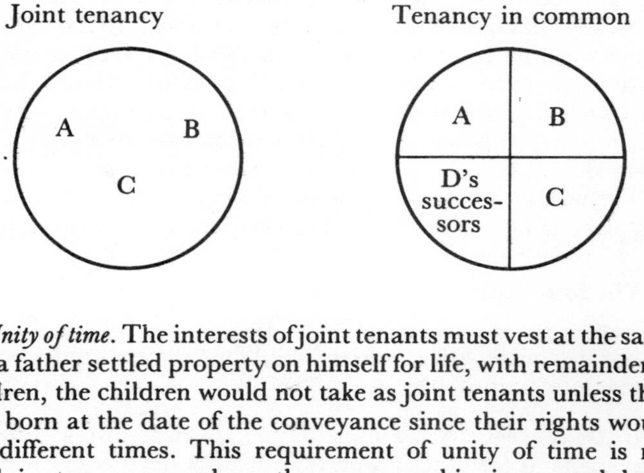

(iv) *Unity of time*. The interests of joint tenants must vest at the same time. If a father settled property on himself for life, with remainder to his children, the children would not take as joint tenants unless they were all born at the date of the conveyance since their rights would vest at different times. This requirement of unity of time is not essential in two cases: where the co-ownership is created by a conveyance to uses (see Chapter 8) and where it is created by a disposition in a will.

These four unities are necessary conditions for the existence of a joint tenancy, but they are not sufficient, since even where all four are present, there may be a tenancy in common (see below).

6. Creation of joint tenancy or tenancy in common

Because of the operation of the right of survivorship, the number of joint tenants is likely to reduce until eventually only one remains as sole owner of the property, unless the joint tenancy is converted to a tenancy in common by severance (see below). With the tenancy in common, however, it is likely that the number of tenants will increase rather than fall with each death. In Figure 9.1b the successors taking D's share on his death might well be his wife and four children, increasing the number of co-owners to eight. Tenants in common need not take equally, although they will often hold in equal shares. Figure 9.2 shows the shares which are taken where property is originally held by four tenants in common in equal shares, and D then dies intestate so that his wife W takes two thirds of his share and his four children E, F, G and H the remainder between them. Because of the difficulties for conveyancing this could cause—on a sale all the tenants in common would have to be unanimous in wishing to sell, and the title of each would have to be separately investigated—and for other reasons relating to feudal services and incidents, the common law preferred a joint tenancy. Equity, however, leant against the joint tenancy, since the right of survivorship was capable of producing unfair results. There are cases, therefore, in which equity would require legal joint tenants to hold upon trust for themselves as equitable tenants in common: *Elliot* v. *Brown* (1791). This occurs in three cases set out in Section 8, below.

Figure 9.2: Fragmentation of shares in tenancy in common

a. While D is alive *b. On D's death*

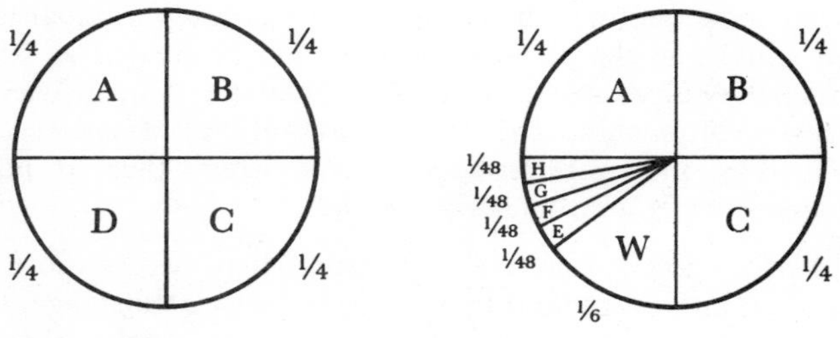

7. The terms of the disposition

Wherever two or more persons were together entitled to possession, the common law presumed a joint tenancy. But this presumption could be rebutted by the terms of the disposition. An express direction by the grantor that the grantees were to take as tenants in common would be effective in the absence of mistake or fraud. Even if there was no express direction, a tenancy in common would be indicated by *words of severance*, these being words suggesting a notional division of ownership into shares, which is inconsistent with a joint tenancy. Expressions which would operate in this way include "to be divided between" (*Crozier* v. *Crozier*, 1843); "share and share alike" (*Mill* v. *Mill*, 1877); and "in equal shares" (*Jury* v. *Jury*, 1882). The words of severance could be negated by a clear intention to create a joint tenancy, and equally the disposition construed as a whole may indicate a tenancy in common: *Bray* v. *Jennings* (1902).

8. Preference for tenancy in common in equity

The three special cases in which legal joint tenants will hold upon trust for themselves as equitable tenants in common are:

(i) *Unequal contributions to purchase price.* Where two or more persons together purchase property, the terms of the conveyance may make them legal joint tenants. If, however, they provided the purchase price in unequal shares, then it is presumed that they intended to take beneficially as tenants in common in shares proportionate to their contributions, and equity will impose a trust to achieve this: *O'Connell* v. *Harrison* (1927). If they contribute equally, the presumption is that they intend to take as joint tenants. These presumptions may be rebutted by the circumstances of the acquisition or the terms of the conveyance: *Fleming* v. *Fleming* (1855).

(ii) *Joint business undertaking.* Where land is acquired pursuant to a joint business venture, then whether or not the participants contributed equally to the acquisition, they will be treated as tenants in common in equity since the right of survivorship is inconsistent with a business relationship: *Lake* v. *Craddock* (1732); *Hawkins* v. *Rogers* (1951). This presumption applies even where there is no formal partnership: *McCarthy* v. *Barry* (1859).

(iii) *Money lent on mortgage.* Similarly, where two or more persons acquire an interest in land by lending money on mortgage, they will be presumed tenants in common in equity. Again, the right of survivorship is inconsistent with the commercial nature of the transaction: *Petty* v. *Styward* (1632); *Morley* v. *Bird* (1798).

Where a tenancy in common is not indicated by either the terms and circumstances of the conveyance, or by one of the three special cases above, then the co-owners will take as joint tenants, provided that the four unities are present. If the unity of title, time, or interest is absent, the co-owners must be tenants in common.

9. Severance of joint tenancy

Severance is the process by which the rights of one joint tenant are converted into a distinct share of ownership, so making him a tenant in common. There are several ways in which they may occur.

(i) *Alienation.* If a joint tenant alienates his interest to another person by way of sale or gift, then this will effect a severance, for it destroys the unity of title. The donee or purchaser derives his rights under a separate title from the remaining tenant or tenants: *Connolly* v. *Connolly* (1866). While it was recognised that a joint tenant could sever during his lifetime, he could not do so by will, for here the right of survivorship prevailed to deprive a joint tenant of any property to give by will: *Cockerill* v. *Gilliland* (1854). A joint tenant desiring to create himself a tenant in common can do so by conveying to another to the use of or upon trust for himself: *Cray* v. *Willis* (1729). An alienation operating in equity only (and a specifically enforceable contract would amount to an alienation in equity) will sever a joint tenancy in equity: *Gould* v. *Kemp* (1834). It is possible for a joint tenant to surrender his interest to the other joint tenants. In this case there is no severance but instead the other joint tenants are entitled as if the tenant surrendering was dead.

(ii) *Acquisition of a further interest.* In the original grant of a joint tenancy, one of the joint tenants may be given a further interest in the property. For instance, land could be conveyed to A and B for life with remainder to B in fee simple. However, if subsequently to the original grant one of the joint tenants acquired a further interest, this interest would *merge* with his existing interest, so destroying the unity of interest and making him a tenant in common: *Flynn* v. *Flynn* (1930). So, in the above example, if A acquired the fee simple from B, A and B would become tenants in common. Merger only applies where the interest a joint tenant acquires is consecutive to his existing interest. So if land were given to W for life, with remainder in fee simple to A, B and C as joint tenants, A's interest would be severed if he acquired W's life estate. It would not be severed if he acquired C's interest (although such an alienation by C would sever C's share).

(iii) *Homicide.* Because of the principle that a person may not profit by his own crime, where one joint tenant kills another, he will be prevented in equity from benefiting from the right of survivorship. Severance will take place in equity to the extent necessary to prevent the wrongdoer from profiting from his crime (*Rasmanis* v. *Jurewitsch*, 1969); alternatively, the surviving joint tenant will hold half the property on a constructive trust for his victim's estate (*Schobelt* v.

Barber, 1966). In Northern Ireland relief from the principle of forfeiture may be available under the Forfeiture (N.I.) Order 1982.

(iv) *Mutual agreement* A mutual agreement among joint tenants that they will hold as tenants in common will amount to a severance in equity: *Williams* v. *Hensman* (1861). The agreement need not be specifically enforceable. It "serves as an indication of a common intention to sever": *Burgess* v. *Rawnsley* (1975).

(v) *Course of dealing*. According to Sir William Page Wood V.-C. in *Williams* v. *Hensman* (1861), "there may be a severance by any course of dealing sufficient to intimate that the interests of all were mutually treated as constituting a tenancy in common. When the severance depends on an inference of this kind without any express act of severance (*e.g.* an alienation of a share), it will not suffice to rely on an intention, with respect to the particular share, declared only behind the backs of the other persons interested." The conduct of the co-owners may provide evidence from which a mutual agreement to sever can be inferred (*Wilson* v. *Bell*, 1843), but the final words of Page Wood V.-C. in the passage cited appear to envisage the possibility of severance taking place in equity by virtue of a unilateral declaration of a desire to sever. This view has received some support in England in a number of cases, notably *Re Draper's Conveyance* (1969) and *Burgess* v. *Rawnsley* (1975) although the point cannot by any means be considered settled, and it has been criticised, for instance by Walton J. in *Nielson-Jones* v. *Fedden* (1975).

10. An unseverable joint tenancy

Before 1883, when land was transferred to a husband and wife in such a way that they would have taken as joint tenants were they unmarried, then they took as *tenants by entireties*. A tenancy by entireties was a form of joint ownership in which the husband and wife were treated as one so that while they were both living neither could dispose of any interest in the property without the concurrence of the other: *Crofton* v. *Bunbury* (1853). The tenancy could not be converted into a tenancy in common by severance, and any rents and profits were payable to the husband while both he and his wife were alive: *Chamier* v. *Tyrell* (1894). On the death of one of the spouses, the other succeeded to the whole property by virtue of the original transfer under which the husband and wife were treated as one, rather than by survivorship. The Married Women's Property Act 1882 prevented the creation of any new tenancies by entireties since 1883. This type of co-ownership is therefore defunct.

In *Bedson* v. *Bedson* (1965), however, Lord Denning M.R. suggested that as between husband and wife, a joint tenancy could not be severed and neither spouse could sell his or her interest separately. "If he or she could do so it would mean that the purchaser could insist on going into possession himself—with the other spouse there—which is absurd. It would also mean that one of them could, of his own head, destroy the right of survivorship which was the essence of the joint tenancy. That cannot be correct." Russell L.J. in the same case completely rejected this view. "The proposition is, I think, without the slightest foundation in law or in equity." Plowman J. in *Re Draper's Conveyance* (1969) aligned himself with the views of Russell L.J. and there has been no case in which Lord Denning's opinion has been supported. Much the same result is achieved in the Republic, however, by the Family Home Protection Act 1976. By section 3:

> "Where a spouse, without the prior consent in writing of the other spouse, purports to convey any interest in the family home to any person except the other spouse, then, [subject to certain exceptions] the purported conveyance shall be void".

"Conveyance" and "interest" are widely enough defined to include any alienation of a share by a joint tenant or tenant in common (s.1).

It may also be noted that it has been held in some U.S. cases that

> "Joint occupancy of property, particularly residential property, obviously demands reasonable restrictions on the right of each joint occupant either by himself or through another to exercise full control over the property at all times regardless of the wishes of another joint occupant present on the premises. A joint occupant's right of privacy in his home is not completely at the mercy of another with whom he shares legal possession." (*Tompkins* v. *Superior Court of San Francisco*, 1963).

There may also be difficulties in obtaining a court order for shared possession: see *Tubman* v. *Johnston* (1981).

11. Determination of co-ownership

There are three ways in which co-ownership may be brought to an end. The first is by sale. If all the co-owners consent to a sale, the property may be sold, and the purchaser will then take it free from the rights of the joint tenants or tenants in common, whose interests will shift to the purchase price. The sale of the entire property by all the co-owners will not in itself amount to a severance of a joint tenancy. As O'Connor L.J. said in *Re Hayes Estate* (1920) "a mere agreement by persons entitled as joint tenants to convert their property from one species to another does not operate to work a severance." See also *Byrne* v. *Byrne* (1980). The co-ownership ends only so far as the property sold is concerned; the co-ownership continues in the proceeds of sale and in any substituted investment.

A second way in which co-ownership may be determined is by partition, that is, by a division of the property. Subject to any requisite Land Purchase Acts or Land Act consents, the land may be physically divided with one part going to each co-owner. This may be achieved voluntarily, or by order of the court under the Partition Acts 1868 and 1876. At common law there was no right on the part of a joint tenant or tenant in common to compel partition. In many cases, as where the property held by co-owners is a single dwelling, it will be more convenient to sell the property and divide the proceeds. In a partition action the court may also, where it is appropriate, order a sale and division of the proceeds. By section 4 of the Partition Act 1868, a co-owner entitled to a half share or more may demand a sale and the court must direct this "unless it sees good reason to the contrary": *Northern Bank Ltd.* v. *Beattie* (1982); *O'D* v. *O'D* (1983).

The third way in which co-ownership will end is where the property becomes vested in one only of the co-owners. With a joint tenancy this will eventually happen through the operation of survivorship, unless severance has taken place. With a tenancy in common or a severed joint tenancy union in a single co-owner will occur only where one tenant acquires the shares of the others by grant, will, or operation of law.

12. Coparceny

The form of co-ownership known as coparceny is now extremely rare. In the past it arose where the owner of real property died intestate leaving no male heir. Under the ancient rules of inheritance an elder male descendant (and any of his issue) was preferred to a younger male descendant (and any of his issue), but where the nearest descendants were female, they took equally as coparceners. The operation of the rules of inheritance is explained more fully in Chapter 12. The rules of inheritance have been replaced by new rules of intestate succession by the Administration of Estates Act (N.I.) 1955 and by the Republic's Succession Act 1965. The only instance in which the rules of inheritance continue to operate is in the descent of an unbarred fee tail (see p. 47). It is therefore still possible for coparceners to succeed to a fee tail general. The special features of coparceny are that although the four unities are normally present and there are no words of severance, the coparceners hold in undivided shares as if they were tenants in common, and the right of survivorship does not apply. Coparceny may be determined in the same way as a joint tenancy or tenancy in common, one difference being that even at common law a coparcener had a right to compel partition, a right not given to other co-owners until the Partition Acts 1868 and 1876.

13. The rights of co-owners to possession and rent

The essence of co-ownership is that during the continuance of the co-ownership each of the tenants has a right to possession of the entire property. It is therefore not a trespass for one tenant to be in sole possession of the whole. However no tenant may evict or exclude the others, and in ousting another he would be guilty of trespass (*Jacobs* v. *Seward*, 1872). He would then be obliged to pay a proportion of the fair rental value of the property to compensate the excluded co-owners: *Dennis* v. *McDonald* 1982. Where there is no question of a co-owner having been excluded from possession, but he simply chooses to live away from the property, he has no right to claim a rent: *Jones* v. *Jones* (1977). So, as will often be the case in Ireland, where a father leaves the family home to his children as joint tenants or tenants in common, but some of the children have emigrated, they will have no claim for a notional rent against the children remaining in Ireland who continue in possession of the home. Moreover, as will be seen in Chapter 13, the co-owners remaining in possession may, after the appropriate period, acquire title against the others by limitation.

If the land subject to co-ownership is producing a net income in the form of profits or rent paid by a third party, that net income must be shared equally between joint tenants, and in proportion to the respective shares of tenants in common. By section 23 of the Administration of Justice Act (Ireland) 1707, a co-owner who has taken more than his share of the net income can be made to account in an action to the others.

14. The rights of co-owners to sell or mortgage

If co-ownership property is to be sold or mortgaged as a whole, the co-owners must be unanimous in concurring in the transaction. The only way of compelling a sale against the wishes of one of the tenants is by seeking an order for sale in a partition action. Without unanimity on the part of the tenants, it is still possible for a joint tenant or tenant in common to sell or mortgage his own share, and such a share may have a judgment mortgage registered against it: *McIlroy* v. *Edgar* (1881). The sale or mortgage by a joint tenant of his share will of course operate as a severance. A purported but ineffective attempt by some only of the co-owners to sell or mortgage the property as a whole will normally be treated as effective in equity to the extent of the vendor's own interest in the land: *First National Securities* v. *Hegarty* (1984). Where, however, the creation of an equitable interest in the land depends upon an agreement being specifically enforceable (as in the case of an agreement to create a mortgage or charge: see Chapter 18), no interest in the land will arise if the court refuses a decree for specific performance on such grounds as hardship to the other co-owners: *Thames Guaranty Ltd.* v. *Campbell* (1984).

Part 3

Transfer of Land

10 Acquisition And Transfer Of Land Inter Vivos

A. Acquisition of Land

1. Acquisition of ownership

Ownership may be acquired in two ways: originally, where ownership is acquired of a thing not previously owned; and derivatively, where ownership is acquired of something previously owned by another. This chapter is concerned with original acquisition, and with derivative acquisition of freeholds through transfers *inter vivos*. Leaseholds are dealt with in Chapter 11. Chapter 12 deals with succession, *i.e.* transfers taking effect on death, and Chapter 13 with the acquisition of title by limitation. Settled Land is dealt with in Chapter 14. Both these latter chapters concern exceptions to the ordinary rule that only transfers by an owner are effective to convey an interest in land.

2. Original acquisition

There is no land in Ireland which is without an owner since the State (in Northern Ireland, the Crown), by virtue of the ancient common law doctrine that all land is held from the Crown (the doctrine of tenure: see Chapter 6), has a residual right to all land which is not in the ownership of some other. In modern times also, the principle that there can never be ownerless land is reinforced by the position of the State as ultimate intestate successor in the Republic of Ireland (see p. 139), and by the Crown's right in Northern Ireland to land as *bona vacantia* on the death of an owner without successors.

New land is created only very rarely. Since land is a space which contains constituents which may change from time to time (see p. 21), even the reclamation of inland lakes does not create new land. It merely changes the physical components of the space. One of the very few cases in which new land arises is through *accretion* at the sea boundary or in a tidal waterway. Accretion is the process of the encroachment of land upon the sea by gradual deposition of sand or silt. The foreshore (the area between high and low tides) belongs to the Crown or State, but where new land rises above the tides, the normal rule is that the accretion belongs to the contiguous inland owner: *Attorney-General* v. *McCarthy* (1911); *Southern Theosophy Inc.* v. *South Australia* (1982). The issue of ownership may, however, depend upon the proper construction of the title deeds of the riparian owners: see *Baxendale* v. *Instow Parish Council* (1981). Where land is created by avulsion, or sudden change, or by deliberate reclamation, in the absence of any statutory provision, the land will belong to the owner of the area previously covered by water, rather than to the riparian owner: at the sea's edge, the Crown or State would therefore benefit.

Another way in which new land arises (or a change can take place in the component elements of the land) is through *accession* where personal property attached to land becomes part of the land. The maxim *quidquid plantatur solo, solo cedit* applies to such fixtures: the owner of the land acquires ownership of the things attached to it (see pp. 22 to 24). In *Wheeler* v. *Stratton* (1911), the plaintiff built on land expecting to acquire a lease. The land was sold to the defendant before the lease was granted. It was held that the defendant was entitled to the buildings without compensating the plaintiff. Other cases have come to similar conclusions, but in appropriate circumstances the doctrine of proprietary estoppel may apply. The effect of this is that where a person expends money on land in the expectation, induced or encouraged by the owner, that by doing so he will acquire some right, the owner will be obliged by a court of equity to give effect to the expectation: see Chapter 15.

B. Transfer of Freehold Land

3. Transfer and creation of interests in land

Much more important in practice than acquisition of title to new land is the process of transferring an existing interest in existing land, or of creating a new interest in such land. The appropriate method depends upon whether a freehold or a leasehold interest is involved, and upon whether title to the land is registered or not. The formal requirements for the transfer or creation of an interest in land do not differentiate between sales and gifts, but there is a difference in the practical procedure adopted. On a sale, it is typically the case that a contract will precede the transfer, and that the vendor's title will be investigated by the purchaser before the closing or completion of the sale by way of transfer. The steps are outlined in the next sections. It is not usual for investigation of title to take place prior to a transfer by way of gift. The creation and transfer of leasehold interests is somewhat different and is dealt with in the next chapter.

4. Contracts for the sale of land

The pattern of an ordinary sale by a beneficial owner, for instance by the owner-occupier of a house is that the transaction will go through several stages. The first, of course, is that the vendor must find a purchaser and make an initial agreement with him. This is frequently done through the services of an estate agent. There may at this stage be an oral or written contract, but often any agreement will be only "subject to contract," awaiting the signing of a formal agreement.

It is at this stage that the parties' solicitors usually first become involved. The vendor's solicitor sends a draft contract to the purchaser's solicitor, generally using the standard printed forms of the Incorporated Law Society of Ireland or of the Incorporated Law Society of Northern Ireland. The purchaser's solicitor may at this point make some pre-contract enquiries, for instance to clarify whether the land is subject to burdens not disclosed in the contract, but this is not the usual practice, although it is becoming increasingly common in Northern Ireland. The purchaser will not, however, sign the contract until he is satisfied that he has the necessary finance (for instance by way of arrangement with a building society for mortgage) and sometimes not until he has had the house surveyed for structural defects. Alternatively, and this is the usual practice in Northern Ireland, the contract will be made conditional upon such matters as the purchaser obtaining a mortgage or a satisfactory surveyor's report or a clear Property Certificate from the District Development Officer. Consent to certain sales is also required under the Land Acts. Once these matters have been attended to, the vendor and the purchaser will then proceed to sign the formal contract, and the purchaser will pay a deposit, normally of between 10 per cent. and 25 per cent. of the purchase price, to the vendor or his solicitor.

5. Contract to conveyance

Once the contract between the parties has been reduced to writing, or made in writing, so that there is the proof required under the Statute of Frauds (Ireland) 1695, the agreement between the parties is legally enforceable, but no legal title has passed. This requires a formal conveyance or transfer, different forms being used for registered or unregistered land. Moreover, it is also the practice for the purchaser to investigate the vendor's title. Again, the method depends upon whether or not title to the land is registered. With both kinds of land, however, the post-contract procedure is similar. The vendor supplies his proof of ownership in the form of a chain of title deeds or a copy of the folio (see Chapter 1, pp. 4 to 5). The purchaser in return sends objections and requisitions on title, generally using a standard Law Society printed form with any necessary supplementary questions added. These requisitions are designed to clear up any doubts arising from the purchaser's examination of the title deeds or copy folio and also to check on a wide range of other matters, such as the services supplying the property, whether it is subject to any charges and incumbrances and so forth. The purchaser will also make various searches, including searches at the Registry of Deeds or Land Registry to ensure priority against any inconsistent dealings with the land occurring between contract and completion. Having received satisfactory replies to his requisitions, and after making the appropriate searches, the purchaser will be ready to proceed to completion.

6. Position pending completion

Even though no *legal* title is transferred until the formal conveyance or transfer, under the equitable maxim, "equity treats as done that which ought to be done," a specifically enforceable contract confers upon the purchaser an immediate equitable interest in the property. This interest is enforceable against third parties, such as subsequent purchasers of interests in the land, subject to the requirements of registration, namely registration of the contract in the Registry of Deeds (see *O'Connor* v. *McCarthy,* 1982) for unregistered land or protection by caution for registered land (Registration of Title Act 1964 s.97; Land Registration Act (N.I.) 1970 s.66) in order to ensure priority against subsequent purchasers for value (see p. 109).

The passing of an equitable interest to the purchaser is said to make the vendor a "trustee" pending completion. He must manage and preserve the property with reasonable care and will be liable if he fails to take care to prevent deprivations by trespassers *(Clarke* v. *Ramuz,* 1891); he will also be bound, as trustee, to account to the purchaser for any sums received upon a sale in breach of contract: *Lake* v. *Bayliss* (1974). Subject to this, the risk of gain or loss, such as an increase in value, or a loss through accidental fire, passes to the purchaser.

The constructive trusteeship, however, is an unusual one, for the vendor retains a substantial interest in the property. For instance, until the date of completion he is entitled to occupy the land and retain any rents and profits for himself. He also has a lien on the land for any unpaid purchase money: see p. 236.

7. Completion

Completion, or the closing of a contract for the sale of land, is essentially an exchange of the document transferring title for the outstanding part of the purchase price. There will also be an apportionment of rent, rates, taxes and other outgoings, balanced against any income from the property; any documents such as title deeds, or discharges of mortgages, will be handed over; and undertakings may be given relating to any outstanding matters.

Completion or closing is not quite the final step in a transfer. Any undertakings made will have to be performed and discharged; and the purchaser will need to see that stamp duty is paid, and the transfer duly registered.

8. Conveyance of unregistered freehold land

None of the old methods of transfer of freehold land have in Ireland been abolished. One author, Josiah W. Smith in *A Compendium of the Law of Real and Personal Property*, lists around 23 different modes of transfer. In practice, only one mode of transfer for freehold land is now used. This is the conveyance by deed. This method of conveyance, which is comparatively simple and straightforward, was introduced by the Real Property Act 1845.

A deed is a document under seal. It is distinguished from other documents by the formalities surrounding its creation: to be effective a deed must be signed, sealed and delivered by the grantor. In past times the seal would have been of sealing wax, nowadays it is generally a red wafer disc. In an English case, *First National Securities Ltd.* v. *Jones* (1978) it was held that a printed circle containing the letters L.S. (meaning *locus sigilli* or place for seal), accompanied by a signature, satisfied the formal requirement of a seal.

The need for delivery of a deed does not mean merely physical delivery: it means that there must have been some act upon the part of the grantor indicating his intention that the deed should become operative. This is most commonly shown by a physical transfer of possession. It is possible for a deed to be delivered conditionally. It is then said to be delivered in *escrow* (from the word scroll). The delivery becomes effective if the condition is satisfied. For instance, the vendor will often execute a conveyance some days before completion and hand it to his solicitor to pass over on receipt of the balance of the purchase price. This will often amount to a conditional delivery making the deed an escrow.

9. Contents of a conveyance

A typical deed of conveyance runs to two or three pages. It names the *parties*, contains a *recital* of the purpose of the deed, and of any necessary history. It then contains the *testatum*, or *operative part* of the deed, in which the vendor or other grantor expresses an intention to convey an interest in land to the grantee. The testatum will include a *parcels clause* identifying the property conveyed, sometimes by reference to a schedule, and a *habendum* defining the extent of the interest taken by the purchaser. Additional clauses inserted may certify value for stamp duty purposes, contain exceptions or reservations, and provide for indemnity against liabilities. The deed concludes with a testimonium and attestation, that is a statement that the deed is executed to witness what it contains, and the signing and sealing. Every person who has made some promise in the deed will need to sign it and seal it, and since the purchaser normally enters into covenants on a sale, his execution of the deed would be essential. A truncated form of deed is given in Form 10.1. In practice the deed would be very much fuller.

10. Words of limitation and words of purchase

It is important to note that not only must a conveyance be in the proper form to be effective, it must also contain the correct wording for the estate being conveyed. These words—defining the estate conveyed—are *words of limitation*. The habendum also contains *words of purchase* identifying the purchaser, that is, the person or persons to whom the interest is being conveyed. As we have already seen in Chapter 3 in relation to the doctrine of notice, any person to whom property is conveyed or given by will is a purchaser, even if he takes by way of gift.

The original common law rule was that if it was desired to convey a fee simple, it was necessary to use words indicating the inheritability of the estate. It became accepted that the only words which would suffice for this purpose in a conveyance to a natural person were "and his heirs." The word "heirs" in the plural was essential, together with the appropriate possessive pronoun. In the absence of such words, the purchaser would take only a life estate, even if some other expression such as "for ever" had been used. The addition of superfluous words, such as "assigns" in the common limitation "his heirs and assigns for ever" is unnecessary but harmless. In a conveyance to a corporation sole (*i.e.* a body politic of perpetual succession and consisting of a single person such as the Taoiseach), the appropriate words of limitation for a fee simple are "and his successors." For a conveyance

Form 10.1: Deed of conveyance

Parties THIS CONVEYANCE is made the first day of April 1984 between Florence McCarthy Knox, of Tory Cottage, Curranhilty, County Cork, Horse Dealer (hereinafter called the vendor) of the one part and Sinclair Yeates of Shreelane House, Curranhilty, County Cork, Resident Magistrate, retired (hereinafter called the purchaser) of the other part

Recitals WHEREAS the vendor is seised in fee simple in possession free from incumbrances of the property hereinafter described and has agreed to sell the same to the purchaser at the price of £50,000

Testatum NOW THIS DEED WITNESSETH that in pursuance of the said agreement and in consideration of the sum of £50,000 paid by the purchaser to the vendor, (the receipt whereof the vendor hereby acknowledges), the vendor as beneficial owner HEREBY CONVEYS
Parcels unto the purchaser ALL THAT property situate and known as
Habendum Ardcarrig, Cluin, County Cork TO HOLD the same unto and to the use of the purchaser in fee simple

Testimonium IN WITNESS whereof the parties hereto have hereunto set their respective hands and seals the day and year first hereinbefore written

Attestation SIGNED SEALED AND DELIVERED
by the said Florence McCarthy Knox
in the presence of

Flurry Knox

Seal

James Canty
Tralagough, Co. Cork,
Farmer

Michael Leary
Skebawn, Co. Cork,
Kennelman

SIGNED SEALED AND DELIVERED
by the said Sinclair Yeates
in the presence of

Sinclair Yeates

Seal

Jerome Hickey
Drumcurran, Co. Cork
Medical Practitioner

Timothy Connor
Shreelane, Co. Cork
Gamekeeper

to a corporation aggregate, such as a limited company, no words of limitation are needed to pass a fee simple, presumably since an estate for the life of the corporation would in effect be perpetual. By the Conveyancing Act 1881, s.51, the use of the words "in fee simple" was permitted as an alternative to the words "and his heirs."

The creation in a conveyance of a fee tail, after the estate was created by the Statute De Donis 1285, likewise at common law required the use of the word "heirs" to denote the heritability of the estate, but the word had to be qualified to indicate that only descendants could take. This was done by the addition of *words of procreation* such as heirs "of his body." Other similar expressions would suffice for this purpose. The estate could be further limited to confine the descent to males only, females only, or to issue of a husband and wife (see Chapter 7, p. 48). Once again a change was made by the Conveyancing Act 1881, s.51. The Act made the use of the words "in tail" suffice for the limitation of a fee tail, and the expressions "in tail male" or "in tail female" for entails confined to male and female issue respectively. As with the fee simple, a failure to use the appropriate words of limitation would result in the grantee obtaining only a life estate. The life estate, therefore, would be granted either where there was an intention that it would pass, or where the use of informal words of limitation (or no words of limitation at all) mean that a grant of a fee simple or of a fee tail fails. This rule presuming the grant of a life estate still remains in force notwithstanding that it is inconsistent with what would ordinarily be the intentions of both grantor and grantee.

Table 10.1 sets out the words of limitation required for the freehold estates.

11. Words of limitation in equity

Equity, following the common law, recognised the same estates of freehold, the fee simple, the fee tail, and the life estate. These estates could be created in equity by way of the trust. Where formal conveyancing language was used, equity followed the law, and required the use of the same words of limitation as required in conveyances operating at common law: *Meyler* v. *Meyler* (1883). A failure to use any words of limitation would result in only a life estate being conveyed unless there were something like a prior contract giving the grantee an "equity" to a fee simple: *Jameson* v. *McGovern* (1934). There are some cases suggesting that informal words showing an intention to convey a fee simple would suffice to pass the fee simple, but these cases were overruled by *Re Bostock's Settlement* (1921) and

Table 10.1: Words of limitation in conveyances inter vivos

	At common law	After Conveyancing Act, 1881
Fee simple	"and his heirs" (natural persons) OR "and his successors" (corporation sole)	"and his heirs" OR "in fee simple" (natural persons) OR "and his successors" (corporation sole)
Fee tail	"and the heirs" with words of procreation; words of gender or speciality if required	"and the heirs" with words of procreation, etc. OR "in tail"; "in tail male"; or "in tail female"
Life estate	presumed	presumed

Jameson v. *McGovern* (above). A failure to use the correct words of limitation where it was intended to pass a fee simple or fee tail can, however, be corrected by means of rectification.

The Court of Appeal in Northern Ireland in *Land Purchase Trustee* v. *Beers* (1925) did not follow *Re Bostock's Settlement* and held that the intention of the settlor will suffice to create an equitable estate under a trust unless technical words of limitation conflict with this intention.

12. The Rule in Shelley's Case

If real property were given "to A for his life, and after his death to his heirs" this could be considered a long-winded way of describing how the fee simple was held under the old rules of inheritance. In other words, the expression "for his life, and after his death to his heirs" is a limitation of the fee simple, and is not intended to confer upon the heirs a life estate upon A's death.

A gift in this form is governed by the rule in *Shelley's Case* (1581). Under this rule, which still remains in force in Ireland;

> "when an estate of freehold is given to a person and by the same disposition an estate is limited, either mediately or immediately,

to his heirs or to the heirs of his body, the words 'heirs' or 'heirs of his body' are words of limitation and not words of purchase" (Megarry and Wade, *The Law of Real Property*).

The rule, which does not yield to a contrary intention, and applies to both deeds and wills, covers two basic kinds of gift. In a disposition "to A for life, remainder to his heirs," a case of an immediate limitation to the heirs, it operates to give A a fee simple (or a fee tail had the remainder been given to the heirs of A's body). The other kind of disposition is one involving an intermediate limitation to some other person, such as a gift "to B for life, then to C for life, remainder to B's heirs." With this disposition, the rule gives B a life estate in possession, and a fee simple in remainder subject to C's life estate. If B disposes of the land during his lifetime, his heirs will receive nothing.

13. Modified estates

The technical rules relating to words of limitation apply only to the creation of the two basic estates of inheritance, the fee simple and the fee tail. No technical rules concerning the manner of words required apply to limitations modifying an estate by making it subject to some condition or determining event.

14. Transfer of registered land

The sale of land, title to which is registered, follows the same pattern as that for unregistered land. The form of transfer, however, is different. Ownership is passed not by deed of conveyance, but by registered transfer. Different forms are used according to the circumstances, but Form 10.2, the form prescribed for transfers of freeholds by a full owner in the Republic of Ireland, is representative.

Forms of transfer of registered land are normally more concise than the corresponding deeds for unregistered land. The registered land transfer, being signed, sealed and delivered, is a deed. Amongst the differences are that a registered land transfer contains no recitals, no testatum, no habendum and no testamonium. The registered land deed is "gutted" to the bare essentials, although as with a deed of conveyance additional clauses may be added if desired or appropriate. Attestation of a transfer is required: in the Republic of Ireland by one witness; in Northern Ireland by two witnesses or a solicitor: Land Registration Rules 1972, r. 54; Land Registration Rules (N.I.) 1977, r. 159.

Words of limitation are not required on a transfer of registered land in order to pass a fee simple. By the Registration of Title Act 1964,

Form 10.2: Transfer of registered land

LAND REGISTRY

County Cork Folio 1234 F
Transfer dated 1st day of April 1984

Florence McCarthy Knox, the registered owner, in consideration of £50,000 (the receipt of which is hereby acknowledged) as beneficial owner hereby transfers all the property described in folio 1234 F of the register County Cork to Sinclair Yeates.

The address of Sinclair Yeates in the State for service of notices and his description are: Shreelane House, County Cork, Resident Magistrate, retired

Signed sealed and delivered
by Florence McCarthy Knox
in the presence of

James Canty
Tralagough, Co, Cork
Farmer

Flurry Knox (Seal)

Michael Leary
Skebawn, Co. Cork
Kennelman

s.123 and the Land Registration Act (N.I.) 1970, s.35 a document of transfer of registered land without words of limitation operates to pass the fee simple, or other the whole estate which the transferor had power to transfer, unless a contrary intention appears in the document of transfer.

15. Conveyance or transfer by way of gift

Conveyances or transfers by way of gift must be made in the same form as upon sale, that is by way of deed of conveyance or by way of registered transfer. The steps from contract to conveyance would, however, be dispensed with.

A voluntary conveyance can give rise to one special problem not associated with a conveyance upon sale. There is an equitable presumption that on a conveyance which is not made for valuable consideration (except for conveyances to close relatives "in consideration of love and affection"), the grantor intends to make the grantee a trustee and to retain the beneficial interest himself. Since the Statute of Uses remains in force, this resulting trust would be executed in favour of the grantor, thus cancelling out the conveyance. This can be avoided by employing some formula, such as the words "unto and to the use of" the grantee, indicating that the grantee is to take the beneficial interest. This time-hallowed expression is often inserted into conveyances on sale, although it is not there strictly necessary, nor is it necessary on a transfer of registered land in relation to which it is provided that a resulting use or trust is not to be implied merely because the property is not expressed to be transferred to the use or benefit of the transferee: Registration of Title Act 1964, s.123; Land Registration Act (N.I.) 1970, s.35.

16. Effect of conveyance of unregistered land

A conveyance of unregistered land vests a legal estate in the grantee. Subject to the rules relating to registration of deeds, the grantee will therefore take an interest in land subject to any existing legal rights, and subject to any existing equitable rights except in so far as he can establish that he is a *bona fide purchaser of a legal estate for value without notice* (see pp. 13–16). Although registration of the deed in the Register of Deeds is not compulsory, it is essential if it is to be ensured that the deed will have priority over any subsequent dealings or purported dealings with the land. The registration of a deed also gives it priority over any previous legal or equitable interests created in writing which have not been registered, except where the purchaser has actual notice of the previous interest. For the rules concerning registration of deeds, see Chapter 3, p. 16.

17. Effect of transfer of registered land

A transfer of registered land requires registration at the Land Registry to become operative to transfer ownership because of the principle that the owner of registered land is always the person recorded in the register: Registration of Title Act 1964, s.51; Land Registration Act (N.I.) 1970, s.34. Until registration the transferee has only an "equity" to apply for registration.

On completion of the transfer by registration, the fee simple vests in the transferee as if the transfer had been a conveyance by deed:

Registration of Title Act 1964, s.52; Land Registration Act (N.I.), 1970 s.34. Where the transfer is a transfer for value, the transferee takes subject to any registered burdens and to what may for convenience be called *overriding interests,* that is interests which by section 72 of the 1964 Act and Schedule 5 to the 1970 Act affect the land even without registration.

Where the transfer is not a transfer for value, the transferee takes subject to all the rights and burdens above, and also subject to all unregistered rights subject to which the transferor held the land transferred. That would include, for instance, an undisclosed trust, or an existing contract for the sale of the land.

Overriding interests are a mixed bag. They include rights being acquired by adverse possession (see Chapter 13), customary rights and rights of the public, and the statutory counterpart of the doctrine of notice, " the rights of every person in actual occupation of the land or in receipt of the rents and profits thereof, save where upon enquiry made of such person, the rights are not disclosed": Registration of Title Act 1964, s.72(1)(*j*). (The Land Registration Act (N.I.) 1970, Sched. 5, Pt. I, para. 15 is in similar terms.) This last category has been held to protect the proprietary rights (*National Provincial Bank Ltd.* v. *Ainsworth,* 1965) of all occupiers, including husbands or wives of registered owners: *Williams and Glyn's Bank Ltd.* v. *Boland* (1980).

18. The registered land "guarantee"

The essence of the system of registration of title is that the State "guarantees" the title of the person registered as owner. This guarantee is of course limited in so far as the unregistered rights referred to above bind a transferee as overriding interests. The guarantee extends also only to the title registered. That registration may be subject to certain burdens, and it may also be that the registration is of less than absolute title. There are four different classes or grades of title.

Absolute title is the best. It means that the estate of the registered owner is subject only to burdens expressly registered, and to those enforceable as overriding interests: Registration of Title Act 1964, s.37; Land Registration Act (N.I.) 1970, s.15. Where there is some doubt concerning the title to land at the time of first registration, perhaps because the title deeds do not extend back for the statutory period, registration will be made with *qualified title.* This has the same effect as registration with absolute title subject to any rights arising under the exception noted on the register by way of qualification: 1964 Act, s.39; 1970 Act, s.18. *Possessory title,* the third class, is registration which offers no guarantee concerning matters arising before the date of first registration, although the register is conclusive concerning dealings after that date; 1964 Act, s.38; 1970 Act, s.17. It would be the appropriate class of title for the registration of a person who had acquired title by adverse possession but could offer no documentary evidence of title to the land prior to his taking possession (see Chapter 13).

The three classes of title referred to above may be used both for freehold land, and also for leasehold land: Registration of Title Act 1964, ss.40, 44, 46, 47; Land Registration Act (N.I.) 1970, ss.19, 20, 22, 23. There is, in addition, a fourth class of title for leaseholds, *good leasehold title*. This has the same effect as registration with absolute title, except that registration does not "affect or prejudice the enforcement of any right adverse to, or in derogation of, the title of the lessor to grant the lease." In other words, no guarantee is offered concerning the title of the landlord: 1964 Act, s.45; 1970 Act, s.21. In Northern Ireland *good fee farm grant title* has a similar effect, operating in the same way as absolute title, except that registration is subject to rights adverse to the grantor's title arising under superior fee farm grants: Land Registration Act (N.I.) 1970, s.16.

There is provision for inferior titles to be upgraded to absolute title (or to good leasehold) where because of the passage of time, or because of new evidence or other reason, the registrar is satisfied as to the new class of title: Registration of Title Act 1964, s.50; Land Registration Act (N.I.) 1970, Sched. 3.

19. Rectification and compensation

Since registration of a person as owner of registered land, subject to the limitations outlined above, is conclusive evidence of ownership, it can sometimes happen that the wrong person is registered as owner, and the "true" owner loses his title. Rectification of the register is permitted only in a limited number of circumstances, for instance where registration has been obtained by fraud, or where there has been an error in the land registry, and all interested parties consent to rectification: Registration of Title Act 1964, ss.31, 32; Land Registration Act (N.I.) 1970, s.69. A person who sustains loss as a consequence of an error in registration, or of the rectification of an error to which he did not consent, is entitled to compensation: 1964 Act, s.120; 1970 Act, s.71. This right to compensation is the "bottom line" of the State guarantee, although the guarantee of compensation is restricted: see, for instance *Re Chowood's Registered Land* (1933); *Re Alice Trainor* (1936); *Re 139 Deptford High Street* (1951).

11 Creation and Transfer of Leasehold Interests

A. General

1. The functions of leases

Leasehold interests are used commercially for two main and disparate purposes: to grant possession of land on a short term basis to a tenant, the landlord retaining both an income and capital appreciation; and to grant possession of land on a long term basis at usually only a nominal rent so that the tenant has in practice ownership of the land, the rights of the landlord being collateral. In the former kind of tenancy, the landlord will usually be liable for repairs and the like; in the latter, the tenant will usually have these obligations. An example of a tenancy of the first kind would be a weekly tenancy, or a student letting for an academic year; in the latter category would be a leasehold fee farm grant. There is no absolute dividing line between the two types of tenancy, and there is an infinite range in between. The threshold at which a lease is treated as making a tenant an "owner" is often considered to be 21 years, a period which is recognised in some statutory provisions. With a few exceptions, however, the same rules apply to tenancies of any duration, so that while this part of the book is concerned with the creation and transfer of ownership, for convenience, the rules concerning the creation and transfer of short-term leases are also discussed.

2. The contractual basis of leases

Leases, it will be recalled, (see p. 36) derived from what were originally considered simple contractual relationships, and it was only late in the development of the law of property that they were recognised as creating proprietary interests. The contractual basis of leases still survives. For instance, Deasy's Act 1860 (the Landlord and

Tenant Law Amendment Act (Ireland) 1860, called Deasy's Act after the Attorney-General for Ireland who piloted the Act through the House of Commons), the Act containing most of the general rules concerning leases in Ireland, provides in section 3 that "the relation of landlord and tenant shall be deemed to be founded on the express or implied contract of the parties." As will be seen, a contract can be sufficient for the creation of a lease without the need for an independent grant, which is essential for the creation or transfer of a freehold. It is also customary for the parties to a lease to set out in considerable detail in their agreement the incidents of their relationship.

B. Creation of Leases

3. Substantive requirements for leases

It is essential to any estate in land that the exclusive right to possession (for brevity, exclusive possession) vests in the tenant. While it is possible for there to be doubt in the context of the freehold estates as to whether a grant confers the right to exclusive possession, the question more often arises in the context of apparent leasehold grants. The question is important in relation to such matters as how far the rights of the grantee can be enforced against third parties such as subsequent purchasers of the land, and to questions concerning some protective legislation. Part II of the Landlord and Tenant (Amendment) Act 1980, for instance, applies only to occupiers "under a lease or other contract of tenancy": see sections 5 and 13; *Gatien Motor Co. Ltd.* v. *Continental Oil Co. of Ireland Ltd.* (1979). A contract or grant apparently creating a lease, but failing to give exclusive possession to the "tenant" will create only a licence (see Chapter 15 where the question of what is meant by exclusive possession is more fully discussed).

In addition to this, the creation of a lease requires an intention to create the relationship of landlord and tenant: *Bellew* v. *Bellew* (1983). This is illustrated by two recent Supreme Court cases. In *Irish Shell and B.P. Ltd.* v. *Costello* (1981) the court had to decide whether there was a tenancy or a licence of garage premises. The court acknowledged that exclusive possession was not conclusive as to the existence of a tenancy. It was necessary to look at the terms of the agreement between the parties. Under this, in return for a hire charge for the use of the petrol pumps, tanks and garage equipment, the plaintiffs allowed the defendants to use the site. No sum was expressed to be payable for the use of the site. The agreement was described as a licence, but this did not determine the answer. It was necessary to look at the substance of the agreement, and in the view of the majority of the court, the substance was that there was a tenancy. The defendants, whom the plaintiffs wished to evict, did have exclusive possession which was a strong indicator of a tenancy, even if not conclusive, and other clauses in the agreement were indicators of a tenancy. Although some of the provisions in the agreement were personal in nature, "what was given to the defendants went far beyond a personal privilege to the occupier of the site, and was in the nature of a tenancy of the site."

By way of contrast, in *Gatien Motor Co. Ltd.* v. *Continental Oil Co. of Ireland Ltd.* (above), the Supreme Court held unanimously that an agreement under which the tenant of garage premises was allowed to remain in possession at the expiry of a lease as a "caretaker" did not amount to a tenancy. Although the tenant had exclusive possession under the caretaker agreement, no rent was payable for the caretaker period, the agreement was drawn up as a licence, and there was no element of sham. "The parties negotiated at arms' length, both were fully legally advised, and the caretaker's agreement . . . expressed the intention of the parties" (Griffin J.). A contract of tenancy could not be implied. See also *Northern Ireland Housing Executive* v. *McCann* (1979).

4. Fines and rent

It is usual, but not essential, for a tenancy to be granted in return for a rent. Although normally in the form of a money payment, rent can also take the form of services or goods: see *Montagne* v. *Browning* (1954). Periodic payments not described as rent, but cloaked under the guise or under the label of payment for hire of equipment may in substance be rent: *Irish Shell and B.P. Ltd* v. *Costello* (1981).

Deasy's Act 1860, s.3 states that "the relation of landlord and tenant . . . shall be deemed to subsist in all cases in which there shall be an agreement by one party to hold land from or under another *in consideration of any rent.*" If interpreted as an exclusive definition of a tenancy (see Kenny J., dissenting, in the *Irish Shell* case, above), then this means that payment of a rent is a prerequisite of a tenancy. The more natural interpretation of the section, however, is that it is inclusive rather than exclusive, clarifying one case in which a tenancy may exist, so that a rent-free holding may be a tenancy. Such holdings are sometimes created by way of mortgage (see Chapter 18) and may be found in family settlements.

Particularly on the grant of long leases, it is common, in addition to rent, or instead of rent, for an initial lump sum, called a *fine* to be payable. Fines are sometimes also popularly referred to as "key money." We have already come across the old practice with perpetually renewable leases of demanding a fine upon each renewal.

5. Formal requirements for the creation of leases

The formal requirements for the grant of a leasehold interest are found in section 4 of Deasy's Act 1860. This provides:

> "Every lease, or contract with respect to lands whereby the relation of landlord and tenant is intended to be created for any freehold estate or interest, or for any definite period of time not being from year to year or any lesser period, shall be by deed executed, or note in writing signed by the landlord or his agent thereunto by him lawfully authorised in writing."

The section does not lay down any formal requirements for the creation of a tenancy at will. This may be created without any formality, and even orally. Similarly, a periodic tenancy: weekly, monthly, quarterly, or even yearly, requires no formalities. So also, a lease for a fixed period of less than a year requires no formality: *Crane* v. *Naughten* (1912). For a tenancy for a fixed period of one year certain, though, the position is unclear. In an Irish case, *Wright* v. *Tracy* (1874), it was held in a different context that a tenancy for a year certain was not less than a yearly tenancy. It would follow that it would not satisfy the exception in Deasy's Act 1860 for tenancies "from year to year *or any lesser period*." The reasoning in the case has been criticised in *Bernays* v. *Prosser* (1963) where the English Court of Appeal refused to follow it, so there is some doubt as to the present position.

For those cases where formalities are required (*i.e.* for leases exceeding one year in duration), either a deed or signed writing may be employed. In practice, a deed is normally used for leases of long duration. An example of a lease by deed is given by Form 11.1.

6. Contracts for leases

Except in the case of grants for leases for long periods, the grant of a lease is not normally preceded by a contract. In the majority of cases, the only agreement made between the parties is for the immediate grant of a lease, although this agreement may well be preceded by extended negotiation over terms. In those rarer cases where the grant of a lease is proceeded by a separate contract (*i.e.* a contract for the grant of a lease at a future date) the procedure adopted is very similar to that adopted on a sale of the fee simple (see Chapter 10). The same

Form 11.1: Lease by deed

Parties	THIS LEASE is made the first day of April 1984 between Florence McCarthy Knox of Tory Cottage, Curranhilty, County Cork, Horse Dealer (hereinafter called the landlord, which expression where the context so admits shall include his heirs and assigns) of the one part and Sinclair Yeates of Shreelane House, Curranhilty, County Cork, Resident Magistrate, retired (hereinafter called the tenant, which expression where the context so admits shall include his executors administrators and assigns) of the other part.
Testatum	NOW THIS DEED WITNESSETH that in consideration of the rents and covenants, on the part of the tenant, hereinafter reserved and contained, the landlord doth HEREBY DEMISE unto the tenant
Parcels	ALL THAT dwelling house situate and known as
Habendum	Ardcarrig, Cluin, County Cork, TO HOLD the same unto the tenant from the first day of April 1984 for the
Reddendum	term of fourteen years PAYING therefor yearly during the said term the rent of £3,600 by equal monthly payments on the first day of each month, the first such
Tenant's covenants	payment to be made on the first day of April 1984 AND the tenant hereby for himself and his assigns covenants with the landlord during the said tenancy: (1) to pay the rent at the appointed times; (2) at his or their own expense to keep the premises in good and substantial repair and condition; (3) to use the premises as a private dwelling-house only; AND ALSO at the expiration or sooner determination of the tenancy to deliver up the premises in such good and substantial repair as aforesaid.
Landlord's covenant for quiet enjoyment	AND the landlord hereby for himself and his assigns covenants with the tenant that the tenant, so long as he shall pay the rent and perform his covenants may hold and enjoy the premises during the tenancy without interruption by the landlord or any person claiming under or in trust for him.

(*Continued*)

Form 11.1: Lease by deed (continued)

Proviso for re-entry

PROVIDED THAT if the rent or any part of the rent (whether demanded or not) shall be in arrear by one month or more, or in the event of any breach of any of the covenants on the part of the tenant, the landlord may re-enter upon the demised premises.

Testimonium

IN WITNESS whereof the parties hereto have hereunto set their respective hands and seals the day and year first herebefore written

Attestation

SIGNED SEALED AND DELIVERED
by Florence McCarthy Knox
in the presence of

James Canty
Tralagough, Co. Cork,
Farmer

Flurry Knox

(Seal)

Michael Leary
Skebawn, Co. Cork,
Kennelman.

SIGNED SEALED AND DELIVERED
by Sinclair Yeates
in the presence of

Sinclair Yeates

Jerome Hickey
Drumcurran, Co. Cork
Medical Practitioner

(Seal)

Timothy Connor,
Shreelane, Co. Cork,
Gamekeeper

is true of the transfer of an existing long leasehold interest, such as a leasehold fee farm grant. A contract for the grant of a lease, not operating in itself as the grant of a lease, is governed not by section 4 of Deasy's Act 1860, but by section 2 of the Statute of Frauds (Ireland) 1695, which requires contracts for the sale of any interest in land to be manifested or proved in writing.

The distinction between grants of and contracts for leases is a subtle one. The distinction is essentially between the creation of the relationship of landlord and tenant (a grant), and a promise to create this relationship (a contract for a tenancy). However, as Deasy's Act makes clear (in ss.3 and 4: see pp. 37 and 115) a contract can operate as the grant of a leasehold interest. It is therefore a question of interpretation in every case whether a contract operates without more to create the relationship of landlord and tenant, or whether it is only a promise to do so. The former may be called a contract of tenancy, the latter a contract for a tenancy. The distinction is narrowed further by the possibility of creating a reversionary lease, *i.e.* a lease to commence at a future date (see p. 55). This is a grant which, without more, creates the relationship of landlord and tenant, but only with effect from a future date.

An example of a contract of tenancy is given in Form 11.2. In practice the contract would be likely to contain covenants similar to those found in Form 11.1.

7. Defective formalities

If the appropriate formal requirements for a purported lease are not met, for instance because although there is a note in writing of a lease for more than a year, it has not been signed by the landlord, the contract between the parties cannot operate to create a legal tenancy (*i.e.* a tenancy enforceable at law according to the terms of the agreement). However, at common law a tenant taking possession under a void lease would be considered a tenant at will, and if rent was paid, a periodic tenancy would arise by implication from the conduct of the parties. The period would depend upon the basis on which rent was paid. If paid on the foot of, say, £40 per month, the implied tenancy would be a monthly tenancy. If, however, the monthly payments were calculated by reference to an annual sum, such as a rent of £480 per annum payable in monthly instalments of £40, the tenancy would be a yearly tenancy. The terms of the defective lease would be incorporated into the implied tenancy in so far as they were not inconsistent with a periodic tenancy: *Richardson* v. *Gillford* (1834). The formal requirements of deed or signed writing do not, of course, apply to periodic tenancies.

Form 11.2: Contract of tenancy

THIS AGREEMENT is made the first day of April 1984 between Florence McCarthy Knox of Tory Cottage, Curranhilty, County Cork, Horse Dealer, and Sinclair Yeates of Shreelane House, Curranhilty, County Cork, Resident Magistrate, retired.

Florence McCarthy Knox, as landlord, agrees to let, and Sinclair Yeates, as tenant, agrees to take, the premises known as Ardcarrig, Cluin, County Cork, from month to month from the first day of April, 1984, at the rent of £300 per month, payable in advance on the first day of each month. The tenancy may be determined at the end of any calendar month by either party giving to the other three calendar months' notice in writing.

AS WITNESS the hands of the parties this first day of April, 1984

Signed by the above-named
Florence McCarthy Knox
in the presence of

Flurry Knox

James Canty,
Tralagough, Co. Cork,
Farmer

Michael Leary
Skebawn, Co. Cork,
Kennelman

Signed by the above-named
Sinclair Yeates
in the presence of

Sinclair Yeates

Jerome Hickey
Drumcurran, Co. Cork
Medical Practitioner

Timothy Connor,
Shreelane, Co. Cork,
Gamekeeper

Equity was prepared to go further. It was prepared to treat a defective lease, if made for valuable consideration, as a contract to grant a lease. Under the maxim "equity treats as done that which ought to be done," a contract to grant a lease, if specifically enforceable, creates an immediate equitable interest in the land. To be specifically enforceable, a contract for a lease must, of course, contain all the essential terms, and either be proved in writing, as required by the Statute of Frauds, or supported by part performance. The way in which equity then intervenes is shown by the case of *Walsh* v. *Lonsdale* (1882). In this case the plaintiff went into possession of a mill under a written contract for a lease. One of the terms to be inserted into the lease, which was never formally drawn up and executed, was that the landlord could demand rent in advance. The plaintiff paid rent in arrears for a year and a half, when the landlord demanded a year's rent in advance. The plaintiff argued that the landlord's demand was inconsistent with the periodic tenancy implied at common law from the payment of rent. This argument was rejected by the court, which held that since the Judicature Act the rules of equity prevail. As Sir George Jessel M.R. said:

> "The tenant holds under an agreement for a lease. He holds, therefore, under the same terms in equity as if a lease had been granted, it being a case in which both parties admit that relief is capable of being given by specific performance. That being so, he cannot complain of the exercise by the landlord of the same rights as the landlord would have had if a lease had been granted . . . merely because the actual parchment has not been signed and sealed."

This rule, that a contract for a lease, if specifically enforceable, created a lease in equity, is known as the rule in *Walsh* v. *Lonsdale*. It applies in Ireland: *McAusland* v. *Murphy* (1881). An equitable lease arising under the doctrine is not, though, as good as a lease granted in proper form: it depends upon the availability of specific performance, and is to that extent discretionary (*Cornish* v. *Brook Green Laundry Ltd.*, 1959); it is not a "conveyance" attracting certain implied rights under section 6 of the Conveyancing Act 1881 (see p. 193); it creates no privity of estate, which is relevant to the enforcement of covenants (see Chapter 17); and being equitable only, it is more likely to lose priority to subsequent legal interests (see pp. 13 to 16).

8. Subleases

A sublease is a lease granted by a tenant out of his own leasehold interest. The rules concerning the creation of subleases are the same as those for the grant of a lease out of a freehold estate, discussed above.

9. Words of limitation

The creation of a leasehold interest for a fixed term of years, and the creation of a periodic tenancy, requires no special form of words, although clearly a lease can create a fixed term only if the dates for the commencement and ending of the term are certain, although the commencement of a term of years may be made conditional upon the occurrence of some event: *Swift* v. *Macbean* (1942). A perpetual lease (*i.e.* a fee farm grant) may be created only by the same words as those appropriate for the conveyance of a fee simple: *Re Courtney* (1981). The effect of informal words not appropriate for the fee simple, and not indicating an intention to create a tenancy for life or for a fixed term of years, is unclear. In *Lace* v. *Chantler* (1944), an English case, a lease "for the duration of the war" was held void for uncertainty, and in some Irish cases, a condition added to a periodic tenancy that the landlord may not determine it so long as rent is paid has been held repugnant to the nature of a periodic tenancy: see *Wren* v. *Buckley* (1904); *March and Clibborn* v. *Wilson* (1895); *cf. Re Midland Railway Co.'s Agreement* (1971). But in other cases, a lease so long as rent is paid or so long as the landlord's interest exists has been held to create a tenancy for the life of the tenant: *Re Coleman's Estate* (1907); *Wood* v. *Davis* (1880); *Stafford* v. *Rosenberg* (1932); but see *Holmes* v. *Day* (1874).

C. Transfer of Leases

10. Assignment

The transfer of the entire interest of a tenant is known as an *assignment*. The person to whom the leasehold interest is transferred is substituted for the former tenant, and holds the land directly from the landlord. In this, it differs from a sublease where the purchaser holds the land as a new tenant under the old tenant. It is a question of construction whether a grant by a tenant amounts to an assignment or to a sublease: *Seymour* v. *Quirke* (1884); *Cork County Council* v. *O'Shea* (1947).

11. Formal requirements for assignment

The formal requirements for the assignment of a tenancy are set out in section 9 of Deasy's Act 1860. These are that except for transmissions on death, and transmission by act or operation of law, such as on bankruptcy, the assignment shall be "by deed executed, or instrument in writing signed by the party assigning or granting the same, or his agent thereto lawfully authorised in writing." The need for a deed or instrument in writing applies even in those cases where the original tenancy was created orally. An assignment of a lease takes substantially the same form as a conveyance of freehold land.

D. Determination of Leases

12. Methods of determination

Except in the rare case of a legal interest defeasible by condition subsequent, the right to the possession of freehold land passes automatically on the determination of any prior estate in the land. This is strictly true even in the case of a fee simple defeasible by condition subsequent, for the occurrence of the condition only gives rise to a right by entry to determine the estate.

For leaseholds also, it is possible for a lease to determine and the right to possession to revert automatically to the landlord. In many cases, though, a lease will determine only as a result of the act of either landlord or tenant. In exceptional circumstances a lease could determine through the operation of the doctrine of frustration: *National Carriers Ltd.* v. *Panalpina* (*Northern*) *Ltd.* (1981).

13. Determination by expiry or notice to quit

A tenancy for a fixed term of years, or for life, or until some event occurs, terminates automatically at the expiry of the term, or when the event occurs, as the case may be. This general rule, though, is modified by protective legislation, such as the Housing (Private Rented Dwellings) Act 1982, giving certain tenants the right to remain in possession even following the determination of their tenancy. A periodic tenancy may be determined by notice to quit of the appropriate duration (see p. 53.) A tenancy for a fixed term may also contain a special condition permitting premature termination by notice to quit. The right to determine a tenancy by notice may once again be limited by protective legislation.

The effect of the termination of a tenancy by expiry or by notice to quit is that the tenancy comes to an end, and the right to possession reverts to the landlord.

14. Surrender, merger and enlargement

If a landlord acquires his tenant's interest under a tenancy, or a tenant acquires his landlord's estate, the tenancy is absorbed into the reversion and is thereby extinguished. This process, where the landlord acquires the interest of the tenant, is known as *surrender*. A surrender is a species of conveyance or transfer, and by section 7 of Deasy's Act 1860 may only be made by deed executed, by note in writing signed by the tenant, or by act and operation of law. Surrender by act and operation of law will occur, for instance, where a tenant takes a new tenancy of the premises from a date before the expiry of the old tenancy: *Conroy* v. *Drogheda* (1894). Any other act indicating an intention that a tenancy is surrendered may be effective on principles of estoppel, provided the intention is clear and acted upon: *Lambert* v. *McDonnell* (1865); *Doran* v. *Kenny* (1869). A tenant may surrender his estate to the landlord only if this is provided for in the tenancy, if the landlord consents, or some special statutory provision permits it: section 40 of Deasy's Act 1860, for instance, permits a tenant, in the absence of contrary provision in the letting agreement, to surrender premises destroyed by accidental fire or inevitable accident.

Merger is the converse of surrender and occurs where the tenant acquires the estate of his immediate landlord. It cannot occur where there is an intermediate estate, as where a subtenant acquires the freehold, but not the estate of his own landlord, a "middleman;" nor where there are mortgages or other incumbrances affecting one of the estates. Nor does merger occur where a tenant acquires his landlord's estate in some different capacity, such as personal representative of the landlord. Moreover, in equity, merger does not take place where no merger is intended, and it is presumed that merger is not intended where it would be against the interests of the person acquiring the two estates: *McIlvenny* v. *McKeever* (1931).

Finally, there are a number of statutory provisions enabling certain tenants to enlarge their interests into a fee simple or fee farm grant: see for instance Conveyancing Act 1881, s.65; Landlord and Tenant (Ground Rents) (No. 2) Act 1978; Leasehold (Enlargement and Extension) Act (N.I.) 1971.

15. Forfeiture and ejectment

Where a tenant fails to observe the terms of the lease or tenancy, the landlord may have a right to forfeit the tenancy. This right may be exercised for a breach of condition, or where a right of forfeiture is expressly reserved in the tenancy. There are also certain statutory provisions enabling a landlord to recover possession of the premises let in some circumstances: for instance where in a tenancy from year to year or any greater period, at least a year's rent is in arrear (Deasy's

Act 1860, s.52). Recovery of possession by the landlord in such a case is known as an *ejectment.*

E. Leases in Registered Land

16. Substantive registration of leases

Under the land registration provisions, both in the Republic of Ireland and in Northern Ireland, leasehold interests are capable of substantive registration: that is, a person with only a leasehold interest in land may be registered as owner. A separate register is kept for the registration of ownership of leasehold interests: Registration of Title Act 1964, s.8; Land Registration Act (N.I.) 1970, s.11. The classes of title with which an owner of a leasehold interest may be registered are similar to those for the registration of freeholds and are set out in Chapter 10, p. 110. The leasehold interests so registrable are terms of years with at least 21 years unexpired at the date of registration (not created by way of mortgage, and interests held at a rent under a lease for a life or lives, or determinable on a life or lives: Registration of Title Act 1964, ss.3, 27; Land Registration Act (N.I.) 1970, s.12, Sched. 2.

17. Leases as registered burdens or overriding interests

Leases which are capable of registration in their own right are also capable of registration as burdens on the registered freehold or leasehold estate out of which they have been created: Registration of Title Act 1964, s.69; Land Registration Act, (N.I.) 1970, Sched. 6. Similarly, a lease for less than 21 years may be registered as a burden affecting registered land if the occupation is not in accordance with the lease: *ibid.* The reason for this provision is that "tenancies created for any term not exceeding twenty-one years or for any less estate or interest, in cases where there is an occupation under such tenancies" are included by section 72 of the Registration of Title Act 1964 and Schedule 5 to the Land Registration Act (N.I.) 1970 in the category of overriding interests affecting registered land without registration. This category and the last are therefore mutually exclusive. It will be remembered, however, that the rights of a person in actual occupation of registered land are binding upon the land without registration (see pp. 16 and 110).

18. Creation of leases by a registered owner

The registered owner of either freehold or leasehold land may create leases as if title to the land had not been registered, and these leases will be binding on him: Registration of Title Act 1964 s.68; Land Registration Act (N.I.), 1970 s.32(2). The leases will also be binding on gratuitous transferees: 1964 Act, ss.68, 52–58; 1970 Act, s.34. Since purchasers for value, however, are bound only by leases which are registered as burdens, or protected as overriding interests, it is prudent for a tenant, certainly where he is not in occupation, to register his tenancy as a burden if it belongs to the category of registrable burdens. This is done by making application to the registrar in the prescribed form.

Registration of a leasehold interest may also be compulsory because the land is in a designated compulsory registration area (Registration of Title Act 1964, s.24; Land Registration Act (N.I.) 1970, s.25), or, in Northern Ireland only, because the grant of the lease is made out of an estate which is already registered. Failure in these cases to register within the prescribed time (six months in the Republic of Ireland, three months in Northern Ireland) renders the grant of the leasehold estate void: 1964 Act, s.25; 1970 Act, Sched. 2, Pt. I.

19. Dealings with registered leases

Where a leasehold interest has been registered in its own right, it is governed by the whole registered land regime. Assignments or transfers must be in the prescribed form, and, like transfers of a registered freehold, do not become effective until registration: Registration of Title Act 1964, s.51; Land Registration Act (N.I.) 1970, s.34. The form of transfer for the Republic of Ireland is given in Form 11.3. It will be seen that it is simply an adaptation of the form used for freeholds, and like them, it would usually have additional clauses and certificates added. In particular, it would be the invariable practice for the usual covenants on the part of the assignee for payment of the rent and performance of the covenants in the lease to be inserted, and it would then be necessary for the assignee to execute the transfer.

Burdens created out of a registered leasehold interest are similarly subject to the registered land rules concerning enforceability in the same way as burdens on registered freehold land (see pp. 109 to 111).

20. Dealings with unregistered leases

A lease or tenancy which is not registered in its own right, even if it is registered as a burden, is an unregistered estate in land and dealings with it are not governed by the land registration rules, but by the unregistered leasehold land rules. By the Registration of Title Act

Form 11.3: Transfer by a registered full owner of a leasehold interest

LAND REGISTRY

County Cork Folio 1234L

Transfer dated the 1st day of April 1984

Florence McCarthy Knox, the registered owner, in consideration of £17,500 hereby transfers all the leasehold interest described in folio 1234L of the register County Cork to Sinclair Yeates

The address in the State of Sinclair Yeates for service of notices and his description are: Shreelane House, Curranhilty, Co. Cork, Resident Magistrate (retired).

Signed, sealed and delivered by
Florence McCarthy Knox
in presence of:
James Canty, Tralagough,
Co. Cork, Farmer.

Flurry Knox.

(Seal)

Michael Leary
Skebawn, Co. Cork,
Kennelman.

1964, s.117, however, registration of a leasehold interest as a burden on registered land exempts the lease itself from registration in the Registry of Deeds, but not other deeds or documents relating to the title to the leasehold interest, such as assignments. For the similar Northern Ireland provisions, see the Land Registration Act (N.I.) 1970, s.72.

12 Succession on Death

A. Administration of Assets

1. General

On a person's death, property to which he was entitled for an interest not ceasing on his death will pass to his successors. His death may also result in the expiry of certain interests in property, the ending of certain incumbrances, or the vesting in possession of contingent or expectant interests. But a person's death is not simply an occasion for succession to property, it is also an occasion for that person's affairs to be wound up, his remains disposed of, and his debts settled. For this reason, property to which a person is entitled for an interest not ceasing on death does not pass automatically to his successors, as it once did in the case of real property. Instead, it passes to his personal representatives who are charged with the duty of paying debts and expenses before passing the surplus on to those entitled by will or intestacy.

A further consideration is that a person is not entitled to dispose freely of all his property on death. Both in Northern Ireland and in the Republic there are restrictions upon a person's freedom of disposition of his property on death designed to protect family and dependants. These restrictions are considered at the end of this chapter.

2. Interests in property ending on death

Property to which a person is entitled only for his own lifetime clearly cannot pass to his successors on his death. His death can, however, have different consequences concerning entitlement to the property. In the case of property held by joint tenants, for instance, the death of one results in the operation of the right of survivorship under which the survivors take the entire property, not as successors to the deceased joint tenant, but by force of the nature of their title: see Chapter 9 and Succession Act 1965, s.4(*c*). Similarly, in the case of settled land, the death of a life tenant will result in the land vesting in the remainderman, not as a successor in title to the life tenant, but independently by virtue of his own estate vesting in possession. If, for instance, Blackacre had been conveyed to A for life with remainder to B in fee simple, on A's death, B will receive the fee simple without, in the case of unregistered land, any need for a further transfer since the estate is already vested in him. In the case of land to which title has been registered, an application to the Land Registry or Registrar of Titles will have to be made to have B entered as full owner since future interests are not registered unless and until they fall into possession: see Registration of Title Act 1964, s.61(1); Land Registration Rules (N.I.) 1977, r.61.

In other cases, a person's death may result in the extinguishment of an encumbrance. The death of a person with a right of residence (see Chapter 15), for instance, will result in the right of residence coming to an end so that the owner of the property over which it could be exercised is freed from the encumbrance. So also if property was charged with the payment of a life annuity (see Chapter 18). On the death of the annuitant the property is freed from the charge.

3. Interests in property not ceasing on death

Property to which a person is entitled for an interest not ceasing on his death is available for the payment of debts and for the benefit of his successors. In the first instance the property vests in the personal representatives of the deceased who will be either the *executors* named in his will, or *administrators* appointed by the court. The personal representatives must obtain a *grant of representation* confirming their authority to administer the estate of the deceased. This grant is called a *grant of probate* where it confirms the appointment of executors, and a *grant of letters of administration* where it appoints administrators. To avoid property being left without an owner pending the appointment of administrators it is provided that in the interim the property of the deceased vests, in the Republic, in the President of the High Court (Succession Act 1965, s.13) and in Northern Ireland in the Probate Judge (Administration of Estates Act (N.I.) 1955, s.3). The provisions do not apply to executors, for the property of the deceased is deemed to vest in them immediately on his death. The grant of probate does not appoint them, but merely confirms their appointment.

With unregistered land, the grant of probate or letters of administration is a document of title proving the right of the executors or administrators to deal with the land of the deceased. In the case of registered land, on the death of a registered full owner, unless a joint tenant survives, only the personal representatives of the deceased owner are recognised as having any powers to dispose of the land, but no registration is made in the names of the personal representatives: Registration of Title Act 1964, s.61; Land Registration Act (N.I.) 1970, Sched. 4.

4. Duties of personal representatives

It is the duty of the personal representatives to administer the estate of the deceased. They must first pay the funeral, testamentary and administration expenses, and then after discharging the other debts and liabilities of the deceased in the prescribed manner (Succession Act 1965, s.46; Administration of Estates Act (N.I.) 1955, s.30), the balance is distributed amongst those beneficially entitled. The personal representatives are given a year (the *executors' year*) in which to administer the estate before they can normally be compelled to distribute although creditors can bring proceedings before the year is out: Succession Act 1965, s.62; Administration of Estates Act (N.I.) 1955, s.4).

The property is transferred to those beneficially entitled by means of an *assent*. An assent of pure personalty may be made without formalities, but an assent must be in writing (although it need not be by deed) in order to pass any estate or interest in land: Succession Act 1965, ss.52–54; Administration of Estates Act (N.I.) 1955, s.34.

B. Testate Succession

5. Testacy

A person is said to die testate if he dies leaving an effective will. If a man he is called a *testator*, if a woman, a *testatrix*. A *will* is a declaration by a person of what he desires to be done after his death, and generally relates to the disposition of his property. A document adding to a will, or otherwise varying its provisions, is called a *codicil* and is treated as part of the will. Wills are by their nature *revocable* at any time before death and are *ambulatory* in the sense that they do not take effect until death, and since the Wills Act 1837 in the sense that they are effective to transfer property of a testator acquired between the date of the will and his death. The Wills Act 1837 remains the principal Act in Northern Ireland governing wills. In the Republic of Ireland it has been replaced by the Succession Act 1965 which has altered the law concerning wills in some respects.

6. Capacity to make a will

In both North and South Ireland, the ordinary minimum age for making a will is 18 years. The testator must also be of sound disposing mind: Wills Act 1837, s.7; Age of Majority Act (N.I.) 1969, s.2; S.R. and O. (N.I.) 1969 No. 327; Succession Act 1965, s.77. In the Republic of Ireland, but not in Northern Ireland, a valid will may also be made by a person under the age of 18 who is or has been married: Succession Act 1965, s.77. In Northern Ireland, but not in the Republic, a valid will may be made by a soldier in actual military service, or a mariner or seaman at sea, even though he may be under the age of 18, and as we shall see, a will in these two cases may be made without the ordinary formalities: Wills Act 1837, s.11; Wills (Soldiers and Sailors) Act 1918.

7. Formal requirements of valid wills

Except in the case of privileged wills, explained below, a will must be in writing, be signed by the testator, and be properly attested by at least two witnesses. These requirements are found in section 9 of the Wills Act, 1837 (for Northern Ireland) and in section 78 of the Succession Act 1965 (for the Republic of Ireland).

8. Will to be in writing

The need for writing is satisfied by any form of writing, including pen, pencil, type or print or any combination of these.

9. Will to be signed by testator

A will must either be signed by the testator, or be signed by some other person in his presence and by his direction. Even initials and a thumbprint have been held sufficient. The signature must appear "at the foot or end" of the will, but as these words, when they first appeared in the Wills Act 1837 were applied strictly by the courts, with the result that many wills were held invalid, the requirement was relaxed by the Wills Act Amendment Act 1852, (the provisions of which are re-enacted for the Republic in the Succession Act 1965, s.78, rr. 3, 4 and 5). The result is in effect that the signature is effective if the will was written before it was signed and the signature is so placed that it appears to have been intended to give effect to the will. Anything written after signature in space or in time will not be treated as part of the will. If the will can reasonably be read in such a way as to make the signature appear at the end of the dispositive part of the will, the courts will do this to validate the will: *In the Goods of Hornby* (1946).

10. Attestation of wills

The formal requirement which is the most often productive of difficulty is the requirement that a will be properly attested. This requires that the testator's signature must have been "made or acknowledged by the testator in the presence of [each of] two or more witnesses present at the same time" and the witnesses must each then sign the will by way of attestation in the presence of the testator: Wills Act 1837, s.9. The words in brackets appear in the version in the Succession Act 1965, s.78.

It is essential that the witnesses are present together simultaneously when the testator signs the will or acknowledges his signature. They do not need to see the signature or to know that the testator is signing a will provided that they see the act of signing, and where the testator acknowledges his signature, the witnesses must have had the opportunity to see it, even if they did not avail of the opportunity: *Cooke* v. *Henry* (1932); *Kavanagh* v. *Fegan* (1932).

Following the signature or acknowledgement of the testator, the witnesses must sign the will in his presence, but not necessarily in the presence of each other. Unlike the signature of the testator, the signatures of the witnesses may be placed anywhere on the will, provided that they are intended to attest (*i.e.* bear witness to) the signature of the testator: *In the Goods of Ellison* (1907). There is no need for a clause (an *attestation clause*) stating that the formalities of attestation have been complied with, but such a clause facilitates the grant of probate. A suitable short form would be "Signed by the testator in the presence of us both present at the same time and then signed by us in the presence of the testator" followed by the signatures of the witnesses.

11. Invalidation of gifts to witnesses

Although both executors and beneficiaries under a will may act as witnesses, a gift in a will to a witness, or to a person who when the will was made, was the husband or wife or a witness, is void. This rule, found in the Wills Act 1837, s.15 and in the Succession Act 1965, s.82 is no doubt intended to guard against undue influence. It applies even where there are at least two witnesses apart from beneficiaries who have signed (*In the Estate of Bravda,* 1968), although the courts have not applied the rule where they have concluded that a beneficiary signed not as a witness, but for some other reason, such as to express approval of the contents of the will: *In the Goods of Shaw* (1944).

12. Privileged wills

Section 11 of the Wills Act 1837, as extended by the Wills (Soldiers and Sailors) Act 1918, permitted wills to be made without any formal requirements whatever by any soldier or any airman in actual military service or any mariner or seaman at sea. This legislation remains in force in Northern Ireland, but not in the Republic. The test of actual military service has been held to be satisfied where a soldier was killed on military patrol in Northern Ireland: *Re Jones* (1981). The word "soldier" includes doctors, nurses, chaplains and others serving in the forces as well as the fighting men and women. A woman typist temporarily ashore between sailings of the *Lusitania* on which she was employed has been held to qualify as a mariner at sea: *In the Goods of Hale* (1915). The expressions "mariner or seaman" are not confined to members of the armed forces.

Where the exceptions apply, the will may take any form, including an oral statement intended as an expression of wishes in the event of death. For instance, in *Re Jones* (above) the soldier concerned said "If I don't make it, make sure Anne gets all my stuff" and in *Re Stable* (1919) the statement of a soldier to his fiancée, "If anything happens to me and I stop a bullet, everything of mine will be yours" was held a valid will. There is no minimum age limit for the making of a privileged will. A privileged will remains in force until it is revoked, even though the privilege may have ceased. It may be revoked by any of the methods outlined below. Whether an informal will can revoke a formal will is uncertain: *Re Gossage* (1921). No provision is made for privileged wills by the Succession Act 1965, for the Republic of Ireland.

13. Revocation of wills

Wills may be revoked in three ways: by subsequent marriage, by formal writing, or by destruction. The marriage of the testator (or testatrix) subsequently to making a will automatically revokes that will, except that a will made in contemplation of a particular marriage is not revoked by that marriage: Wills Act 1837, s.18; Wills (Amendment) Act (N.I.) 1954; Succession Act 1965, s.85. In Northern Ireland the will must itself be expressed to be made in contemplation of marriage, but this requirement does not apply in the Republic.

The revocation of a will by formal writing requires that the writing either takes the form of another will or codicil, executed in the proper way, or of some writing declaring an intention of revoking a prior will, and duly executed in the same manner as a will; Wills Act 1837, s.20;

Succession Act 1965, s.85. The revocation may be of the entirety of a previous will, or of part only. The revocation may also be either express or implied. Most wills commence with an opening statement that all previous wills and codicils are revoked, but the common opening words that "This is the last will and testament" of the testator are not taken on their own as a revocation of previous wills or codicils: *In the Goods of Martin* (1968). Implied revocation takes place where a later will or codicil contains provisions which are inconsistent with or repeat those in earlier wills.

Revocation may also take place by the testator himself or some other person in his presence and by his direction burning, tearing or destroying the will with the intention of revoking it: Wills Act 1837, s.20; Succession Act 1965, s.85. Both the destruction and the intention to revoke are essential. In one case, *Cheese* v. *Lovejoy* (1877) a testator crossed through a will, wrote on it "all these are revoked" and threw it into the waste paper basket. It was retrieved by his housekeeper, who kept it until his death. It was held to be valid since it had not been destroyed by the testator, and his writing did not comply with the formal requirements of revocation by writing.

14. Conditional revocation

Revocation by duly executed writing and revocation by destruction both require that the testator has the intention of revoking his will. This intention may be conditional in the sense that the revocation is to occur only if a certain state of affairs exists. One special form of conditional revocation is known as dependent relative revocation. It occurs where a revocation is conditional upon some new will or provision being substituted for the old, and the new will or gift for some reason fails. For instance a testator may destroy his old will intending to sign a new one later that day, but is killed on the way to the solicitor's office. In that event, if it appears from the circumstances that the testator intended the old will to remain valid until the new one was made, the destruction would not revoke the old will. He might, on the other hand, have intended to revoke his old will in any event, regardless of whether he made a new will. In this case the old will would be revoked: *Re Coster* (1979). See also *Sterling* v. *Bruce* [1973] N.I. 255.

15. Alteration of wills

There are three ways in which the provisions of a will may be altered. First, an alteration made before a will is executed is valid, although proof by means of affidavit evidence may be required to show that the alteration was made before execution. Secondly, an alteration made with the same formalities as required for a will (*i.e.* signature of testator and attestation by two witnesses) will be valid: Wills Act 1837, s.21; Succession Act 1965, s.86. For this purpose the initials of the testator and of the witnesses close to the alteration will suffice. Thirdly, under section 21 of the Wills Act 1837, any alteration which makes the words or effect of a will "not apparent" is valid. Part of the will may, for instance have been cut out, pasted over, covered with typewriter correction fluid or otherwise obliterated or erased. If this makes it impossible to read the will without physically interfering with it, then the alteration will be effective to the extent of expunging the words not apparent. But while pasting a slip of paper over an existing gift in a will may revoke that gift, if a new gift is written in, the new gift must comply with the proper formalities of signature and attestation, although the fact that it is in substitution for the previous gift may lead to the inference that the previous gift was revoked conditionally upon the new one being valid. Thus in *In the Goods of Itter* (1950) the testatrix pasted a slip of paper reading "two hundred pounds" over the words "one hundred and fifty pounds" in a gift in her will. It was held that the revocation of the original gift was conditional upon the higher amount being substituted, so that the gift remained at the original amount.

No express provision is made in the Republic of Ireland for alteration by making words in a will "not apparent." Any alteration or obliteration, if made after the execution of the will, must therefore be separately executed. There is nothing, however, to prevent the partial revocation of a will under the Succession Act 1965, s.85 by destroying part by erasure, cutting or tearing: *In the Goods of Morton* (1887).

16. Revival

A will, or a part of a will, once revoked, can only be revived by re-execution of the will, or by the execution of a codicil showing an intention that the will be revived: Wills Act 1837, s.22; Succession Act 1965, s.87.

17. Lapse

The ordinary rule is that where a beneficiary under a will dies before the testator, the gift to him or her lapses (*i.e.* fails). The testator himself may provide for some other gift in substitution, and there are two statutory exceptions. One of these relates to entails and is of little consequence: Wills Act 1837, s.32; Succession Act 1965, s.97. The other is more important. Where a testator makes a gift by will to a child or other issue of his, the gift does not lapse if the child or issue named himself leaves issue surviving at the testator's death: Wills Act 1837, s.33; Succession Act 1965, s.98. What happens is that the gift is treated as part of the estate of the deceased child or other issue named, and will go under his will or intestacy.

Gifts to children are subject to hotchpot (see Section 27, below).

18. Words of limitation

It is just as important in a will as in a conveyance *inter vivos* that the appropriate words of limitation be used to identify the estate in real property that a beneficiary is to take. The requirements of words of limitation in wills have, however, always been more liberal (and in accordance with modern conceptions of common sense). The common law rule was that in the absence of words of limitation, a gift of land by will was presumed to pass a life estate only, but a fee simple or a fee tail would pass where the will showed an intention that one of these two estates should pass. The presumption of a life estate was reversed by the Wills Act 1837, s.28. This provided that a devise of real estate without words of limitation "shall be construed to pass the fee simple, or other the whole estate or interest which the testator had power to dispose of by will . . . unless a contrary intention shall appear by the will." A further change was made for the Republic of Ireland by the Succession Act 1965. By section 95 the creation of a fee tail now requires the use of the same words of limitation as those required in deeds. For these, see Chapter 10, Section 10 (p. 105).

Before the changes made by the Succession Act 1965, and still, in Northern Ireland, a special rule, known as the rule in *Wild's Case* (1599), applies to a gift expressed to be made "to A and his children." It is not clear in this form of gift whether the word "children" is a word of purchase so that A and his children take the fee simple or life estate jointly (according to whether this is before or after the Wills Act, 1837); or whether the words "and his children" are words of limitation indicating an intention that A should take a fee tail. The solution adopted through the rule in *Wild's Case* is that if at the time when the will was *made*, A had no children, the words were construed as words of limitation. If at that date he did have children, the children living at the death of the testator would take as purchasers. The rule in *Wild's Case* has been abolished for the Republic of Ireland by the Succession Act 1965, ss.89 and 95.

Table 12.1 sets out the requirements for words of limitation in wills.

Table 12.1: Words of limitation in wills

	Before 1837	After Wills Act, 1837	After Succession Act, 1965 (Republic of Ireland)
Fee simple	Intention	Presumption	Presumption
Fee tail	Intention	Intention	"and the heirs" + words of procreation or "in tail"
Life estate	Presumption	Intention	Intention

C. Intestacy in the Republic of Ireland

19. Intestate succession since 1967

A person dies intestate when he dies leaving no will or leaves a will but leaves undisposed of some beneficial interest in his property on death. His property is then divided under the rules which for the Republic of Ireland are found in Part VI of the Succession Act 1965. These rules apply to all property, real and personal, and as the Minister for Justice when introducing them, said:

> "They are simple and uniform and are so framed as to accord due recognition to the important position which the wife occupies in the Irish family."

The intestacy rules in the Succession Act 1965 apply to the estate of a person dying on or after 1st January 1967, the date on which the Act came into operation.

The basic framework of the rules is that any surviving spouse and issue have the first right to the estate, followed by the nearest blood relations, failing whom the property goes to the State.

20. Shares of surviving spouse and issue

Where a person dies intestate with a surviving spouse but no issue, the spouse takes the whole estate. Where the intestate dies with both surviving spouse and issue, the spouse takes two-thirds of the estate and the issue the remainder. Where issue but no spouse survive, the issue take the whole estate: Succession Act 1965, s.67. The expression "issue" is not defined in the Act. It does not include illegitimate children: *In the Goods of Walker* (1984). The only rights of succession they have are under the Legitimacy Act 1931, s.9(1). This gives an illegitimate child, or his issue, the right to succeed to the estate of his mother as if he had been born legitimate where the mother dies wholly or partly intestate and is not survived by any legitimate children or issue. An illegitimate child has no rights of succession to the estate of his father under the Act.

Children legitimated under the Legitimacy Act 1931 at the date of the death of an intestate have the same succession rights as legitimate children, and under section 26 of the Adoption Act 1952, adopted children have the same succession rights after the making of an adoption order as a child of the adopter born in lawful wedlock.

21. Method of distribution among issue

Section 67(4) of the Succession Act provides how the share of issue is to be distributed. Where the issue are in equal degree of relationship to the deceased, the distribution shall be in equal shares among them, *i.e. per capita*. Thus if all four children of an intestate survive him, they will take a one-quarter share each.

Where the issue are not in equal degree of relationship, then distribution is *per stirpes*, according to each stock of descent. Thus in Figure 12.1, if Anne, one of the intestate's four children, has predeceased him, but is survived by her own two children, Edward and Fanny, these two grandchildren "stand in the shoes" of Anne, and take between them the share she would have received had she survived. Edward and Fanny thus take one-eighth each, the surviving children, Barry, Charles and David, one-quarter each. George and Harry take nothing, since Charles, their father, survives, nor do Oliver and Peter take anything since Fanny also survives. If Fanny had predeceased the intestate, Oliver and Peter would have represented her, taking one-sixteenth of the estate each. Children or other issue represent a parent only if he is not alive. See generally the Succession Act 1965, s.3(3). It should also be observed that the shares of children and issue representing them are subject to *hotchpot*: that is, they take account of advancements made to the child during the life of the intestate (see Section 27, below).

22. Shares of parents, brothers and sisters

Where the intestate is survived by neither spouse nor issue, his parents are entitled. If both parents survive, they take equally. If only one parent survives, that parent takes the whole estate: Succession

Figure 12.1: Distribution per stirpes

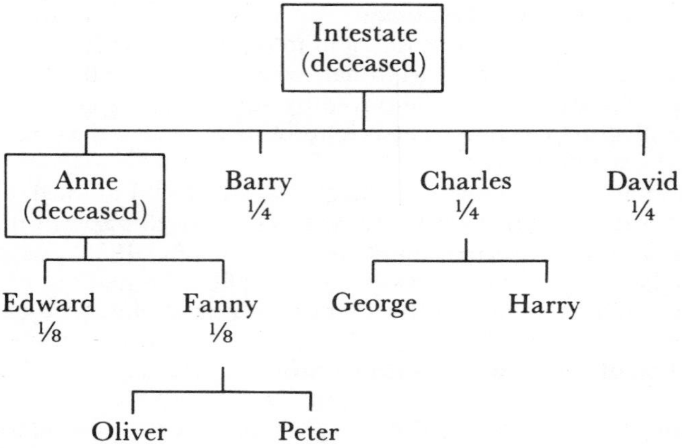

Act 1965, s.68. Where neither parent survives, the estate is distributed between the brothers and sisters of the intestate in equal shares. Children of a deceased brother or sister of the intestate take their parent's share, if any other brother or sister of the intestate survived him. Such children take *per stirpes* the share which their parent would have taken if he had survived the intestate. If the intestate has no surviving brother or sister, the surviving children of his brothers and sisters take equally: Succession Act 1965, s.69.

23. Shares of next of kin

Failing the survival of spouse, issue, brothers and sisters and their children, the estate is divided equally amongst the nearest blood relations, described as the next-of-kin: Succession Act 1965, ss.70 and 71. The degree of relationship is computed by calculating the number of generations dividing the intestate from his ancestor or other relative. Thus a grandfather is two degrees removed. Where the relative is not a direct lineal ancestor, it is necessary to count upwards to the nearest common ancestor and then down to the relative. An uncle is thus three degrees removed: two degrees to the grandfather, the nearest common ancestor, and then one degree down. A great grandfather is also three degrees removed, but the Succession Act provides that relatives, such as uncles, who are not direct lineal ancestors are to be preferred to direct lineal ancestors even though they are in the same degree of relationship. See also the Administration of Estates Act (N.I.) 1955, s.12. In tracing relationships, relatives of the half-blood take equally with relatives of the whole blood in the same degree: Succession Act 1965, s.72; Administration of Estates Act (N.I.) 1955, s.14.

24. Right of State

Where no other person is entitled under the rules outlined above, the State takes as ultimate intestate successor: Succession Act 1965, s.73.

25. Outline of succession rights

Table 12.2 shows in tabular form the order of entitlement on intestacy under the Succession Act 1965. It should be remembered that division between issue and between brothers and sisters and their children is not necessarily in equal shares.

26. Partial intestacy

Where a person dies leaving a will which disposes of some, but not all, of his estate, the gifts by will take effect first, and the undisposed of balance of the estate is distributed under the intestacy rules: Succession Act 1965, s.74. Gifts under the will do not have to be taken into account in computing shares on intestacy.

27. Hotchpot

In computing the shares of children of an intestate, the children must bring into account as between themselves any advancement received from the intestate during his lifetime. This would include gifts of money or other property intended as permanent provision for a child. Thus if on his death an intestate had four children, but no surviving spouse, and left a net estate valued at £50,000, the children would each be entitled to £12,500 if they had received nothing during the lifetime of the intestate. If the eldest had already received £10,000 on coming of age, but no similar payment had been given to the others, the three younger children would take £15,000 each and the eldest only £5,000 since when added to the £10,000 he has already received, this means he will have had the same as the others. See the Succession Act 1965, s.63.

This hotchpot rule applies both to total and partial intestacy, and also to gifts by will except where the deceased has made it clear that the lifetime gift was intended to be in addition to anything a child would receive on his death.

Table 12.2: Order of entitlement on intestacy

Surviving spouse	Surviving issue	Surviving parents	Surviving brothers and sisters	Surviving children of brothers and sisters	Surviving next-of-kin	State
Whole estate	None					
Two-thirds of estate	One-third of estate					
None	Whole estate					
None	None	Whole estate				
None	None	None	Whole estate children representing deceased parent			
None	None	None	None	Whole estate		
None	None	None	None	None	Whole estate	
None	None	None	None	None	None	Whole estate

Note: The word "None" means no person in this category survives. Where a block remains blank, it signifies that it is irrelevant whether a person in this category survives.

28. Intestate succession before the Succession Act 1965

Prior to the Succession Act 1965 intestate succession in the Republic of Ireland was governed, in the case of real property, by the ancient rules of inheritance, and in the case of personal property, by rules of succession laid down by the Statute of Distributions (Ireland) 1695. These rules were only modified to a minor extent by subsequent statutes.

29. Rules of inheritance

The rules of inheritance, which were abolished by the Succession Act 1965, except so far as regards the descent of entails, contained three chief rules. These were the rules of male preference, primogeniture and preference for issue. If a person entitled to real property died, that real property passed to his heir. This would be his first-born son if that son survived. If the son did not survive, any of that son's children or other descendants would stand next in line to succeed. Failing any issue of the first-born son, the second son would be entitled, then his issue, and so on. Only if there were no sons or their issue would daughters be entitled, and they took as coparceners if there was more than one of them (see Chapter 9). If no issue at all survived, the heir could be traced amongst the lineal ancestors and their issue. The nearest familiar analogy with the rules of inheritance is the order of entitlement to the British Crown. Figure 12.2 shows the order of entitlement of an heir based upon an hypothetical example.

Figure 12.2: Ascertainment of heir

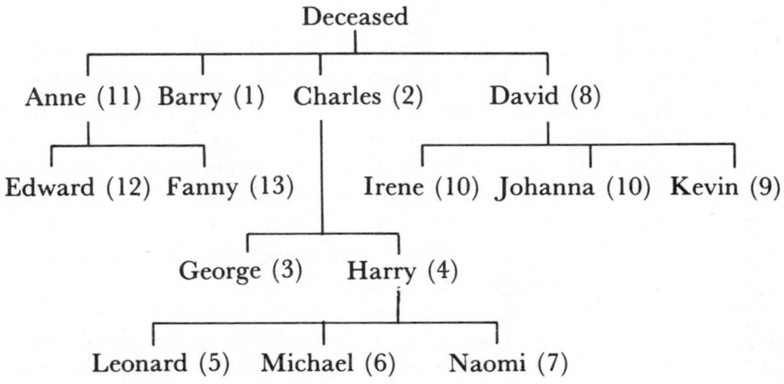

The rights of an heir were subject to certain limits. One was that the widow of a landowner had a right of quarantine under *Magna Carta*, which was a right to remain in the chief house of her husband for 40 days. She also had a right to dower, which was a right to a life estate in one-third of the fee simple or fee tail estates of her husband provided that the birth of issue of the marriage capable of inheriting had been possible. A wife's right to dower was lost, however, where her husband had disposed of land during his lifetime or by will, or where he had made a declaration barring dower under the Dower Act 1833.

A husband, conversely, had a right to a tenancy by the curtesy, being a right to a life estate in the entire heritable real property of his deceased wife, provided in this case that issue capable of inheriting had in fact been born, although such issue need not have survived. The right of curtesy was lost where the wife disposed of property *inter vivos* or by will.

30. Devolution of personalty before 1967

Personal property, including leasehold land, did not pass to the heir on an intestacy. Instead it went to the personal representatives of the deceased, who after meeting "all debts, funeral charges and just expenses" distributed the "surplusage" in the way laid down by the Statute of Distributions (Ireland), 1695. In brief, this meant that if the deceased was survived by a widow and issue, the widow took one-third of the estate, the remainder being distributed among the issue *per stirpes*. Where a widow but no issue survived, the widow took half of the estate, the remainder being distributed amongst the next-of-kin of the husband (*i.e.* those most nearly related to him by blood). The widow took the entire estate if there were no next-of-kin. Where a woman was survived by her husband, he took the whole personal estate under his common law right as husband. This was so whether or not there were issue. Failing the survival of a husband, the balance after paying the share of the widow (if any) was distributed first among the issue *per stirpes*, and failing any surviving issue to the father, and failing him, to the mother, brothers and sisters equally (children of a brother or sister representing their parent if dead), and failing these, to the next-of-kin, being those most closely related by blood. For a table of the method of distribution see McGuire and Pearce, *The Succession Act 1965*, (2nd ed.), App. A.

Registered land which had been bought out under the Land Purchase Acts, although real property for most purposes, devolved as if it were personal property: Local Registration of Title Act 1891, ss.84 and 85.

31. Statutory legacy of widow prior to 1967

The rules outlined above for the devolution of real and personal property were modified by the Intestates Estates Act 1890. Under this Act a widow, where no issue survived, was entitled to the entire estate, real and personal, of an intestate if this amounted to £500 or less. If the value of the estate exceeded this sum, she was entitled to a first charge of £500 with interest, charged rateably (*i.e.* proportionately) upon the real and personal property. She was then entitled to a half share in the residue of the personal estate, the other half passing to the next-of-kin of the husband, or to the wife if he had no next-of-kin. The widow also retained her right to dower out of the remaining real estate. The 1890 Act was replaced by the Intestates Estates Act 1954 which increased the statutory legacy to the widow to £4,000.

D. Legal Rights of Spouse and Children in the Republic

32. Protection of spouse and children

The Succession Act 1965 contains important provisions designed to protect the spouse and children of a testator from disinheritance. These provisions operate by conferring on a surviving spouse a minimum fixed share of the estate, the "legal right share," and by conferring on children a right to apply to court for better provision than a testator has made for them by will. Both forms of right apply only where "a person dies wholly or partly testate:" Succession Act 1965, s.109(1). This restriction is sensible enough in relation to a surviving spouse since the right of a spouse on intestacy always exceeds the legal right share. In relation to the right of children to apply to court for proper provision the restriction operates perversely since judicial decisions indicate that in special circumstances proper provision for a child can exceed the equal share a child would receive under the intestacy rules. It was almost certainly for this reason that Carroll J. in *R.G.* v. *P.S.G.* (1981) held that a person who by his will made his wife his sole executrix (*i.e.* personal representative) and sole beneficiary died "testate" under section 109 even though she had predeceased him so that his will was wholly inoperative at the date of his death.

33. Legal right share of spouse

Where a testator leaves a spouse and children, the spouse has a legal right to one third of the estate. Where the testator leaves a spouse and no children, the spouse has a legal right to one half of the estate:

Succession Act 1965, s.111. It should be noted that the size of the share depends upon whether or not there are *children*. The size of a spouse's intestate share depends upon whether there are *issue*. Apart from this distinction, the legal right share is half of the share a surviving spouse would take on intestacy. A spouse may renounce his or her legal right in writing before the death of the testator: Succession Act 1965, s.113. The right can also be disclaimed after the testator's death. As a transitional provision, permanent provision made by a testator for a spouse during his lifetime and before the Succession Act came into operation is to be taken into account in computing the legal right share.

A testator may, by his will, make a gift to the spouse which is in addition to the legal right share, but it is presumed that a gift by will is intended to be in satisfaction of the legal right share unless it is expressed in the will to be in addition: Succession Act 1965, s.114.

In some cases it is necessary for a spouse to elect to take the legal right share. This is so where the deceased died wholly testate, making a gift to the spouse which is not expressed to be in addition to the legal right share, or where the deceased dies partly testate. In both of these cases, unless the spouse elects to take the legal right share, he or she takes only under the will or the will and partial intestacy. The spouse has twelve months from the date on which the personal representatives obtained a grant, or six months from being served notice of the right to elect by the personal representatives, whichever is the later: Succession Act 1965, s.115. A spouse has no need to elect, and takes the legal right share automatically, where the testator died wholly testate, but making no gift to the spouse, or where the testator makes a gift by will to the spouse expressed to be in addition to the legal right share.

34. Provision for children

Under the regime in force in the Republic of Ireland, children are not given an absolute right to any part of a testator's estate. An application to the court is necessary, and the court may order whatever provision it considers just to be made out of the estate. The rules are found in section 117 of the Succession Act 1965. The test for the court in deciding whether provision should be made is whether the testator "has failed in his moral duty to make proper provision." This is to be tested from the point of view of a just and prudent parent. The court is not permitted to make provision for a child which interferes with the legal right share of a surviving spouse, nor with a gift by will or share on intestacy of a parent of the child.

The court's decision consists of two stages. The first is that the court must decide whether the testator has failed in his moral duty to make proper provision for a child. Only if he has failed to do so does the court proceed to the second stage, which is to decide what provision it will order to be made.

The first reported case in which section 117 was invoked was *F.M.* v. *T.A.M.* (1970). The guidelines laid down by Kenny J. in that case have been generally followed since, although they have been much enlarged upon by the numerous subsequent decisions. The majority of these cases are reviewed by Cooney in "Succession and Judicial Discretion in Ireland: the Section 117 Cases" (1980) 15 Ir. Jur. (N.S.) 62.

It would seem from the decisions that a testator does have a moral duty to make proper provision, although that duty may have been discharged by gifts to a child during his lifetime, and "proper provision" does not always require that each child should receive something. The comparative circumstances of all the testator's children are relevant, and even though illegitimate children may not themselves be able to assert a claim for proper provision (since they are not "children" within the meaning of the Act), nevertheless the testator may owe moral obligations to them. These moral obligations, and any other moral obligations of the testator, such as to aged and infirm parents, must be taken into account in deciding whether he has made proper provision for his legitimate children at least in so far as the moral claims upon the testator are provided for in his will: *L.* v. *L.* (1978); *M.P.D.* v. *M.D.* (1981).

Nor must the children of a testator necessarily have been provided for equally by him, indeed a prudent and just parent would treat his children unequally according to their needs and circumstances: see *L.* v. *L.* (above). Relevant circumstances include the age and financial position and prospects in life of children (although even a 32 year old first mate in the merchant navy has made a successful claim: *F.M.* v. *T.A.M.*, above), the mental capacity of a child and the child's health. The conduct of a child has also been treated as relevant. A dutiful child is more likely to be successful than one who has not behaved in a proper filial manner. However, in one case where a father had behaved harshly, cruelly and neglectfully towards his children, he was held to have a moral duty to help in the rehabilitation of a son who had served six years in prison for receiving stolen goods: *Re F.F.*; *H.L.* v. *Bank of Ireland* (1978).

The standard of provision which the court expects a testator to make clearly depends to a very great degree upon the means of a testator. If he is well-off, his duty to make proper provision will normally extend beyond simply providing for the maintenance of his infant children, and may require the provision of a lump sum by way of advancement for them in life: *Re N.S.M., B.S.M.* v. *R.J.W.* (1971). Conversely, a testator of limited means cannot be expected to make such generous provision.

There are a number of factors which may operate to reduce the extent to which a testator must make proper provision for his children by will. Provision during his lifetime, or otherwise, is expressly to be taken into account. Sums received from others by a child, such as gifts from grandparents or other relatives, are to be taken into account (*Re N.S.M.*, above), but the value of indirect, contingent or expectant benefits will have to be discounted to take into account the fact that it may prove that the benefit is not as large as anticipated: see *M.P.D.* v. *M.D.*, above.

In determining whether a testator has failed in his moral duty to make proper provision, the courts have asserted that a judgment must be made on the basis of the facts existing at the date of death, although the choice of this date can give rise to inconveniences which Kenny J. in *Re N.S.M.* (above) was able to avoid only by crediting to a testator an extraordinary degree of prescience enabling him to foresee not only that litigation would follow his death, but also that this litigation would render a residuary gift to a child virtually worthless.

Once (but only if) the court has decided that a testator has failed to make proper provision, it may itself order provision to be made out of the estate. The same factors are taken into account in assessing the quantum of provision in this second stage as in the first stage. Changes between the death and the hearing are, however, taken into account, it would seem (see *M.P.D.* v. *M.D.*, above), and in making provision, the court will be concerned to interfere as little as possible with the testator's will consistently with making an order which is just and fair. For this principle, and its limits, see *W.* v. *D.* (1975).

Any application by or on behalf of a child seeking an order for provision must be made within 12 months of a grant of representation first having been taken out: *M.P.D.* v. *M.D.* (above).

E. Intestacy in Northern Ireland

35. The history of intestate succession

The modern rules now governing intestacy in Northern Ireland are found in the Administration of Estates Act (N.I.) 1955 and 1971, as amended by the Administration of Estates (N.I.) Order 1979. These rules first came into force in 1956 replacing the old rules of inheritance and intestate succession described in Sections 28 to 31 above, although of course the variation of the statutory legacy of a widow made by the Intestates Estates Act 1954 did not apply to Northern Ireland.

36. Intestate succession since 1955

The rights of the surviving spouse and other relatives of an intestate in Northern Ireland depend on who survives the intestate. The surviving spouse (if any) takes the whole estate if there are no surviving issue of the intestate, nor surviving parents, brothers, sisters or their issue. Where there are survivors in the categories just mentioned, the surviving spouse takes the "personal chattels," a fixed sum, and a proportion of any residue of the estate. "Personal chattels" are elaborately defined by the 1955 Act and include basically the household furniture and effects, but not chattels used for business or professional purposes, nor money.

The fixed sum to which a surviving spouse is entitled is, since 1981 (see Administration of Estates (Rights of Surviving Spouse) Order (N.I.) 1981) £40,000 where there are issue, and £85,000 where there are no issue but there are surviving parents, brothers, sisters, or their issue. The fixed sums were originally £1,500 and £5,000 respectively, but these sums have been varied from time to time. The proportion of the residue which the surviving spouse takes is one-half where the higher fixed sum is due, or where only one child or the issue of one child of the deceased survives. Where two or more children (again with surviving issue representing a deceased child) survive, the fraction taken by the surviving spouse is only one-third.

Subject to the rights of the surviving spouse (if any), the order in which the residue of the estate is distributed is that children take first, issue of a deceased child representing him or her and taking *per stirpes*. The parents are next entitled, and then brothers and sisters of the intestate, issue of a deceased brother or sister representing *per stirpes* that sibling. All the relations in these categories will take the half share of the residue (two-thirds where two or more children or their issue survive) where there is a surviving spouse, or the whole of the estate where no spouse survives. Failing any relations in the categories already enumerated, the whole of the estate passes to the next-of-kin, who are the nearest blood relations ascertained as described in Section 23 above. A difference is that a deceased uncle or aunt (*i.e.* a brother or sister of a parent of the intestate) will be represented by his or her issue who will take *per stirpes*, if issue survive the intestate. Failing next-of-kin, the entire estate passes to the Crown as *bona vacantia*.

A further difference with the law in the Republic of Ireland is that illegitimate children have full rights of inheritance from their parents (and vice versa), although these rights of inheritance do not extend to other relations: Family Law Reform (N.I.) Order, 1967 (applies to deaths from January 1, 1978).

37. Hotchpot and partial intestacy

Advancements made to a child, or to a grandchild to whom the intestate stood *in loco parentis*, but not to remoter issue or other relatives, must be brought into account in the distribution on intestacy (see Section 27, above). In Northern Ireland, hotchpot does not apply to gifts by will, but it does apply to a child's share on partial intestacy: Administration of Estates Act (N.I.) 1955, ss.17 and 18.

In a partial intestacy, after meeting any dispositions by will, the residue of the estate is distributed as if the deceased died intestate leaving no other estate: 1955 Act, s.18.

38. Outline of succession rights

Table 12.3 sets out in tabular form the order of entitlement on intestacy in Northern Ireland. Representation by issue is admitted in the case of children, brothers and sisters, and uncles and aunts of the intestate. In all of these cases issue representing a deceased child, brother, sister, aunt or uncle, as the case may be, take *per stirpes*: see Section 21 and Figure 12.1, above.

F. Protection of Family and Dependants in Northern Ireland

39. Protection of family and dependants

The Inheritance (Provision for Family and Dependants) (N.I.) Order, 1979 extends to Northern Ireland provisions substantially similar to those in force in England and Wales for the protection of family and dependants. Unlike the provisions in the Republic of Ireland, the 1979 Order applies on intestacy as well as where the deceased died testate. Family and dependants have no right to a fixed share of a deceased's estate; instead they may apply for a court order on the grounds that they did not receive from the estate of the deceased "reasonable financial provision." Application must be made within six months of representation to the estate being taken out, or later with the permission of the court. Irrespective of whether or not a grant has been taken out, an application for financial provision can only affect the deceased's severable share in property held under a joint tenancy if it is made not later than 18 months from the date of death. Considerable latitude is given to the court as to the manner in which it may order that provision be made.

Table 12.3: Order of entitlement on intestacy in Northern Ireland

Spouse	Children		Parents	Brothers and sisters (or issue)	Next-of-kin	Crown
	One only (or issue)	Two or more (or issue)				
Whole estate	None		None	None		
Personal chattels £40,000 + ½ residue	½ residue					
Personal chattels £40,000 + ⅓ residue		⅔ residue				
Personal chattels £85,000 + ½ residue	None		½ residue			
Personal chattels £85,000 + ½ residue	None		None	½ residue		
None	Whole estate					
None	None		Whole estate			
None	None		None	Whole estate		
None	None		None	None	Whole estate	
None	None		None	None	None	Whole estate

Note: The word "None" signifies that no person in this category survives. Where a block remains blank, it signifies that it is irrelevant whether a person in this category survives.

40. Protection of family

The members of a deceased's family who may make application for provision are a surviving spouse or former (*e.g.* divorced) spouse who has not remarried, a child, and any person treated as a child of the family (*e.g.* children of a second wife by her first husband). Included in the category of children are illegitimate and adopted children.

Where application is made by a spouse "reasonable financial provision" means such provision "as it would be reasonable in all the circumstances of the case for a husband or wife to receive, whether or not that provision is required for his or her maintenance." The age of the applicant and the duration of the marriage are two of the special relevant circumstances. Probably the most important consideration for a surviving spouse, though, is "the provision which the applicant might reasonably have expected to receive if on the day on which the deceased died the marriage, instead of being terminated by death had been terminated by a decree of divorce." This statutory provision is intended to avoid spouses doing better on divorce than on death. But see *Re Besterman* (1984).

General considerations, which apply in the other cases too, include the means and needs of the applicant, any other applicant, and beneficiaries of the estate, and the moral obligations of the deceased to them; the value of the estate, and the conduct of the applicant or any other person where this is relevant.

Where the applicant is not a surviving spouse, the appropriate test is whether the provision is such as it would be reasonable in all the circumstances of the case for the applicant to receive for his maintenance. Special relevant circumstances here include the manner in which the child was, or could expect to be, educated or trained.

41. Provision for dependants

Application to court may be made not only by members of the deceased's family, but also by a person who immediately before the death of the deceased was being maintained wholly or partly by the deceased. This will be so only "if the deceased, other than for full valuable consideration, was making a substantial contribution in money or money's worth towards the reasonable needs of that person." Reasonable financial provision in this case, as for children, is confined to provision for maintenance, and special relevant circumstances are the extent to which the deceased assumed responsibility, and the length of time for which he discharged that responsibility.

13 Adverse Possession

1. Transfers by non-owners

It is not normally possible to acquire ownership of land through a transfer by a non-owner. As with personal property, the basic rule is "*nemo dat quod non habet*"—no one may give what he does not have. It is because of this that a purchaser of land goes through the procedure of checking the vendor's title. The process of investigation of title will normally ensure that the vendor does, indeed, have a right to convey the land.

There are a number of exceptions to the *nemo dat* rule. In these cases a transfer by a non-owner can be effective. Exceptions explained elsewhere include a sale by a mortgagee under a power of sale conferred by the mortgage (see p. 224), and a sale by a tenant-for-life under the powers contained in the Settled Land Acts (see Chapter 14). In addition a person may be given an express right by way of a power of attorney to conclude a sale or other dealing concerning land on behalf of the owner. In appropriate circumstances, the owner of land may also be bound to a deal made by another under a principle of estoppel. For instance, in *Spiro* v. *Lintern* (1973) the sole owner of a family home was the husband. He and his wife decided to sell. All the correspondence concerning the sale was conducted by the wife, and it was she who finally authorised the estate agents to sign a contract with the plaintiff. Over the following four weeks the plaintiff employed an architect to undertake certain functions on his behalf connected with the house, he visited the house and saw the husband three times, and he had certain building work carried out. At no time did the husband demur or dissent from the plaintiff being treated as purchaser. It was held that, by his conduct in allowing the plaintiff to incur expenditure in the belief that he had a binding contract of purchase, the husband was estopped from asserting that the contract had been entered into without his authority. For other examples of estoppel see Chapter 15.

Another instance of the acquisition of title against the will of the owner arises in the case of registered land. Because of the rule that registration of a person as owner of land is proof of his title (Registration of Title Act 1964, s.31; Land Registration Act (N.I.) 1970, s.11) even a registration procured by fraud vests an estate in the land in the registered owner except where he himself is party or privy to the fraud (1964 Act, ss.37 *et seq.*, 30(2); 1970 Act ss.15 *et seq.*, 83(2)). The "true" owner thereby deprived of title is protected by the provisions for rectification and indemnity. Another example still where title to land may be acquired against the will of the owner is through the process of limitation. It is this process which is the primary concern of this chapter.

2. Acquisition of title to land by limitation

The importance of possession at common law has already been referred to (see p. 3). Even a person in possession without any claim of right is treated as having a right to the land which prevails against all except those who can demonstrate a superior title. Acquisition of title to land by limitation is founded on the notion of adverse possession. A person entering into possession of land without the consent of the owner is a trespasser and may be evicted by the true owner. Against others he has a possessory title—a right to the land based on his possession. By holding the land to the exclusion of the true owner for a sufficient period, the right of action of the "paper owner" is lost and his title extinguished. This happens because just as under the Statutes of Limitations a person with a contractual right ceases to be able to enforce it after a period of years, normally six, from the date on which his cause of action accrued, so also a person with a claim to land loses the right to enforce his claim after the expiry of the appropriate period of limitation.

3. Operation of Statutes of Limitations

The method of acquiring title to land by limitation arises in two different kinds of case: that of the deliberate taking of land known to belong to another; and that of innocent encroachment upon land not known to belong to another. Examples of the latter kind arise not infrequently where a developer of land builds houses which are not located exactly in accordance with the layout indicated on the site plan. These changes may occur because of a surveying error or for reasons associated with conditions on the site. If the builder's changes are not communicated to the solicitor preparing the conveyances, it can happen that the boundaries of the plot conveyed do not correspond with the boundaries as laid out on the ground. The operation of the Statutes of Limitations provides a convenient solution to this lack of correspondence. Some English decisions, however, show a reluctance to extend the benefit of the doctrine of adverse possession to a possessor who has deliberately taken possession of land which he knows belongs to another. It has yet to be seen whether the Irish courts will be influenced by the distinction between "wrongful" and "innocent" adverse possessors.

4. The limitation period

The period within which claims to recover land must be brought is normally 12 years: Statute of Limitations 1957, s.13; Statute of Limitations (N.I.) 1958, s.17. Other periods apply for special cases. The period is 30 years for actions by a State authority or the Crown to recover land, and 60 years where the claim relates to the foreshore, or 40 years (30 in Northern Ireland) from the date on which land ceased to be foreshore but remained in the ownership of State or Crown: *ibid.* For claims made under a will or an intestacy there is, in the Republic, a special limitation period of six years: Succession Act 1965, s.126. McMahon J. has held in *Drohan* v. *Drohan* (1981) that this shorter limitation period does not apply to claims brought by the personal representatives of a deceased.

5. When time begins to run

In the usual case, time (under the limitation period) begins to run from the date at which a cause of action accrues and there is some person in whose favour the period of limitation can run: Statute of Limitations 1957, s.18; Statute of Limitations (N.I.) 1958, s.22; *McDonnell* v. *McKinty* (1847). For there to be some person in whose favour the period of limitation can run the true or "paper" owner must either have been dispossessed or he must have given up possession and possession must then have been taken up by another.

6. Adverse possession

We can, for convenience, call the person in whose favour the limitation period can run a *squatter*. Some special cases aside, he can only benefit from the Statutes of Limitations if his possession is adverse to that of the paper owner for otherwise the paper owner will have no cause of action against him. This requirement of *adverse possession* gives rise to difficulties which are most explored in the English caselaw.

It may first be observed that where a person is in possession by the leave or licence of the true owner, his possession does not become adverse until the leave or licence has terminated: see for instance *Bellew* v. *Bellew* (1983); *Hyde* v. *Pearce* (1982). The same is true of a tenant in possession by virtue of a lease, except that in the case of a tenancy at will, the tenancy is, for the purposes of the Statute of Limitations in the Republic of Ireland, but not in Northern Ireland, deemed to have been determined one year from its commencement, if not already determined: 1957 Act, s.17; and see *Bellew* v. *Bellew* (above). Periodic tenancies without a lease in writing are deemed to determine at the expiration of the first year or other period, although time runs afresh from the receipt of any payment of rent: 1957 Act, s.17; 1958 Act, s.21. The possession of a tenant at sufferance (*i.e.* a tenant after the expiry of his lease) is adverse since he does not in reality have a lease at all.

7. Inconsistent acts

Even though a squatter may not be in possession with the express consent of the paper owner, he will not be treated as in adverse possession if his use of land is so casual as not to be considered to amount to possession, or if his acts of possession are not inconsistent with the right of the true owner. As Kenny J. put it in the Supreme Court in *Murphy* v. *Murphy* (1980), "adverse possession means possession of land which is inconsistent with the title of the true owner: this inconsistency necessarily involves an intention to exclude the true owner, and all other persons, from enjoyment of the estate or interest which is being acquired." See also *Powell* v. *McFarlane* (1977).

What acts and intention will amount to adverse possession depend largely upon the circumstances of each case. In *Murphy* v. *Murphy* (above) a son and his mother were each entitled to adjacent farm lands. For many years the son farmed all the lands as a single unit, and for nearly as long he had treated all the lands as his own, banking the entire income in his own name, and mortgaging the whole of the lands as security for a bank loan. This was held to amount to adverse possession of the mother's lands. It was inconsistent with and in denial of the mother's rights as legal owner. On the other hand, in *Browne* v. *Fahy* (1975) a licence had been given to graze cattle by the owners of land. Kenny J. held that planting trees, fencing along a road, draining and manuring, were all consistent with the licence and did not amount to acts of adverse possession.

The English courts have treated one kind of case as special. This is where the paper owner has no immediate use for the land, but does have a specific use to which he intends to put the land at a later date. Possession by a squatter which is not inconsistent with this future purpose has been held not to amount to adverse possession. This principle derives from the case of *Leigh* v. *Jack* (1879). The use by a squatter of a strip of land for storing heavy materials was held not inconsistent with the intentions of the owner to dedicate the land in the future as a highway. The principle has recently been applied in *Wallis's Cayton Bay Holiday Camp Ltd.* v. *Shell-Mex and B.P. Ltd.* (1975) where using land for farming and later for recreational space for a holiday camp was held not to be adverse possession, the owner of the land intending to develop it as a filling station fronting a new road which had not yet been built.

Where the paper owner has no specific intention in relation to the future use of land, adverse possession is more easily established: see *Treloar* v. *Nute* (1976). This case, however, was one in which the squatter incorrectly believed he had title to the land in question. In the *Wallis* case, by contrast, the squatter knew full well the land was not his.

8. Implied licence

In the *Cayton Bay Holiday Camp* case (above) Lord Denning MR put forward the proposition that a person knowingly taking possession of the land of another would be prevented from acquiring the land by limitation by being treated as having an implied or hypothetical licence from the owner. This proposition was adopted in some later cases, but has now been largely rejected by legislation in England and Northern Ireland. A licence is not to be implied as a matter of law, but there may nevertheless be cases in which the implication of a licence is justified on the actual facts of a case. It is unlikely that the courts in the Republic would accept the fiction of the licence implied by law, but again a licence could be implied on the facts.

9. Possession of co-owners

In the ordinary case the paper owner has a cause of action against the person in adverse possession. One exception to this is of particular importance in Irish conditions. It relates to co-ownership. By virtue of the unity of possession of co-owners, where one co-owner is out of possession, he has no cause of action against the others in possession unless they have ousted him. Nevertheless, under section 21 of the Statute of Limitations 1957 (s. 25 of the N.I. Statute) time runs in favour of a co-owner in possession against others who are not in possession. This provision is important in view of the frequency with which on a person's death, particularly in a rural area, a child or children will remain in possession of the family home without ever taking out representation, while other children who would have been entitled to a share on intestacy as tenants in common may be living elsewhere or abroad. See also Succession Act 1965, s.125.

In Northern Ireland if a child entitled under an intestacy seeks to plead the Statute of Limitations against other children so entitled, he may be debarred from doing so on the ground that he is an executor *de son tort*: *Molony* v. *Molony* (1894). This problem is probably avoided in the Republic by the provisions of section 125 of the Succession Act 1965.

10. Extending the limitation period

The ordinary limitation period of 12 years can be extended where at its commencement the true owner was suffering from a disability such as infancy or unsoundness of mind. In such cases the limitation period may be extended until six years from the ending of the disability up to a maximum of 30 years from the accrual of the cause of action: Statute of Limitations 1957, ss.48, 49; Statute of Limitations (N.I.) 1958, ss. 49, 50.

Where a cause of action is based on fraud, or is concealed by fraud, time does not run until the plaintiff could have discovered the fraud: 1957 Act, s.71; 1958 Act, s.70. This deferment of the limitation period does not apply where a claim is brought against a bona fide purchaser for value without notice of the fraud.

11. Limited interests

Where the paper owner is only a tenant or other person with a limited interest in the land, time runs only against him and not against the reversioner or remainderman. Time begins to run against the person next entitled only on the determination of the prior interest. If the prior interest was a lease, the limitation period applicable to the interest of the landlord is twelve years from the determination of the lease: 1957 Act, s.15; 1958 Act, s.19. Where the prior interest was a life estate or other limited estate under a settlement, the reversioner or remainderman has twelve years from the date of the squatter taking possession, or six years from the determination of the prior interest, whichever is the longer, in which to bring action: *ibid.*

12. Starting time running again

Once time has started running against a paper owner, nothing he does subsequently by way of disposing of his title to land affects the running of the limitation period. To "stop the clock," the paper owner must assert his title by retaking possession of the land, or by taking legal proceedings. Before the limitation period has run in full, a written and signed acknowledgment of the paper owner's title can interrupt the limitation period and start time running again: 1957 Act, ss.50–60; 1958 Act, ss.51–60.

13. Successive squatters

Provided that land remains continuously in adverse possession, the limitation period can run in favour of a series of successive squatters. For instance where A in 1970 is dispossessed by B, time begins to run against A. If in 1975 B conveys to C, time continues to run against A who will lose his title in 1982. The result would be the same, so far as A is concerned, if B had not conveyed to C in 1975 but had been dispossessed by C although C would not in this case extinguish B's title until 1987, 12 years from the date on which C entered into possession. Had C not dispossessed B, but taken possession some time after B had abandoned possession, time would have run against A in favour of C only from the date on which C took possession.

14. Tenants as squatters

During the subsistence of the tenancy, possession by a tenant of the land demised does not amount to adverse possession. If the tenant encroaches upon other land (belonging to the lessor or to a stranger) and remains in adverse possession for the requisite period, the land so acquired is considered to be an accretion to the lease so that the lessor is entitled to it at the end of the lease. This will be so unless the circumstances make it clear that the tenant intended to annex the land for his own benefit exclusively: see *Meares* v. *Collis* (1927); *Kingsmill* v. *Millard* (1855).

15. Extinguishment of title of landlord

If a tenant fails to pay the rent due under a lease, arrears of rent cease to be recoverable six years after they became due, but this does not affect the landlord's title to recover rent which is not six years in arrears, or to recover possession on the determination of the lease: 1957 Act, s.28; 1958 Act, s.32. Similarly although the failure of a landlord to exercise a right of forfeiture for 12 years results in the extinguishment of that right, this is without prejudice to his right to possession on the natural expiry of the lease: 1957 Act, s.16; 1958 Act, s.20.

It is different where a tenant pays the rent to a person other than the landlord or his agent. If the rent due under a lease in writing exceeds £1 per year and is paid for a period of 12 years to a person wrongfully claiming to be entitled without any rent being paid to the landlord, the right of action and title of the landlord are extinguished: 1957 Act, s.17; 1958 Act, s.21.

16. Effect of limitation

When a cause of action relating to land becomes time expired under the Statutes of Limitations, the cause of action of the paper owner is lost, and his title is extinguished, but there is no "parliamentary conveyance." What this means is that although the squatter cannot be sued by the paper owner, he does not acquire the title of the paper owner. The squatter's title is based independently on his possession and is enforceable against others on the basis that *de facto* possession confers a right to possession which is good against anyone who cannot show a better title. The estate a squatter holds is a fee simple, for it has the potentiality to last for ever, even if it is liable to be defeated by the true owner before the expiration of the limitation period. The squatter does, however, hold subject to any burdens affecting the land, such as easements or restrictive covenants unless, in the latter case, he is a bona fide purchaser for value of a legal estate without notice: *Re Nisbet and Potts' Contract* (1905).

There can be difficulties where the person a squatter has dispossessed is only a tenant. Although the squatter extinguishes the title of the tenant, he does not acquire the tenant's estate, nor are any of the landlord's rights affected: see *Tichborne* v. *Weir* (1892), the leading English case which it is generally thought would be followed in Ireland. The result is that the tenant cannot enforce any of the covenants in the lease against the landlord, nor can the landlord directly enforce any covenants against the tenant. The landlord, however, has a right to possession on the natural expiry of the lease and retains any right he has to forfeit a lease for breach of condition: *Tickner* v. *Buzzacott* (1965); *Perry* v. *Woodfarm Homes Ltd.* (1975). The landlord's right of entry for breach of condition means that the squatter is indirectly obliged to perform the covenants in the lease.

In a decision of the English House of Lords, *Fairweather* v. *St. Marylebone Property Co. Ltd.* (1963), it was held that even though the title of a tenant had been extinguished as against a squatter who had remained in adverse possession for over 12 years, the tenant could surrender the residue of his lease to the landlord with the result that the lease was determined prematurely. The landlord could therefore recover possession immediately from the squatter.

The decision in the *Fairweather* case has been subject to some academic criticism, and has not been followed in the Republic of Ireland. In *Perry* v. *Woodfarm Homes Ltd.* (above) the Supreme Court held that once the title of a tenant has been extinguished by adverse possession, he is not in a position to deal effectively with his leasehold estate at all and therefore he has nothing to surrender and nothing to assign. In the case a squatter remained in adverse possession of a plot of ground for over 12 years. The land was held under a lease for 999 years. The tenant assigned his interest to the plaintiff, who subsequently acquired the fee simple. It was held that the leasehold and fee simple estates did not merge in the hands of the plaintiff to enable him to recover possession from the squatter.

17. Registered land

The Statutes of Limitations apply to claims to recover registered land, although there are some special provisions contained in the land registration legislation: see Registration of Title Act 1964, s.49; Land Registration Act (N.I.) 1970, s.53. One difference is that the nominal title of the paper owner is not extinguished simply by virtue of adverse possession because of the principle that the person whose name appears on the register is the owner. The rights of a person acquired or in the course of being acquired under the Statutes of Limitation are, however, overriding interests which bind the land even if not registered, so that a registered proprietor and any successor in title will always hold subject to the rights of a squatter: Registration of Title Act 1964, s.72(1)(*p*); Land Registration Act (N.I.) 1970, Sched. 5, Pt. 1, para. 14.

The Land Registration Acts in both Northern Ireland and the Republic of Ireland provide that where a person has acquired an estate in registered land by adverse possession, he may be registered as owner: Registration of Title Act, 1964, s.49; Land Registration Act (N.I.) 1970, s.53. The practice in both the Province and in the Republic is for registration to be made in the same folio as that of the dispossessed paper owner, thus in effect achieving a forced conveyance: see *Perry* v. *Woodfarm Homes Ltd.* (above), *per* Walsh J. In England the practice is for a new title to be opened in respect of the estate of a squatter and for the title of the paper owner to be closed: see *Spectrum Investment Co.* v. *Holmes* (1981). This seems more in accord with the negative effect of the Statutes of Limitations.

14 Settled Land

1. Settlements of land

We have already seen how the concept of estates in land permits the creation of a number of successive interests. Interests in land of limited duration, with the exception of leasehold interests, have never been used commercially to any significant extent. Where estates such as the life estate and the fee tail have been most employed is in family settlements. A testator in his will, for instance, might well leave the family home to his widow for life, and direct that on her death his eldest son is to have the fee simple.

2. Strict settlements

A *strict settlement* was a special form of settlement employing the fee tail. It was designed to retain land within the family. The original owner, A, by a deed executed *inter vivos*, would confer upon himself a life estate, with remainder to his eldest son, B, for life, and then after providing for B's widow and younger children, with remainder to B's first and other sons successively in tail. Until B's first son attained his majority, the fee tail could not be barred, and even then, the disentailment would require the consent of A or B, whoever of the two was entitled in possession, if the disentailing assurance was to convey a fee simple. The operation of the strict settlement in keeping land within the family was reinforced by means of resettlement each generation. Under the strict settlement B's son would not derive any income from the land until A and B died. Until then, their life estates entitled them to the income. On B's son coming of age, he would be persuaded, in return for a suitable annuity, to relinquish his fee tail for a life estate. With the consent of the person in possession, B's son would bar the entail and immediately resettle the land with limitations substantially similar to those in the previous settlement except that he would take a life estate and the entailed interest would be given to his children.

3. Disadvantages of settlements

Strict settlements of the classical form are now very rare, in part because of the effects of capital taxes. Even the simpler modern forms of settlement though, share some of the disadvantages of the strict settlement.

One of these is the problem of inalienability. Because of the principle *nemo dat quod non habet* it is not normally possible for a person to confer on others any greater interest in property than he has himself. A person with a life estate cannot, at common law, sell and convey a fee simple, and even if he grants a lease, it will only be derived out of his life estate and will not bind the holder of the fee simple. In practice, therefore, settled land can only be sold or let at common law with the consent of all those with an interest in it, present or future. Since some of those entitled to a future interest might be infants, or not even born, it might be impossible to obtain the concurrence of all those involved.

Another problem related to improvements. The person entitled in possession to settled land had, at common law, no right to the capital value of the land, but only to the income, and he had no power to mortgage the land itself, but only to mortgage his own interest. If he desired to make any improvements to the land, they would have to be financed out of income.

Finally, the strict settlement locked wealth into land. The land could not be sold and the proceeds reinvested in some other form. While this was not a serious drawback while land was one of the few permanent income-producing investments, it became an increasing disadvantage as the industrial revolution and the growth of the market in stocks and shares provided alternative investments.

4. Statutory reform

A solution to the disadvantages associated with settlements was for the settlor to incorporate express powers of sale and management into the deed of settlement. Express powers of sale became commonplace by the middle of the nineteenth century. Statutory reforms were also introduced in the eighteenth and nineteenth centuries, culminating in the Settled Land Acts 1882–1890 which still remain in force in both parts of Ireland.

The scheme of the Acts is to leave unchanged the beneficial interests arising under a settlement. However, extensive powers of disposition, capable of overreaching and binding successors, are given to the person designated *tenant for life*. Certain controls restrain the improper exercise by the tenant for life of his powers, these controls being chiefly given to the *trustees of the settlement*.

5. Application of the Settled Land Acts

The Settled Land Acts 1882–1890 apply to settled land. By the Settled Land Act 1882, s.2(3), settled land is defined as being "land, and any estate or interest therein, which is the subject of a settlement." "Settlement" is defined by section 2(1). A settlement exists where under any instrument or instruments "any land, or any estate or interest in land, stands for the time being limited to or in trust for any persons by way of succession."

This definition contemplates two possibilities: where land is conveyed so as to confer on the beneficiaries successive legal estates in the land; and where land is conveyed to trustees to hold for beneficiaries successively entitled in equity. Where land is conveyed to trustees upon trust for sale, that is, with an express direction to the trustees that they are to sell the land and to hold the proceeds of sale upon trust for the beneficiaries, special rules apply. Although land held upon trust for sale is deemed to be settled land (Settled Land Act 1882, s.63), the powers conferred upon the tenant for life can only be exercised with the leave of the court. Until then the trustees named in the settlement have the powers of disposition conferred upon them by that settlement: Settled Land Act 1884, s.7. These special rules are designed to prevent concurrent conflicting powers.

There is also special provision for land held by an infant. By section 59 of the 1882 Act where the person entitled in possession to land is an infant, the land is deemed to be settled land, even though there may be no successive interests. The infant is deemed to be tenant for life, but by section 60 the powers normally exercisable by a tenant for life are, where he is an infant, exercisable by the trustees of the settlement. These provisions overcome the difficulty that although an infant may own land, any dispositions he makes of it during his infancy are voidable within a reasonable time of him attaining his majority.

6. The tenant for life

The tenant for life of settled land is the person who is for the time being entitled to possession. In the commonest case this will be the person having a life estate in possession: Settled Land Act 1882, s.2(5). A number of others who may be tenant for life in the sense of having the powers of a tenant for life are catalogued in section 58 of the 1882 Act. These include a tenant in tail, the holder of a base fee, a tenant *pur autre vie*, a tenant in fee simple with an executory limitation, gift, or disposition over, and others. The special case of an infant entitled in possession to land has already been referred to in the last Section. There can sometimes be cases where no tenant for life can be identified, as for instance in the case of discretionary trusts, *e.g.* where under the terms of a will settlement trustees are to apply the income for the benefit of such of the children of the testator as the trustees may select. The Acts make no provision for such cases.

Leases for lives at a rent, formerly very common in Ireland, are excluded from the ambit of the Settled Land Acts because section 58 of the 1882 Act confers the powers of a tenant for life only on tenants for years determinable on life, or for the life of another, who do not hold "merely under a lease at a rent." The payment of rent therefore takes a lease out of the settled land legislation: see *Re Drew's Settled Estates* (1911).

7. The trustees of the settlement

The trustees of the settlement play an important role in the scheme of the Settled Land Acts. As will be seen later, the trustees of the settlement hold capital money, and have some control over the exercise by the tenant for life of his powers. In some cases they may themselves exercise the powers of a tenant for life.

The persons who are trustees of the settlement are (i) those persons who are trustees with a power of sale or of consent to sale of the settled land, or if there are none such, then (ii) those persons who are declared by the settlement to be trustees for the purposes of the Settled Land Acts: Settled Land Act 1882, s.2(8).

Where there are no trustees under either of the first two heads then the trustees are (iii) those persons who are trustees with a power of sale over any other land comprised in the settlement and held on the same terms, or who hold such land upon trust for sale, or whose consent is required for the sale of such land; or if there are no such persons, then (iv) those persons who are trustees with future power of sale, or under a future trust for sale or whose consent is required to a future power of sale: Settled Land Act 1890, s.16.

If there are no trustees of the settlement under the preceding four heads, then, where a settlement is made by will, the personal representatives of the testator (provided that they are at least two in number) are to be the trustees of the settlement until other trustees are appointed: Succession Act 1965, s.50(3); Administration of Estates Act (N.I.) 1955, s.40(5). Special provision is also made for the case of an infant becoming entitled to land on intestacy. By section

58 of the Succession Act 1965 and section 38 of the Administration of Estates Act (N.I.) 1955 a settlement is deemed to subsist notwithstanding the absence of any instrument, and the trustees of the settlement are such persons as are trustees for the infant of the other property he receives from the deceased.

In the event of none of the above provisions producing trustees of the settlement, there is a general saving provision in section 38 of the Settled Land Act 1882 enabling the court, on application, to appoint trustees of the settlement.

8. Powers of tenant for life

The tenant for life is given, by the Settled Land Acts, a number of powers exercisable over the entire estate or interest in land comprised in the settlement, and not exercisable only in relation to his own interest. Chief among these powers are the power of sale and the power to lease.

The power of sale is found in section 3 of the 1882 Act. Under this section, a tenant for life "may sell the settled land, or any part thereof, or any easement, right or privilege of any kind, over or in relation to the same." In exercising this power of sale, the tenant for life is under a duty to obtain the best price that can reasonably be obtained: 1882 Act, s.4; and see *Wheelwright* v. *Walker* (1883).

The power to lease is found in section 6 of the 1882 Act. Under this section, a tenant for life may lease the settled land for a maximum term of 99 years in the case of building leases; 60 years in the case of a mining lease; and 35 years (see 1882 Act, s.65(10)) in the case of any other lease.

The grant of leases by the tenant for life is subject to a number of conditions. Any lease under the statutory powers must be made by deed, and a counterpart (*i.e.* duplicate) executed by the lessee and delivered to the tenant for life (writing only is required for a lease not exceeding three years: Settled Land Act 1890, s.7); the lease must take effect in possession within twelve months; must provide for forfeiture for non-payment of rent; and must reserve the best rent reasonably obtainable, taking account of any fine paid: Settled Land Act 1882, s.7. Sections 8 to 11 of the 1882 Act contain further special provisions applicable to building and mining leases.

In addition to these primary powers of sale and to lease, a tenant for life is given other statutory powers. These include the power to accept surrenders of leases (1882 Act, s.13); the power to raise money by mortgage for certain limited purposes such as enfranchisement or discharging incumbrances (1882 Act, s.18; 1890 Act, s.11); and the power to enter into contracts concerning the settled land (1882 Act, s.31).

9. Restrictions on powers of tenant for life

The powers of a tenant for life may be added to or extended by the express terms of the settlement: 1882 Act, s.57. A tenant for life may, for instance, be given the power to grant leases for periods longer than the statutory maxima, or his power to raise money by mortgage may be extended.

The statutory powers of a tenant for life may not, however, be restricted. Any attempt to exclude or to restrict the powers of the tenant for life is void: 1882 Act, s.51. This prohibition covers any provision:

> "purporting or attempting, by way of direction, declaration or otherwise, to forbid a tenant for life to exercise any power under this Act, or attempting, or tending, or intended, by a limitation, gift, or disposition over of settled land, or by a limitation, gift, or disposition of other real or any personal property, or by the imposition of any condition, or by forfeiture, or in any other manner whatever, to prohibit or prevent him from exercising, or to induce him to abstain from exercising, or to put him into a position inconsistent with his exercising, any power under this Act."

As can be seen the prohibition is fairly comprehensive. It should be observed, though, that it renders a provision void only in so far as it has the effect of fettering the powers of the tenant for life. For instance, a gift over of the settled land in the event of the tenant for life ceasing to reside upon the property is void in so far as it would tend to prevent the exercise of his statutory powers to sell or to lease (*Re Fitzgerald*, 1902; *Re Adair*, 1909), but the provision is capable of operating if the tenant for life ceases to reside for any reason other than the exercise of his statutory powers: *Re Haynes* (1887).

Just as the settlor can do nothing to restrict the powers of the tenant for life, so also the tenant for life can do nothing to restrict his own powers. By section 50 of the 1882 Act a tenant for life cannot assign or release his powers, nor can he contract not to exercise any of his powers. Even where a tenant for life assigns his beneficial interest under a settlement, he retains his powers, except that he normally requires the consent of an assignee for value of his interest before he can exercise his powers in a way which would affect the assignee. In some cases, where a tenant for life surrenders his interest to the person next entitled under the settlement, he thereby ceases to be tenant for life so that the powers become exercisable by the person next entitled: *Re Bruen's Estate* (1911).

10. Exercise of powers by tenant for life

The tenant for life in the exercise of his powers is to have regard to the interests of all parties entitled under the settlement and is deemed to be a trustee for them in relation to the exercise of the powers: Settled Land Act 1882, s.53. He is not, though, a trustee of the land itself, so that he may use the land to his own best advantage within the limitations of the rules of waste; nor can he be compelled to exercise his Settled Land Act powers; but if he does exercise those powers, he is accountable to the other beneficiaries if he does so improperly. He would thus be liable for any difference between the best price reasonably obtainable on a sale, and the price in fact received, if he sold at an undervalue. He may also be restrained from the improper exercise of his powers, such as in one case where a total abstainer sought to lease a public house on terms that no intoxicating liquor should be sold there: *Re Earl Somers* (1895).

11. Notices and consents

Before exercising the majority of his powers, the tenant for life is obliged to give one month's notice of his intention to do so to the trustees of the settlement: 1882 Act, s.45. Except in relation to the exercise of the power of mortgage, the notice may be in general terms, and the necessity for serving notice may be waived by the trustees of the settlement: Settled Land Act 1884, s.5. The object of requiring notice to be served is to enable the trustees of the settlement to intervene to prevent an improper exercise of a tenant for life's powers. The trustees of the settlement are, though, under no obligation to act, and are expressly exempted by section 42 of the 1882 Act from any liability for not taking action. A person—for instance a tenant or purchaser—dealing in good faith with the tenant for life is not concerned to enquire whether notice has been served upon the trustees of the settlement: 1882 Act, s.45(3).

There are some powers which a tenant for life may exercise without having first to notify the trustees of the settlement. An example is the power under section 7 of the Settled Land Act 1890, to grant leases for a term not exceeding 21 years at the best rent that can reasonably be obtained without taking a fine, and where the lessee remains liable for waste.

Conversely, in some other cases, the *consent* of the trustees of the settlement is required for the exercise of a power by the tenant for life.

Consent, for instance, is required for a disposition of the principal mansion house (if any) and the pleasure grounds and park and lands (if any) usually occupied therewith: Settled Land Act 1890, s.10. No definition is given of a principal mansion house, but two cases are excluded: where a house is usually occupied as a farmhouse, and where the site and grounds usually occupied with a house do not exceed 25 acres. In the vast majority of modern settlements there will therefore be no principal mansion house.

12. Capital money

The tenant for life is entitled to retain any receipts from the settled land of an income nature, subject to any contrary direction in the settlement. The tenant for life is not, however, entitled to any capital money such as money received on a sale, fines on the grant of leases and money raised by mortgage. By section 22 of the 1882 Act, capital money is to be paid to the trustees of the settlement or into court. For this purpose there must be two trustees (1882 Act, s.39) unless the settlement authorises payment to a single trustee, or in Northern Ireland, where payment may be made to a trust corporation acting alone: Trustee Act (N.I.) 1958, s.14. The capital money is applied or invested in accordance with the Settled Land Acts: see 1882 Act, s.21.

13. Overreaching

A disposition made in exercise of the powers of the tenant for life, and in accordance with the Settled Land Acts, has overreaching effect. That is, the beneficial interests of those entitled under the settlement shift from the land and into the proceeds of the disposition. Thus on a sale by the tenant for life under his statutory power of sale the purchaser takes an estate in the land free from any interests under the settlement. The claims of those entitled under the settlement attach instead to the purchase price received. Similarly on a lease the interests of the beneficiaries under the settlement cannot be enforced against the tenant, but only against any fine or rent paid.

To overreach the interests under the settlement, however, a disposition must comply with any applicable statutory requirements. The disposition must be within the powers of the tenant for life, and any capital money must have been paid to the trustees of the settlement or into court. A purchaser is however protected if he deals in good faith with the tenant for life without any knowledge of any improper dealing, for by section 54 of the 1882 Act he is then, as against all parties entitled under the settlement,

> "conclusively taken to have given the best price, consideration, or rent, as the case may require, that could reasonably be obtained by the tenant for life, and to have complied with all the requisitions of this Act."

It seems that a purchaser will be protected, provided he is in good faith, even where he is not aware that he is dealing with a tenant for life: *Re Morgan's Lease* (1972).

14. Powers exercisable by trustees

In some cases the powers of a tenant for life are exercisable by the trustees of the settlement. Of the three more important instances, one has already been mentioned: where the tenant for life is an infant. The powers of the tenant for life are also exercisable by the trustees of the settlement where the tenant for life seeks an exercise of the powers in his own favour: Settled Land Act 1890, s.12. This special provision overcomes any difficulty which might otherwise arise from the position of the tenant for life as trustee in the exercise of his powers. The third instance is where the settlor has expressly conferred powers on the trustees of the settlement already enjoyed under the Settled Land Acts by the tenant for life. The trustees may then exercise these powers only with the consent of the tenant for life: Settled Land Act 1882, s.56(2).

15. Common law powers

The existence of the Settled Land Act powers does not affect the common law rights of disposition of those entitled under the settlement. For instance, rather than sell the settled land under his statutory power in that regard, a tenant for life can dispose of his own estate; and if he were a tenant in tail, he could, by means of a disentailing assurance, enlarge the fee tail into a fee simple on a conveyance. Similarly, a remainderman, who has no powers under the Settled Land Acts, may still dispose of his own interest under the settlement. The Settled Land Acts do not affect the beneficial interests under the settlement, or the devolution of ownership, except in so far as the beneficial interests are overreached upon an exercise of the statutory powers.

16. Registered land

The Settled Land Acts apply to registered land as they do to unregistered land, but subject to the provisions of the relevant Acts relating to registered land. Only the title of the tenant for life is registered, but instead of being registered as *full* owner, as he would be if he were entitled to the entire fee simple or leasehold estate, the tenant for life is registered as *limited* owner: Registration of Title Act 1964, s.27; Land Registration Act (N.I.) 1970, s.12. The details of the settlement are not disclosed on the register, but the names of the trustees of the settlement may be recorded: 1964 Act, s.99; 1970 Act, s.56.

On the determination of the interest of a limited owner, the person next entitled under the settlement will be registered as owner upon application made by him or by the trustees of the settlement: 1964 Act, s.61; 1970 Act, Sched. 4. Registration will be as full or limited owner as the case may require. On a sale by a tenant for life under his Settled Land Act powers, the purchaser will be registered as owner in the ordinary way, except that the Registrar will require evidence that the capital money has been properly paid to the trustees of the settlement.

Part 4

Rights in the Land of Another

15 Licences

A. General

1. Possession without ownership

Ownership normally carries with it possession, or the right to possession, but there are cases where ownership and possession (or in some cases simply occupation) part company. In such cases the right to possession may be seen as a right in the property of another, although it may also be property in its own right. We have already seen how difficult it is, however, to speak of ownership in land law and how this may be illustrated by reference to leases (see p. 18). A short-term lease, such as a weekly tenancy, is an example of possession without ownership. We would consider the landlord to remain owner despite having parted with possession. As the duration of the lease grows longer, and the tenant's right to possession more secure, we reach a point where we begin to consider ownership of the land to be in the tenant, and the landlord's right to rent being little more than a charge upon the tenant's ownership.

2. Rights to possession

For convenience, the rules concerning leases have already been discussed, because many urban properties are owned in Ireland on a leasehold basis. It is, however, possible for a person to be on land, or even to be in possession of land, with the consent of the owner, without being a tenant of the owner. A person who is, thus, lawfully upon land without being a tenant, is said to be there by way of *licence*. He is therefore a *licensee*, a title which will be familiar to students of the law of tort. In land law the title licensee is wider than in tort for it includes both licensees and invitees as those terms are used in relation to occupiers' liability.

3. Licences

The expression "licence" lacks precision. A person is a licensee if he has a right to occupy another person's land, but his right does not fit into any other recognised legal category such as a legal or equitable life estate, fee tail, fee simple or leasehold estate. Licences are therefore a residuary category. They do, however, cover a wide spectrum of rights, from the implied permission a customer has to enter a shop to a right to occupy a room in a house for the rest of one's life.

The term licence is used not only in relation to rights of occupation, but also in relation to rights of enjoyment falling short of occupation, such as the right to post bills on the gable wall of a house. Once again, though, a right will be a licence only if it does not fall into another recognised category, such as, in this context, easements, profits, and restrictive covenants.

4. Categorisation of licences

The nature of the rights which a person may have by licence is almost infinite. The problems which most frequently arise, however, can be resolved to three main issues. These are how far a licensee is protected against the revocation of his licence; whether the benefit of the licence can be assigned; and how far the licensee can enforce his licence against successors in title of the landowner. The most helpful categorisation of licences is therefore one which helps to provide a solution to these three main issues. It is not possible, having characterised something simply as a licence, to attribute to it fixed characteristics. The relationship is not identical in all cases. The incidents of licences may vary according to the circumstances. It is well to bear in mind the warning given by Lord Wilberforce in *National Provincial Bank Ltd.* v. *Ainsworth* (1965) that it is not legitimate to describe a legal relationship as a licence, and then to ascribe to it incidents which are defined by reference to other kinds of licences: "that is an argument *per saltum.*"

The rights of a licensee in relation to the issues mentioned above depend to a large extent upon the circumstances surrounding the creation of the licence. Three main categories embrace the overwhelming majority of licences. These categories comprise bare licences; contractual licences; and licences by estoppel. In addition to these chief categories, four other kinds of licence mentioned later may have a claim to recognition.

B. *Creation of Licences*

5. Creation of bare licences

A *bare licence* is a mere permission, unsupported by any contract or equity or other circumstance protecting the licence. It matches the description of licences given by Vaughan C. J. in *Thomas* v. *Sorrell* (1673) that it "properly passeth no interest, nor alters or transfers property in any thing, but only makes an action lawful, which without it had been unlawful." A gratuitous invitation to a friend's room for a drink would be a bare licence. But the permission need not be express. It can also be implied. For instance, the open door of shop or garage premises constitutes "an invitation to all persons having business with the owners of the premises to go to the premises and to enter the premises" (*Davis* v. *Lisle* 1936).

Bare licences are a residual category of licences in that a licence does not belong to this category if there is anything in the circumstances to confer protection upon the licensee beyond the minimum protection which the law affords to all licences.

6. Creation of contractual licences

Contractual licences comprise all licences which originate from a term, express or implied, in a contract. The granting of the licence need not have been the primary purpose of the contract. The purchase of a cinema ticket confers a contractual licence to enter to view the film, and that is the primary purpose of the contract. But the right of a building contractor to enter and use a building site during construction will also be a contractual licence, even though the erection of a building was the primary purpose of the contract.

7. Contractual licences and leases

It can sometimes be difficult to distinguish between a contractual licence and a lease in view of the contractual basis of both arrangements. At one time it was thought that any arrangement conferring exclusive possession (or the right to it) on the "tenant" amounted to a lease: see *Lynes* v. *Snaith* (1899). That view no longer represents the law: *Cobb* v. *Lane* (1952); *Bellew* v. *Bellew* (1983). It is now accepted that a contractual licence can confer a right to exclusive possession, although a person cannot be a tenant unless he has the right to exclusive possession. Exclusive possession in this context means the right to the sole occupation of premises, with the right to exclude all other persons from the premises, including the right generally to exclude the landlord. It is not inconsistent with a person having an exclusive right to possession for the landlord to reserve the right to carry out repairs to the demised premises and to enter for that purpose: *Bradley* v. *Baylis* (1881), nor for the landlord to retain general superintendence of a building including control of access. A person could still have exclusive possession of a unit within that building, as for instance a unit inside an enclosed shopping centre: see *Joel* v. *International Circus and Christmas Fair* (1920). On the other hand, if a landlord retains a general right to enter premises, the occupier does not have exclusive possession. A lodger or hotel guest is therefore only a licensee.

The absence of a right to exclusive possession characterises an agreement as a contractual licence and not a tenancy. Where exclusive possession is given, then whether there is a licence or a tenancy depends upon the intention of the parties, as gathered from the substance of the agreement. The label put by the parties on their relationship is not conclusive for the true relationship of the parties "is determined by the law and not by the label which they choose to put on it:" *Facchini* v. *Bryson* (1952). If the occupier is given a right to exclusive possession, this is a strong circumstance in favour of the view that there is a tenancy as opposed to a licence, and in many of the cases where an occupier has been held to be a licensee "there has been something in the circumstances, such as a family arrangement, an act of friendship or generosity, or such like, to negative any intention to create a tenancy:" *ibid.* (see also p. 113).

8. Creation of estoppel licences

Licences can arise through the operation of the doctrine of estoppel. The essence of the doctrine of estoppel is that where one person has led another to act upon a particular belief, he will not be permitted to contradict that belief.

There are a number of forms of estoppel. The most ancient is the common law and equitable doctrine of estoppel by representation. It arises where one person makes a representation to another which is acted upon by the latter to his detriment. For instance, in *Hopgood* v. *Brown* (1955) the defendant, the owner of a plot of land, employed his neighbour, a building company, to build him a garage. The garage projected slightly over the boundary onto adjoining land owned by the company. It was held that the company and its successors in title were prevented from alleging that the defendant was trespassing because by its conduct the company had impliedly represented that the defendant could safely proceed to build as he planned.

9. Proprietary estoppel

The doctrine of estoppel by representation is rarely invoked in cases involving licences. Much more important is ***proprietary estoppel***, sometimes called estoppel by encouragement or acquiescence. It is a purely equitable doctrine. Although it has antecedents of some antiquity, it has received considerable development in English cases in recent years. A classic statement of the doctrine is given by Lord Kingsdown in *Ramsden* v. *Dyson* (1866):

> "If a man, under a verbal agreement with a landlord for a certain interest in land, or, what amounts to the same thing, under an expectation, created or encouraged by the landlord, that he shall have a certain interest, takes possession of such land, with the consent of the landlord, and upon the faith of such promise or expectation, with the knowledge of the landlord, and without objection by him, lays out money upon the land, a court of equity will compel the landlord to give effect to such promise or expectation."

The gist of the principle is that where the owner of land encourages another to act to his detriment in reliance upon some expectation, induced by the owner, of having an interest, then it will be inequitable for the owner to fail to honour the expectation. The doctrine is a flexible one, and the court will grant such relief as it considers just and equitable in the circumstances. Unlike other forms of estoppel, the doctrine of proprietary estoppel can be used assertively, as a cause of action, and not merely as a defence.

10. Applications of proprietary estoppel

The doctrine of proprietary estoppel has been applied in a wide range of English and Commonwealth cases. For instance in *Inwards* v. *Baker* (1965) a son wished to build a house. He could afford either the cost of a site, or the cost of building, but not both. His father offered to allow the son to build his house upon the father's land. This the son did, and lived there for many years. Some years after the father's death the trustees to whom the father had left his land by will sought to evict the son. The court held that the son could not be evicted. By building the bungalow in the expectation, created by his father, that he would be allowed to live there, an equity arose in favour of the son. The court considered that the appropriate way to satisfy the equity was to order that the son had a right of residence in the house so long as he desired to use it as his home.

In other cases the doctrine has been used to give a person a right of way (*Crabb* v. *Arun District Council*, 1976); an indefinite and irrevocable right to use a jetty (*Plimmer* v. *Wellington Corporation*, 1884); an irrevocable right to take sand and gravel (*Woods* v. *Donnelly*, 1982); and a right to the conveyance of the fee simple of a house (*Pascoe* v. *Turner*, 1979). In an appropriate case the court might permit a landowner to resile from an expectation he has induced where he repays an occupier any expenditure which the latter has incurred in faith of the expectation: see *Dodsworth* v. *Dodsworth* (1973).

11. Proprietary estoppel in Ireland

The doctrine of proprietary estoppel has been considered in two reported Irish cases. The first was *Cullen* v. *Cullen* (1962). This case was decided before *Inwards* v. *Baker* (above), the case which represents the beginning of the modern development of the doctrine. In *Cullen* v. *Cullen*, Mrs. Cullen won a fully furnished portable home in a competition in the *Sunday Press*. She gave it to Martin, one of her sons. He began to prepare a site for it on his own lands, but Mrs. Cullen requested him to erect it nearer to her on her husband's lands and to that end sought permission from Mr. Cullen. Relationships with Mr. Cullen were at that time strained, and as part of a resolution of the family differences Mr. Cullen was proposing to make over his lands to Mrs. Cullen. In his reply to Mrs. Cullen's request, Mr. Cullen through an intermediary, indicated that since the lands would be given to the mother, she could put the mobile home where she liked. Martin accordingly put the house on his father's land at a cost of about £200 and with his own labour. Kenny J. was "convinced that the plaintiff [Mr. Cullen] knew at all times that Mrs. Cullen had given the house to Martin and that the house was being erected for Martin to live in." Family relations subsequently worsened and Mr. Cullen in court proceedings sought to exclude Martin from his land.

Counsel for Martin, in the High Court, sought to rely upon the case of *Ramsden* v. *Dyson* (above). Kenny J. rejected the argument based on this case which, he said, could only support a claim where a person expended money upon land mistakenly believing himself to be the true owner. Since Martin knew that the land belonged to his father, he could not rely upon the principle of *Ramsden* v. *Dyson*.

Kenny J's narrow view of the effect of *Ramsden* v. *Dyson* is clearly inconsistent with the subsequent English authorities and with *Plimmer* v. *Wellington Corporation*, a case to which Kenny J. was not referred. It is submitted that Kenny J.'s restrictive view of *Ramsden* v. *Dyson* is incorrect: see also Brady (1970) Ir. Jur. This submission is supported by the more recent case of *McMahon* v. *Kerry County Council* (1981) where Finlay P. indicated that in his view the case of *Ramsden* v.

Dyson was merely an instance of a broader underlying equitable principle which he applied to prevent the owner of land from recovering possession where "it would truly be unconscionable and unjust" for him to do so. In that case the County Council had erected two houses on the plaintiffs' land without the plaintiffs' knowledge, but in circumstances where there was a "combination of factors . . . which are many and possibly in their combination unique" leading to Finlay P.'s conclusion that the McMahons should not be given an order for possession.

Furthermore, although Kenny J. in *Cullen* v. *Cullen* took an unduly narrow view of *Ramsden* v. *Dyson*, by different means he reached the same result as a broader interpretation would have achieved. He held that on the basis of the principle in *Central London Property Trust Ltd.* v. *High Trees House Ltd.* (1947), Mr. Cullen "is estopped by his conduct in giving consent to the erection of the house . . . when he knew that the house had been given to Martin and that the plaintiff [Mr. Cullen] cannot now assert any title to the site on which the house has been erected." Kenny J. would have liked to order Mr. Cullen to transfer the site to Martin, but thought he had no jurisdiction to do so, a result compelled by his reliance upon the *High Trees* principle of promissory estoppel. Instead, he considered that Martin could not be evicted in any court proceedings, and at the expiry of 12 years, would have acquired a title to the site by adverse possession. It is highly doubtful whether Martin's possession could truly be considered adverse in view of Mr. Cullen's giving of consent (see p. 153), but this circuitous form of relief was adopted also by Finlay P. in *McMahon* v. *Kerry County Council*. In the latter case, however, the relief granted to Kerry County Council was made conditional upon them compensating the McMahons for the loss of their site.

What, then, is the position of the doctrine of proprietary estoppel in Irish law? The view generally taken by practitioners is that the doctrine of proprietary estoppel is part of Irish law. The doctrine was applied by Finlay P. in *McMahon* v. *Kerry County Council* in a decision giving the doctrine an unprecedented scope; and it is at the least arguable that Kenny J.'s decision in *Cullen* v. *Cullen* amounts to an application of the doctrine of proprietary estoppel, although he traced the doctrine to an unconventional pedigree. What remains to be seen is whether, in a case where there is full reference to the more recent English and Commonwealth cases, the Irish judiciary will continue to apply the doctrine with its present Hibernian idiosyncracies.

12. Benefit and burden

It is an ancient principle that he who takes the benefit of a deed cannot disregard any burdens imposed on him by the deed. From this ancient principle, two branches to the doctrine of benefit and burden have emerged: see *Tito* v. *Waddell* (*No. 2*) (1977). One is the principle of conditional benefits, where the enjoyment of some benefit is made conditional upon assuming a burden. The other principle, which can be called the pure principle of benefit and burden, requires a man to submit to the burden of an arrangement when he enjoys the benefit of it, even though the benefit and burden are independent in the sense that the benefit is not qualified by the burden.

The principle of benefit and burden is generally associated with the case of *Halsall* v. *Brizell* (1957). In the case a question arose as to the obligations of the owner of a house to contribute towards the cost of maintaining roads and drains. Such payments could not normally be enforced, being a positive covenant (see Chapter 17). Upjohn J., applying the principle that he who takes the benefit of a deed must also submit to the burden, held that the owner of the house was not entitled to take advantage of the trusts contained in a deed giving him the benefit of the roads and sewers without undertaking the obligation the deed imposed to contribute towards the cost of maintenance.

E.R. Ives Investment Ltd. v. *High* (1967) is an example of the application of the doctrine to licences. The foundations of a newly built block of flats encroached upon neighbouring land. The neighbour allowed them to remain on terms that he be given a right of way. The agreement was informal, but it was held by the Court of Appeal that both parties must continue to shoulder their burden. The principles of proprietary estoppel and of mutual benefit and burden were invoked.

13. Derogation from grant

Another ancient principle is that a man may not derogate from his grant. This principle is generally encountered in relation to the creation of implied easements under the rule in *Wheeldon* v. *Burrows* (1878) (see Chapter 16). The doctrine can operate in some cases to protect licences by converting them into easements and can, it seems, create rights incapable of creation as easements: see *Pwllbach Colliery Co. Ltd.* v. *Woodman* (1915).

14. Licences arising by operation of law

Most licences arise from the grant of a permission by the owner of land, but there are a number of cases where a person, even without any express or implied permission, may have the right to enter or use land. An example is the right of one spouse to live in a family home owned by the other spouse. The exact nature of this right has not been fully determined, but it does appear to subsist throughout the duration of the marriage (see Shatter, *Family Law in Ireland* (2nd ed., p. 317). Statutory and common law rights to use the land of another also fall within this category.

15. Licences coupled with an interest

A number of old cases support the concept of a licence coupled with an interest. These could be explained as being instances of *profits à prendre* (see Chapter 16) were it not for modern cases adopting the concept which cannot be explained on this basis: see for instance *James Jones & Sons Ltd.* v. *Earl of Tankerville* (1909). The modern cases suggest that this category comprises licences coupled with or granted in aid of a chattel interest or an interest in realty, such as a sale of cut timber with the right to enter to remove it. Where a purchaser obtains such an interest, then his licence may be protected on foot of the principle, already mentioned, that a man may not derogate from his grant: *Woods* v. *Donnelly* (1982). There are some cases which go further, but it is submitted that their reliance on the concept of a licence coupled with an interest does not withstand careful scrutiny: *Vaughan* v. *Hampson* (1875); *Hurst* v. *Picture Theatres Ltd.* (1915).

16. Informal grants

A licence may be created not through any deliberate intention to create a licence, or because the nature of what it is intended to create is capable of existing only as a licence, but because there has been a failure to observe some formal requirement in the grant of some other interest. Thus the creation of a legal life estate requires the use of a deed to convey the estate. If no deed is used an arrangement may give rise to a licence giving the licensee a right of residence for life: *Inwards* v. *Baker* (above); *Piquet* v. *Taylor* (1978). It should not be forgotten, however, that in equity "a contract is as good as a grant." A contract to create a legal interest, such as a life estate or an easement, is treated as the grant of an equivalent estate or interest in equity, provided that the contract is supported by consideration: *Frogley* v. *Earl of Lovelace* (1859); *Mason* v. *Clarke* (1955).

C. Revocation of Licences

17. Revocation in general

It is used to be said that, with the exception of a licence coupled with an interest, licences were by their very nature revocable, regardless of how they were created. The leading case for this view was *Wood* v. *Leadbitter* (1845). That position no longer commands acceptance. The view now taken is that the revocability of a licence depends upon the kind of licence involved, and the terms upon which it was granted.

18. Revocation of bare licences

Of bare licences it is true that the licence is revocable at will. The permission the licensor has given may be withdrawn at any time, except that he must either give reasonable notice of revocation, or give the licensee a sufficient period of grace to remove himself: *Robson* v. *Hallett* (1967).

19. Revocation of contractual licences

The view now taken of contractual licences is that their revocability depends upon the terms of the contract: *Woods* v. *Donnelly* (1982). Where there is no express term concerning the duration of the licence, the courts may consider that the licence can be revoked on reasonable notice: *Winter Garden Theatre (London) Ltd.* v. *Millenium Productions Ltd.* (1948). Where the licensor attempts to revoke a licence in breach of contract the licensee will normally be able to restrain him by means of an injunction or a decree for specific performance: *Verrall* v. *Great Yarmouth Borough Council* (1981). If the licensor succeeds in turning out the licensee, the licensee will be entitled to damages for breach of contract (*Kerrison* v. *Smith*, 1897), and if force was used to remove him, to damages for assault (*Hurst* v. *Picture Theatres Ltd.*, 1915).

20. Revocation of estoppel licences

Where a person's occupation or use of land is protected by proprietary estoppel, his licence cannot be revoked so long as the "equity" generated in his favour by the estoppel continues (*Williams* v. *Staite*, 1979). In *Cullen* v. *Cullen* (above) Kenny J. only went so far as to say that Martin Cullen was protected from eviction by court proceedings, leaving open the possibility that his father could lawfully recover possession without recourse to the court. As has already been submitted, however, the decision in that case was based upon an incorrect view of the scope of the principle in *Ramsden* v. *Dyson* (above) and of the powers of the court.

D. Licences and Third Parties

21. Transfer of the benefit of licences

Some licences are purely personal, and are therefore clearly incapable of transfer. This would be true, for instance, of an invitation to a private dinner, or of a personal right of residence: see, for instance *Inwards* v. *Baker* (above). Where the licence is not personal in nature, there would seem to be no reason in principle why the benefit of the licence should not be transferred. If the licence is contractual, it should be transferable as a *chose in action* (see *Clore* v. *Theatrical Properties Ltd.* 1936); and in an Australian case it was held that the benefit of a right arising by proprietary estoppel was assignable: *Hamilton* v. *Geraghty* (1901). In some cases the benefit of a licence will be annexed to land so as to run with the land to a purchaser without any need for an express assignment: see *Ives* v. *High* (above).

22. The running of the burden of licences

A question which has assumed increasing importance with the growing incidence of licences, is the extent to which licences are enforceable against successors in title of the licensor. It is generally agreed that bare licences are not enforceable against successors in title of the licensor. Even here it may be that a purchaser from the licensor who expressly agrees to take subject to the rights of a licensee may find himself bound to give effect to the licence by way of a constructive trust: see *Binions* v. *Evans* (1972); *Bannister* v. *Bannister* (1948); and see below.

In relation to contractual licences, it cannot be assumed that simply because the licensor may not revoke the licence in breach of contract, the licence will bind any successor in title. The legal position is in fact very far from clear: see *National Provincial Bank Ltd.* v. *Ainsworth* (1965). On the one hand it is argued that a contractual licence does not create an interest in the land, but merely a personal contract which is only enforceable among parties between whom there is privity of contract: *Clore* v. *Theatrical Properties Ltd.* (above); *King* v. *David Allen & Sons Billposting Ltd.* (1916). On the other hand, in *Errington* v. *Errington and Woods* (1952), Denning L.J., having said that the common law doctrine that licences were revocable at will had been altered for contractual licences by the interposition of equity, continued,

> "This infusion of equity means that contractual licences now have force and validity of their own and cannot be revoked in

> breach of contract. Neither the licensor nor anyone who claims through him can disregard the contract except a purchaser for value without notice."

In that case the Court of Appeal held that a contractual licence was enforceable, after the death of the licensor, against his widow, to whom he had left the property in question. The reasoning in the case has been severely criticised.

In a subsequent case, *Binions* v. *Evans* (above) Lord Denning M.R. in a minority opinion held that where the purchasers of a house agreed to take it on condition that the widow of an estate worker be permitted to live there rent free for the rest of her life, and paid less in consequence,

> "In these circumstances, this court will impose on the purchaser a constructive trust for her benefit, for the simple reason that it would be utterly inequitable for the purchaser to turn the widow out contrary to the stipulation subject to which he took the premises."

This use of a contractive trust was adopted by Dillon J. in *Lyus* v. *Prowsa Developments Ltd.* (1982).

23. The burden of estoppel licences

A licence protected by the common law doctrine of estoppel by representation will bind not only the person initially making the representation, but also any of his successors in title and others claiming through him: *Hopgood* v. *Brown* (1955). The equitable doctrine of proprietary estoppel gives rise to rights which can be enforced against the original landowner and against all others claiming under or through him, except a bona fide purchaser of a legal estate for value without notice: *Inwards* v. *Baker* (1965); *Ives* v. *High* (1967).

E. Rights of Residence

24. Rights of residence in Ireland

Rights of residence are common features of testamentary provision in Ireland. A father, leaving a farm to his son, will frequently provide that his widow is to have a right of residence for her life. The classification of this right can give rise to problems, particularly in homedrawn wills. The judicial attitude to these rights of residence has not been uniform, although the courts have been consistent in enforcing the rights in question.

25. Analysis of rights of residence

Two main analyses of the right of residence are possible. The first is that a right of residence may confer a life estate upon the beneficiary, but like all estates in land, the life estate requires that the tenant has a right to exclusive possession. The analysis is not, therefore, possible where the beneficiary has only a general right of residence, being a right to share the occupation of the house in question. But in *National Bank Ltd.* v. *Keegan* (1931) the Supreme Court held that an agreement under which the owner of a house gave his aunt "during her life the exclusive use of the drawing-room an bedroom over same" conferred upon the aunt an equitable life estate which took priority over a later equitable mortgage. The difficulty with this solution is that it has the inconvenience of making the beneficiary a tenant for life under the Settled Land Acts (see Chapter 14).

The second analysis is to treat a right of residence as being in the nature of a lien or charge. The concept of the lien is normally used only in relation to obligations to pay money and there are considerable difficulties in applying it to a right of residence. It is, however, the analysis of rights of residence supported by the Irish caselaw where the beneficiary does not have a right to exclusive possession: see *Kelaghan* v. *Daly* (1913). It is also the analysis applied to registered land in the Republic by section 81 of the Registration of Title Act 1964. In *Kelaghan* v. *Daly* it was held that the lien was capable of binding a successor in title who took with notice, but it is possible that a right of residence can be discharged by a money payment. In *Re Shanahan* (1919) a marriage settlement expressly provided for a life annuity to be paid in the event of the person given a right of residence deciding to leave the lands, or in case of a disagreement. In *National Bank* v. *Keegan* Kennedy C.J. said that a "general right of residence charged on a holding is a right capable of being valued in moneys numbered at an annual sum, and of being represented by an annuity or money charge." Johnston J. at first instance went further and said that "when it becomes necessary to sell such property a Court of Equity has power and authority to ascertain the value of such charge, so that the purchaser may get the property discharged from the burden."

If a right of residence can be commuted involuntarily into a money payment, the purpose of the right is in large measure diminished, and the difficulties of valuing the right are considerable. These difficulties do not arise in relation to rights of residence in registered land in Northern Ireland. By section 47 of the Land Registration Act (N.I.) 1970, rights of residence are in effect treated as licences *sui generis*: they are deemed to be personal to the person entitled, but if registered as a burden against the land are binding on the registered owner and his successors in title.

F. Conacre and Agistment

26. Conacre and agistment contracts

Conacre and agistment contracts are both short-term hiring contracts for the use of land: conacre for the growing of a crop; agistment for grazing. The contract is normally confined to a single season, and hence the contract is sometimes called a letting on the eleven-month system, but it is possible for a conacre or agistment contract to be granted for a number of successive seasons: *Re Moore's Estate* (1944).

Like the Irish treatment of rights of residence, conacre and agistment contracts are distinctively treated in Ireland. They are undoubtedly a special form of licence. It has been held that they amount neither to a letting nor to a parting with possession: *Booth* v. *McManus* (1861); *Dease* v. *O'Reilly* (1845). The questions of whether a conacre or agistment contract may be prematurely revoked, the benefit assigned, or the burden enforced against successors in title have yet to be resolved. For a good discussion of conacre lettings see *Maurice E. Taylor Merchants Ltd.* v. *Commissioner of Valuation* (1981).

16 Servitudes

A. *General*

1. The nature of servitudes

A servitude is a right enjoyed for the benefit of one piece of land (the dominant tenement), and enforceable against another piece of land (the servient tenement). Easements and profits are the main kinds of such rights. Although restrictive covenants could be classified as servitudes, they are normally considered separately and are discussed in Chapter 17. It is also possible for rights similar to easements and profits to be enjoyed by way of licence.

2. The nature of easements

An easement is a right over the land of another such as a right of way, a right to cross another's land with drains, or a right to take water from the land of another. Beyond this it is difficult to give any definition, for it is only by analogy with previous cases that it is possible to decide whether a right has the characteristics of an easement. In the case of *Re Ellenborough Park* (1956) it was suggested that a right to use a park for recreation was an easement. In deciding whether it was, the court indicated that there were four essential characteristics: (1) there must be a dominant and a servient tenement; (2) an easement must accommodate the dominant tenement; (3) the dominant and servient owners must be different persons; and (4) the right claimed must be capable of forming the subject-matter of a grant.

3. Dominant and servient tenements

The combined effect of the first and second requirements is that an easement cannot exist *in gross* (*i.e.* independently). It must be for the benefit of nearby land: *Scott* v. *Goulding Properties Ltd.* (1972). The use of a car parking space, or of a helicopter landing pad, could not be an easement unless annexed to nearby land which it benefits: *Dowty Boulton Paul Ltd.* v. *Wolverhampton Corpn.* (*No. 2*) (1976). Two cases concerning the right to use a wall for advertising purposes illustrate the need for a dominant tenement. In *Moody* v. *Steggles* (1879) it was held that the right to affix a signboard to a roadside building to advertise the Grosvenor Arms in Newmarket, which was located down a side alley, was an easement, since the public house was the dominant tenement. But in *Clapman* v. *Edwards* (1938) it was held that an unrestricted right to place advertisements on the walls adjoining a filling station was not an easement. The right did not "accommodate" or benefit the filling station since it was a right to use the walls for general advertising purposes which could have been unconnected with the garage.

It can be very difficult to decide when a particular right accommodates the dominant tenement, especially with land used for business purposes. The classic example is *Hill* v. *Tupper* (1863), where the plaintiff had been given by a canal company a lease of land adjoining the canal together with "the exclusive right or liberty" of using and hiring out pleasure boats. This right was held not to be an easement. Evershed M.R. in *Re Ellenborough Park* (above) explained:

> "what the plaintiff was trying to do was to set up, under the guise of an easement, a monopoly which had no normal connexion with the ordinary use of his land, but which was merely an independent business exercise. So far from the right claimed subserving or accommodating the land, the land was but a convenient incident to the exercise of the right."

The dominant tenement need not necessarily be contiguous to the servient tenement, but there must be a sufficient degree of proximity for the benefit to be real. A right of way across land in Belfast could not be considered to benefit land in Dublin: *Bailey* v. *Stephens* (1862); *Todrick* v. *Western National Omnibus Co.* (1934).

The third of the *Ellenborough Park* requirements, that the owners of the dominant and servient tenements must be different persons, only prevents a man having an easement over his own land. It does not prevent the existence of easements exercisable by or against a tenant, even if the freehold is in common ownership: *Flynn* v. *Harte* (1913); *Hanna* v. *Pollock* (1900).

4. Easements must lie in grant

The fourth of the *Ellenborough Park* requirements for easements is that they must be capable of forming the subject-matter of a grant.

That is, they must be capable of being created by deed. There is a degree of circularity in this requirement, since only rights recognised as easements will become easements if granted by deed. No number of deeds would have improved the exclusive right in *Hill* v. *Tupper* into an easement. It was simply a licence, whether created by simple contract or by deed.

What is involved in this requirement is first, that what claims to be an easement can be sufficiently clearly defined to be capable of express creation without being unenforceable through uncertainty. Second, the right must be within the general nature of rights traditionally recognised as easements. While this second branch does not prevent the creation of new easements, it certainly impedes their development.

Among those rights which have been recognised as easements are rights of way (*Gaw* v. *C.I.E.*, 1953), rights to the access of light to windows (*Scott* v. *Goulding Properties Ltd.*, 1972), rights to the support of buildings (*Latimer* v. *Official Co-Operative Society*, 1885), and rights to take water from or across a neighbour's land (*McCartney* v. *Londonderry and Lough Swilly Railway Co.*, 1904). Many other less common rights have been held to be easements, including in one case the right to use a lavatory: *Miller* v. *Emcer Products Ltd.* (1956).

Conversely the right to a view and to the uninterrupted flow of air have been held too broad to be easements: *Aldred's Case* (1610); *Bryant* v. *Lefever* (1879). Other rights which have been rejected as incapable of existing as easements are rights which require expenditure by the servient owner, such as the right to a supply of hot water (*Regis Property Co. Ltd.* v. *Redman*, 1956); the right to shade and shelter from a hedge (*Cochrane* v. *Verner*, 1895) or from the wall of a house (*Giltrap* v. *Busby* 1970, but see *Bradburn* v. *Lindsay*, 1983), and rights which give the dominant owner exclusive possession or occupation (*Copeland* v. *Greenhalf*, 1952). A claim to exclusive possession amounts to a claim of ownership, not to a claim to a servitude.

5. The attributes of easements

What is special about easements, as compared with simple contractual rights, is that both the benefit and burden of easements pass with the dominant and servient tenements respectively and they are irrevocable. A legal right to an easement can also be acquired through long usage (prescription), which is considered later. These characteristics are shared also by profits, which are discussed next.

6. The nature of profits

A *profit* (or, in full, a *profit à prendre*) is a right to enter upon the land of another and to remove from it some part of the natural produce. Included are the right to take minerals, such as coal or gravel (*Staples* v. *Young*, 1908); the right to take turf, known as a profit of turbary (*Convey* v. *Regan*, 1952); the right to graze animals, called a profit of pasturage (*Tyrringham's Case*, 1584); the right to take fish, or a profit of piscary (see *Moore* v. *Attorney-General*, 1934); and a right to take game (*Radcliff* v. *Hayes*, 1907). That list is by no means exhaustive, but somewhat oddly, the right to take the cultivated or artificial produce of land is not properly classified as a profit, and can be only a licence.

A profit can exist in gross, independently of any dominant tenement. It is not, then, of course, a servitude, but creates an independent object of property. This is reflected in the land registration legislation. A separate register is maintained for the registration of the ownership of profits and other incorporeal hereditaments held in gross: Registration of Title Act 1964, s.8; Land Registration Act (N.I.) 1970, s.10. A profit held in gross may authorise the taking of a limited quantity of the produce of the land, or an unlimited amount. In the latter case it is said to be *without stint*. The profit may also be an exclusive right to a particular kind of product, in which case it is a *several* profit, or it may be a right, in common with others, to share the produce. It is then a *right of common*.

As well as existing in gross, profits may exist as true servitudes, being annexed to a dominant tenement. Certain rights of common of pasturage, arising on a grant of arable land within a manor made before Quia Emptores 1290, are *appendant* to the land, having been created by operation of law, and are governed by some special rules: *Davies* v. *Davies* (1975). The overwhelming majority of profits annexed to land are *appurtenant* to that land, having been created by an express or implied grant. A profit which is appurtenant to land must be limited to the needs of the dominant tenement: *Anderson* v. *Bostock* (1976). A common of fishery appurtenant to a house gives a right to catch fish limited to the needs of that house, and does not authorise the catching of fish for sale: *Lord Chesterfield* v. *Harris* (1908).

7. Natural Rights

Some rights similar to easements exist as natural rights, that is, as rights automatically annexed to land without the need for creation by express or implied grant. One such natural right is the right to have one's land supported at its natural level by adjoining and nearby land: *Latimer* v. *Official Co-operative Society* (1885). This right is infringed if a neighbour by excavation or mining withdraws support, although he is under no obligation to take positive acts to maintain the support. The natural right does not extend to a right to the support of buildings, which must be acquired by express or implied grant, but if the natural right is infringed, the measure of damages can include compensation for damage to buildings: *Stroyan* v. *Knowles* (1861).

Another natural right is the right of a riparian owner to take water from a river or other watercourse flowing in a defined channel: *Thompson* v. *Horner* (1927). This right is infringed if the river is dammed or diverted: *McClone* v. *Smith*, 1888.

8. Public and local customary rights

Some public rights, that is, rights enjoyed by the public as a whole, are similar to easements. One public right is the right of the general public to fish in tidal rivers up to the point of the ebb and flow of the tide; another is the right to pass and repass along a highway (*i.e.* a public right of way). The exercise of a public right is open to all, irrespective of the ownership of any land.

Local customary rights, that is, rights exercisable by the members of a local community, may also exist. These are the rights of the inhabitants of a village or other community to do some thing by virtue of the exercise of those rights since time immemorial, or by express or implied grant from the Crown: *Daly* v. *Cullen* (1958); *Mahoney* v. *Neenan* (1966). The kind of rights which have been held to be exercisable on this account have been the right of locals to play games upon land; of the fishermen of a parish to dry their nets upon private land; and of the inhabitants of a place to enjoy a fishery.

B. Creation of Easements and Profits

9. The need for a grant

It is a basic principle that apart from easements and profits created by statute, easements and profits may be created only by way of a grant. Such a grant may be express, implied, or presumed. Easements conferred by statute need not conform to the ordinary rules concerning easements, such as the need for a dominant tenement (see Garner (1956) 20 Conv. (N.S.) 208).

10. Express grant

An easement may be created expressly by the use of a grant, either independently, or as part of a conveyance of an estate or interest in land. Easements and profits must ordinarily be created by deed, but easements and profits may also be validly created if the requirements of Deasy's Act 1860 are complied with. This permits the letting of an easement or profit appurtenant to land, or the letting of a profit in gross to be made by deed or signed writing, or even orally, if the letting is from year to year or any lesser period (see p. 115; and *Bayley* v. *Conyngham*, 1863). No special words of grant are required, but the appropriate words of limitation should be used, since an easement or profit can subsist for any of the freehold or leasehold estates. It is also advisable to identify the appropriate dominant tenement expressly, although in the absence of express identification the court will examine all the relevant circumstances to identify the dominant tenement: *Johnstone* v. *Holdaway* (1963).

Where a grant does not comply with the essential formalities to create a legal title to the easement or profit, it can nevertheless create an easement or profit in equity if it was given for value and evidenced in writing or supported by part performance. Equity will then treat the informal arrangement as a specifically enforceable agreement, which will operate as a grant of the easement or profit in equity: *McManus* v. *Cooke* (1887).

11. Implied grant

Even where an easement is not created expressly, there are certain cases in which the grant of an easement will be implied in favour of a purchaser on a conveyance of land forming part of a larger area owned by the vendor. The implication of an easement in such cases is based upon the intention of the parties.

An intention to create an easement can easily be found in a case of necessity. If land is conveyed in circumstances where it is incapable of any beneficial use unless an easement is implied over the land retained, then the purchaser will have an easement of necessity. For instance if land is sold which has no means of access to a public road or to other land owned by the purchaser, a way of necessity over the vendor's retained land will be implied: *Donnelly* v. *Adams* (1905). No easement of necessity will arise if the parties expressly exclude the implication of such an easement: *Nickerson* v. *Barraclough* (1981).

In other cases an implied easement can arise under the principle that a man may not derogate from his grant. Where it is the common intention of vendor and purchaser that the land shall be used in some particular way, which is possible only if a certain easement is granted, then that easement will be implied: *Pwllbach Colliery Co. Ltd.* v. *Woodman* (1915). For example, in *Wong* v. *Beaumont Property Trust Ltd.* (1965) basement premises were leased for use as a Chinese restaurant. Under public health regulations the basement could only be used for this purpose if the kitchens were vented to roof level. It was held that there was an implied easement (described in the case as an easement of necessity) to install a ventilation duct through the upstairs floors retained by the landlord.

12. The rule in Wheeldon v. Burrows

An application of the rule that a man may not derogate from his grant has become known as the rule in *Wheeldon* v. *Burrows* (1879). According to Thesiger L.J. in that case:

> "on the grant by the owner of a tenement of part of that tenement as it is then used and enjoyed, there will pass to the grantee all those continuous and apparent easements (by which, of course, I mean *quasi* easements), or, in other words, all those easements which are necessary to the reasonable enjoyment of the property granted, and which have been and are at the time of the grant used by the owners of the entirety for the benefit of the part granted."

It is unclear from the judgment in *Wheeldon* v. *Burrows* whether the two tests put forward of "continuous and apparent" and "necessary to the reasonable enjoyment of the property granted" are alternative requirements for the creation of an easement, or whether they must both be satisfied. The issue has been dodged in subsequent cases, in which both tests have been held to be satisfied. The test of "continuous and apparent," which may well be a borrowing from French law, seems only to require that the existence of the easement can be discovered by an inspection of the land, for instance where there is a made-up road or path running from the land sold over the land retained: *Borman* v. *Griffith* (1930); *McDonagh* v. *Mulholland* (1931). An underground drain would almost certainly be continuous and apparent if its existence was disclosed by inspection covers: see *Pyer* v. *Carter* (1857).

The rule in *Wheeldon* v. *Burrows* elevates a thing which was being enjoyed by the owner before sale by virtue of his common ownership of the lands sold and retained into a full easement: a legal easement if the grant is a conveyance of a legal estate; an equitable easement if the grant takes effect only in equity.

13. Conveyancing Act 1881, s.6

The benefit of an existing easement passes automatically on the transfer of the dominant tenement without any need for the mention of the easement in the conveyance. In the cautious fashion of lawyers, however, it has always been the practice to refer expressly to them.

The Conveyancing Act 1881 contained a number of word-saving provisions, of which section 6 is one. These provisions were automatically implied into conveyances, in some cases subject to any contrary stipulation, and saved conveyancers inserting some long clauses which had formerly been customary. Section 6(1) of the Conveyancing Act 1881 provides:

> "A conveyance of land shall be deemed to include and shall by virtue of this Act operate to convey, with the land, all buildings, erections, fixtures, commons, hedges, ditches, fences, ways, waters, watercourses, liberties, privileges, easements, rights, and advantages whatsoever, appertaining or reputed to appertain to the land, or any part thereof, or at the time of the conveyance demised, occupied, or enjoyed with, or reputed or known as part or parcel of or appurtenant to the land or any part thereof."

This provision carries, on a conveyance of land, the benefit of any existing easements and profits. It has also been held, in certain cases, to create new easements or profits: *Henry Ltd.* v. *McGlade* (1926). To operate in this way there must have been diversity of ownership or occupation before the conveyance (*Long* v. *Gowlett*, 1923), the grantor must have had power to create the easement, and the right must be in its nature capable of existing as an easement or profit. A permissive right which an occupier is enjoying by licence pending completion can thus be elevated to an easement: see *Goldberg* v. *Edwards* (1950). Here the landlord of a flat allowed a tenant into possession before the lease was signed. The tenant was allowed to use a secondary means of access to the flat over land retained by the landlord. It was held that when the lease was signed, this licence was turned into an easement. Similarly, a right enjoyed by permission by an existing tenant over land belonging to his landlord can become an easement on the grant of a new lease: *International Tea Stores Co.* v. *Hobbs* (1903); *Jeffers* v. *Odeon* (*Ireland*) *Ltd.* (1953). Some "rights" enjoyed by a tenant may, however, be so precarious as to be incapable of conversion into an easement. Where a tenant of shop premises asked for permission from his landlord every time he wished to make a delivery through a rear passageway the landlord retained, it was held that no easement arose in his favour on the grant of a new lease. All he had was "a purported right of way for such periods as the servient owner may permit one to use it," which is a right without substance: *Green* v. *Ashco Horticulturist Ltd.* (1966).

The effect of section 6 of the Conveyancing Act 1881 can be excluded by a contrary intention: *Steele* v. *Morrow* (1923).

14. Prescription

Long and uninterrupted enjoyment of an easement or profit as of right can give rise to an irrebuttable presumption of legality. The rules are judge-made, but have been modified by statute. They operate on the basis that a valid grant of the right has been made, although there will in fact rarely have been such a grant.

Enjoyment or *user* of an easement or profit as of right requires that the use should have been *nec vi, nec clam*, and *nec precario*—without force, secrecy or permission. Prescription is based upon acquiescence —the servient owner must know of the acts, be able to take steps to prevent them, but fail to do so. Repeated objections to the use by the servient owner may sufficiently preclude prescription.

The rules concerning prescription are most unsatisfactory. There is no single prescription period, and three different cases have to be distinguished: common law prescription, the fiction of the lost modern grant, and statutory prescription.

15. Common law prescription

At common law, user from time immemorial gives rise to a conclusive presumption that a right has a lawful origin. Following a statute of Henry VIII (32 Henry VIII, Chap. 2), the date "from time whereof the memory of men runneth not to the contrary" (*Coke on Littleton*, p. 170) has been arbitrarily fixed at the year 1189. The difficulty of proving continuous use of a right since that date has been mitigated by the willingness of the courts to accept proof of a minimum of twenty years user, or of a lifetime's enjoyment as evidence of user since 1189: see *O'Brien* v. *Enright* (1867). A claim will however be defeated if it is shown that the right must have been of more modern origin, for instance because it relates to a building which did not exist in 1189 or because the land has at some time since then been in common ownership: *Wilson* v. *Stanley* (1861).

16. Lost modern grant

The failure of prescription at common law in relation to rights first exercised after 1189 led to the development by the courts of the fiction of the lost modern grant. Under this doctrine, where an easement has been enjoyed for 20 years, but it could not have been enjoyed from time immemorial, it will be presumed to have a legal origin in the form of a modern grant of the right which has been lost, and so cannot be produced in evidence: *Bryant* v. *Foot* (1867). The presumption canot be rebutted by evidence that a grant was never in fact made (*Tehidy Minerals Ltd.* v. *Norman*, 1971), but the presumption will not be made if during the period of user there was no person capable of making a grant (*Daniel* v. *North*, 1809) or if a grant would otherwise have been impossible, for instance because the right claimed was incapable of being an easement (see *Bryant* v. *Lefever*, 1879). As with prescription at common law, user must have been as of right: *Hanna* v. *Pollock* (1900).

17. Statutory prescription

Some of the difficulties of common law prescription were tackled by the Prescription Act 1832, an Act which was described by the English Law Reform Committee in its 14th report in 1966 as "one of the worst drafted Acts on the Statute Book." The Act was extended to Ireland by the Prescription (Ireland) Act 1858. The Act makes special provision for rights of light, and these will be discussed separately later. For other easements and profits, the Act distinguishes between a short period of user (20 years for easements, 30 years for profits) and a longer period of user (40 years and 60 years for easements and profits respectively).

In relation to the shorter period, the Act provides that an easement enjoyed as of right and without interruption for a period of 20 years (30 years for a profit) next before some suit or action cannot be defeated by proof only that user began after 1189.

In relation to the longer period, the same user without interruption for a period of 40 years (60 years for a profit) next before some suit or action makes the title to an easement or profit "absolute and indefeasible," unless it has been enjoyed by written consent. In computing this longer statutory prescription period, the period may include periods of incapacity on the part of the owner of the servient tenement; such periods of incapacity may not form part of the shorter period. Furthermore, user for the 40 or 60 year period is deemed to be as of right notwithstanding any oral permission given by the servient owner before the commencement of this period. For common law prescription and the shorter statutory period, any consent, written or oral, is fatal since it means that user is permissive: *Gardner* v. *Hodgson's Brewery Co. Ltd.* (1903). The statutory exception concerning oral permission and the longer period applies only at the commencement of the 40 year or 60 year period. Oral consent given during the period interrupts it because it negatives user as of right: *Healey* v. *Hawkins* (1968).

18. Prescriptive right to light

The Prescription Act 1832 treats easements of light (*i.e.* the right to the access of light to a defined aperture or window) differently from other easements and profits. Under the Act, where the access of light to a building is enjoyed without interruption for 20 years next before some suit or action, the right becomes absolute and indefeasible. There is no requirement that the access of light be enjoyed as of right, and the right to light may be acquired despite any oral consent, or payment of rent, whether made before or during the period. Only if consent was given in writing or by deed is a claim defeated.

19. "Without interruption . . . next before some suit or action"

It is a requirement of all the statutory periods of prescription that they should have been enjoyed "without interruption . . . next before some suit or action." Even after 20, 30, 40 or 60 years have passed, as the case may be, an easement or profit is not acquired under the statute. The right to it remains inchoate until established in legal proceedings and will be lost if there is a subsequent interruption. The statutory period must therefore run up to the date of the action. The action may be of any kind: an action seeking a declaration; an action for infringement; or an action by the servient owner.

The 1832 Act gives a special meaning to the words "without interruption." An interruption will only break the statutory prescription periods if it is "submitted to or acquiesced in for one year after the party interrupted shall have had or shall have notice thereof, and of the person making or authorising the same to be made." Thus if the owner of the servient tenement interrupts a right of way by erecting a fence across it, this will not prevent the owner of the dominant tenement establishing his right if within a year he breaks down the fence, protests at the interruption, or commences an action: *Claxton* v. *Claxton* (1873).

In the case of an easement of light, the way in which the servient owner must establish an interruption in the Republic of Ireland is by erecting a screen or a hoarding or permanent building in such a position as to obstruct the flow of light to the dominant tenement. The same method may be used in Northern Ireland, but the servient owner may alternatively invoke the provisions of the Rights of Light Act (N.I.) 1961. This enables a servient owner to register a notional obstruction in the Statutory Charges Registry after notifying the dominant owner and making advertisements. Registration has the same effect as a physical obstruction.

20. Prescription by and against tenants

The rules concerning prescription by and against tenants are unsettled and appear arbitrary. See generally Delany (1958) 74 L.Q.R. 82 and Chua (1964) 15 N.I.L.Q. 489.

A tenant may acquire an easement by prescription against a stranger. Where he does so, the easement will enure for the benefit of the fee simple estate in the dominant tenement if the claim is made on the basis of immemorial user or under the Prescription Act 1832: see *Wheaton* v. *Maple & Co.* (1893). It is probably the case that a tenant can prescribe for an easement against other land held by his landlord under the longer statutory prescription period (*Fahey* v. *Dwyer*, 1879), but he cannot prescribe against his landlord under the shorter period or under the doctrine of lost modern grant: *Macnaghten* v. *Baird* 1903.

Where the servient tenement is in the possession of a tenant, all forms of prescription are possible if user began against an owner in fee simple: *Palk* v. *Shinner* (1852). Where user began only against the tenant or limited owner, prescription is possible only under the longer of the statutory periods (*Beggan* v. *McDonald*, 1878) and under the doctrine of lost modern grant: *Deeble* v. *Linehan* (1860). If there is no evidence of acquiescence by the landlord of the servient tenement, the easement prescribed for may be limited to the term of the servient owner's tenancy: see *O'Kane* v. *O'Kane* (1892). Where prescription is claimed under the longer (40 year) statutory period, the term of any lease for life or tenancy exceeding three years is to be deducted in computing the period if, but only if, a claim is brought by the reversioner within three years of the end of the term: Prescription Act 1832, s.8. An easement may therefore be acquired which is good against the tenant, but liable to be defeated by his landlord or other reversioner: *Beggan* v. *McDonald* (1877) 2 L.R. Ir. 560.

Where one tenant seeks to prescribe against land held by another tenant under the same landlord, his claim is admissible under the longer statutory period (*Fahey* v. *Dwyer*, above) and probably also under the doctrine of lost modern grant: *Hanna* v. *Pollock* (1900).

Acquisition of an easement of light under the special statutory provisions of the Prescription Act 1832 is possible in all the cases enumerated above.

21. Express reservation of easements

An owner who is selling only part of his land may wish to retain, for the benefit of the part he keeps, an easement over the part he sells. Strictly speaking such an easement cannot be excluded or excepted from the grant of land as it has no existence during common ownership. There are, however, two methods whereby it is possible to create an easement by reservation. The first is that if a purchaser executes a conveyance which reserves an easement to the vendor, this will take effect as a regrant of the easement. In other words, the conveyance will be seen as doing two things: as first conveying an estate to the purchaser, who then out of this estate conveys back an easement to the vendor: *Wickham* v. *Hawker* (1840). This seemingly bizarre analysis means that in the event of any doubt about the extent of the right granted, the doubt will be resolved against the purchaser: see *Johnstone* v. *Holdway* (1963). In the event of a failure on the part of the purchaser to execute the conveyance, the doctrine in *Walsh* v. *Lonsdale* (1882) would apply: see page 120. The vendor would have an equitable right to compel the purchaser to execute the conveyance, with the result that the reservation, under the principle "equity treats as done that which ought to be done," would operate to create an equitable easement: *May* v. *Belville* (1905). In Northern Ireland, by virtue of section 40 of the Land Registration Act (N.I.) 1970, execution by the purchaser is not required in a deed reserving a right exclusively over registered land.

The second method of reservation is that by the combined effect of the Statute of Uses (Ireland) 1634 and the Conveyancing Act 1881, s.62(1) the vendor can convey the land to the use that the vendor shall have an easement or profit, and subject thereto to the use that the purchaser shall have the fee simple. The uses are then executed into legal rights and estates.

22. Implied reservation

The reservation of an easement will only exceptionally be implied. The rules in *Wheeldon* v. *Burrows* and the Conveyancing Act 1881, section 6 do not operate. Only in cases of necessity or clear common intention will a reservation be implied: *Brown* v. *Maguire* (1922).

23. Extent of easements and profits

The extent of an easement or profit depends upon the mode of its creation. Where the right is created expressly, its extent will depend upon the interpretation of the grant, which will be construed *contra proferentem*, but taking account of all the relevant circumstances such as the nature of the dominant tenement: *Neill* v. *Duke of Devonshire* (1882); *St. Edmundsbury and Ipswich Diocesan Board of Finance* v. *Clark (No. 2)* (1975). If on its proper interpretation the grant is of an unrestricted right, it may be exercised even if there is a change in the use of the dominant tenement.

An easement based upon the common intention of the parties is limited in its extent to the minimum required to give effect to that common intention (*Pwllbach Colliery Co. Ltd.* v. *Woodman*, 1915), and similarly, an easement of necessity is limited to the circumstances of the necessity existing at the time of the grant: *Browne* v. *Maguire* (1922).

An easement or profit acquired by prescription permits user which is measured by the extent of the user during the period of acquisition. The user of a right of way acquired by prescription may increase provided that there is no radical change in the nature or character of the dominant tenement. Thus a right of way to a caravan site may still be exercised if the number of caravans is increased (*British Railways Board* v. *Glass*, 1965), but a right acquired by agricultural user would not permit use for access to a factory (*Williams* v. *James*, 1867).

In the case of a right to light acquired by prescription, the dominant owner is entitled not to have the access of light reduced below such a level as is needed for the comfortable use of the premises for ordinary purposes: *Smyth* v. *Dublin Theatre Co.* (1936). What is ordinary will depend on the nature of the building and the purposes for which it is adapted. The satisfactory use of a greenhouse will require a higher degree of light than the satisfactory use of a warehouse: *Allen* v. *Greenwood* (1979). There is no set or scientific test for the amount of light: *McGrath* v. *Munster and Leinster Bank Ltd.* (1959). The dominant owner cannot increase the burden on the servient tenement by increasing the size of his windows or adding additional ones until the right to the extra light has been acquired by prescription: *Scott* v. *Goulding Properties Ltd.* (1972) (*cf. Re London, Tilbury & Southend Railway and the Trustees of the Gower's Walk Schools* (1889)). A right to an exceptional amount of light may be acquired by prescription where to the knowledge of the servient owner at all material times the dominant tenement has been used for purposes reasonably requiring the exceptional amount of light: *Allen* v. *Greenwood* (above).

C. Extinguishment of Easements and Profits

24. Discharge and modification of easements

Although an easement may be extinguished by compulsory acquisition under statutory powers, and other legislation may affect easements, there is no statutory procedure in the Republic of Ireland under which easements which have become redundant or obstructive may be modified or extinguished. In Northern Ireland easements and profits can be modified or extinguished under the Property (Northern

Ireland) Order 1978. Apart from those rare cases in which an easement is extinguished under statutory powers, the only way in which an easement can be extinguished is by release or unity of possession and title.

25. Release

The way in which an easement is discharged by private act is by release. Release may be either express or implied. An express release, to take effect at law, must be made by deed. However, a specifically enforceable agreement to release an easement will, on general equitable principles, operate as a release in equity. The doctrine of proprietary estoppel can also apply so that where the dominant owner has led the servient owner to believe that he will not exercise his easement, and the servient owner has changed his position in reliance on this, the dominant owner will be prevented from claiming that the right still exists: *Davies* v. *Marshall* (1861).

An implied release will occur where the dominant owner abandons the easement or profit: that is, he ceases to enjoy the right with the intention of giving up the right permanently. A mere failure to exercise the right is not sufficient, but an intention to release will normally be implied from twenty years desuetude, although this may be negatived by the circumstances. The circumstances may also show an intention to abandon even before this: *Moore* v. *Rawson* (1824).

26. Unity of possession and title

An easement or profit is automatically extinguished where dominant and servient tenements are in common ownership and occupation, for one of the essential requirements of an easement is thereby lost: *Buckley* v. *Coles* (1814); *Wilson* v. *Stanley* (1861). There will not, though, be any extinguishment if although there is a union of the fee simple estates there is no unity of possession because one of the tenements has been let: *Richardson* v. *Graham* (1908). Nor will there be any extinguishment if there is unity of possession without unity of fee simple title; the easement will simply be suspended during the concurrent possession: *Thomas* v. *Thomas* (1835).

D. Registered Land

27. Easements and profits in registered land

The rules concerning easements and profits apply to registered land with few modifications. As has already been observed, title to profits à prendre in gross is registered in a separate register (see p. 189). The benefit of an easement or profit appurtenant to registered land may be recorded by an entry on the folio relating to the dominant tenement (Registration of Title Act 1964, s.82; Land Registration Act (N.I.) 1970, s.51) and such entry is conclusive evidence of the existence of the right: 1964 Act, s.31; 1970 Act, s.11.

Easements and profits, unless created by express grant or reservation after the first registration of the land, fall into the category of overriding interests, that is of interests affecting the registered servient tenement without the need for registration: 1964 Act, s.72; 1970 Act, s.38, Sched. 5. Easements and profits created by express grant or reservation after the first registration of the land are registrable as burdens against the servient tenement: 1964 Act, s.69; 1970 Act, Sched. 6, Pt. 1.

Even if the benefit of an easement or profit is not recorded on the folio, it will pass on a transfer of the dominant tenement by operation of law: 1964 Act, s.52; 1970 Act, s.34; Conveyancing Act 1881, s.6.

Easements and profits may be created in and over registered land in the same way as over unregistered land.

17 Covenants

A. General

1. Obligations concerning land

It will often be the case that on the transfer of an interest in land, the vendor will wish the purchaser to undertake certain obligations, or *vice versa*. For instance, the owner of a house with a large garden selling part of the garden as a building site may wish to ensure that no more than one house is erected on it, or that it is not used for business purposes. Similarly, the tenant of a flat may wish the landlord to keep the roof in good repair, and to clean and maintain those parts shared with other tenants.

An agreement made between vendor and purchaser in the transfer, or at the same time, will be enforceable as a contract (provided that it is supported by a deed or by consideration). But contracts are normally enforceable only where there is privity of contract. The question thus arises as to the position of successors in title. If the agreement creates an easement or a profit it is clear that both benefit and burden pass to successors in title. What is the position concerning obligations which are not capable of existing as easements or profits? An initial distinction here has to be made between obligations entered into between landlord and tenant, and other obligations. It will also be necessary later to distinguish between positive covenants and restrictive covenants for as we shall see the intervention of equity has enabled covenants restrictive in nature to be more widely enforced than covenants positive in nature.

2. Meaning of "covenant"

Strictly speaking, a *covenant* is a promise under seal, that is, a promise made by deed. Since most of the obligations with which we are concerned are made as part of a conveyance of an interest in land, and most conveyances are made by deed, it is inevitable that most promises will be covenants in the strict sense. In general, however, the same rules apply to contractual promises which are not contained in a deed, such as the "covenants" contained in a contract of tenancy.

3. Covenants as contracts

It must not be forgotten that covenants are contracts, and that most of the ordinary rules relating to contracts apply to them. The main reason for considering covenants specially is that in certain cases, by way of exception to the ordinary contract rules, the benefit or burden of covenants, or both, may run to successors in title. There is no need to resort to the special rules, however, where a question arises between the original contracting parties. With one exception concerning leases, mentioned below (see p. 204) a covenant entered into between the original parties remains enforceable between them and their personal representatives, as it would if it bore no relation to land; and on ordinary contractual principles the benefit of most covenants can be expressly transferred by way of assignment.

B. Covenants in Leases

4. Common covenants in leases

The relationship between landlord and tenant is unlike that between vendor and purchaser of a freehold estate in fee simple. The transaction is not a once-off deal, but creates a continuing relationship between the parties. This is reflected in the provisions commonly found in leases and contracts of tenancy. Depending upon the length of the term, the lease or contract is likely to contain provisions concerning repair, rent, use, and other matters (see, for example, Form 11.1 on p. 116). Even where there are no express covenants, some covenants will be implied by common law or statute.

5. Implied covenants in leases

Implied covenants on the part of the landlord, unless there is express provision to the contrary, are that he has good title to make the lease, and that the tenant will enjoy quiet possession during the term of the lease: Deasy's Act 1860, s. 41. At common law there is an implied covenant that furnished premises (but not unfurnished premises) are fit for human habitation at the commencement of the lease. Apart from these general covenants, further covenants may be implied in special cases, such as a letting falling within the provisions of the Housing (Private Rented Dwellings) Act 1982.

Implied covenants on the part of the tenant include a covenant to pay the rent, and to give up peaceable possession on the determination of the lease, subject, of course, to any statutory restrictions on the landlord's right to possession, such as under the rent restriction legislation: Deasy's Act 1860, s. 42.

6. Express covenants in leases

It is not uncommon for a landlord to covenant expressly to carry out certain repairs and maintenance of the demised premises, such as the repair and maintenance of parts used in common with other tenants, and of the roof and exterior. In some cases the landlord may also undertake to provide services such as heating and security or supervision. There can sometimes, but only exceptionally, be an implied obligation on the part of the landlord to carry out repairs and maintenance: see *Liverpool City Council* v. *Irwin* (1977).

Express covenants on the part of the tenant, which are generally more numerous than those on the part of the landlord, are likely to include a covenant to pay rent, rates, and other outgoings; to carry out internal repairs or decorations; to use the premises only for certain purposes; not to use the premises in a way which may cause a nuisance or offence; not to carry out any alterations without the landlord's consent; and not to assign or sublet without permission.

7. Liability between original landlord and tenant

At common law, covenants between landlord and tenant being contracts, they were enforceable between the original parties even though the landlord might have sold the reversion, and even though the tenant might have sublet or assigned the lease. The original landlord and tenant were, in a sense, guarantors to each other that the covenants in the lease would be duly performed: see *Stuart* v. *Joy* (1904).

To safeguard against being held liable for the acts of others, the landlord or tenant, on an assignment, would obtain from the assignee a covenant of indemnity. This would mean that if the original covenantor were found liable, he would be able to recover from the assignee any sums paid.

The common law position holds good today, with one major statutory modification. By section 16 of Deasy's Act 1860, a tenant who assigns his lease with the consent of the landlord is released and discharged from future liability under the lease.

8. Liability of assignees at common law

Covenants in leases have long been recognised as exceptions to the rule that contracts may normally only be enforced where there is privity of contract. At common law, leasehold covenants were enforceable between assignees only if there was *privity of estate* between the plaintiff and the defendant, and if the covenant in question *touched and concerned* the land.

Privity of estate exists where the parties stand in the relationship of landlord and tenant to each other. If, for instance the tenant T assigned his lease to A, then the landlord L and A would stand in privity of estate. But if A then assigned to B, there would no longer be privity of estate between L and A. There would instead be privity of estate between L and B. If, instead of assigning to A, T had sublet to S, T would remain in privity of estate with L, and there would be privity of estate between T and S, but no privity either of estate or of contract between L and S.

A covenant touches and concerns land if it affects the landlord in his normal capacity as landlord or the tenant in his normal capacity as tenant (see Cheshire and Burn, *Modern Law of Real Property* (13th ed.), p. 430). Examples would be covenants by the tenant to repair (*Martyn* v. *Clue*, 1852), to manure the land (*Sale* v. *Kitchingham*, 1713) or to insure against fire (*Vernon* v. *Smith*, 1821), and covenants by the landlord to supply the house let with water (*Jourdain* v. *Wilson*, 1821) or not to build on neighbouring land (*Ricketts* v. *Enfield Churchwardens*, 1909).

At common law, subject to some conditions, both the benefit and burden of covenants touching and concerning the land pass to an assignee of a tenant: *Spencer's Case* (1583). It was not until the Statute of Reversions (Ireland) 1634, however, that the benefit and burden of all covenants touching and concerning land was made to pass on an assignment of the landlord's reversion. This statutory modification was re-enacted in an improved form by sections 10 and 11 of the Conveyancing Act 1881.

9. Position of assignees under Deasy's Act, 1860

A parallel set of rules concerning the running of covenants in leases was introduced by Deasy's Act 1860. The relationship between these rules and the common law rules, as modified by the Conveyancing Act 1881 remains unclear: see *O'Leary* v. *Deasy* (1911).

By section 12 of Deasy's Act 1860, covenants contained or implied in a lease or tenancy agreement, or incident to the tenancy can be enforced against a successor in title of the tenant by the landlord or his successors in title. There is no express requirement that the covenant should "touch and concern" the tenancy (see *Lyle* v. *Smith*, 1909; *Liddy* v. *Kennedy*, 1871), but it may be doubted whether the section could be effective to transfer either benefit or burden of a covenant clearly personal in nature, such as a covenant for personal services.

Section 13 of Deasy's Act provides that covenants contained or implied in a lease may be enforced against the successors in title of the landlord by a tenant or his successors in title. It is here necessary for the covenants to be "concerning the land" which, it may be thought, imports the common law concept of "touching and concerning" land: but see *Burrowes* v. *Delaney* (1889).

The provisions in sections 12 and 13 of Deasy's Act apply only to assignees of the landlord and tenant. They create no liability between a landlord and subtenant.

10. Position of assignee following assignment

The right of an assignee to sue upon, and his liability under, covenants in a lease depends upon privity of estate, and so the general rule is that he cannot sue, or be sued upon covenants after an assignment. This is because the assignment destroys the privity of estate. This general rule is modified by sections 14 and 15 of Deasy's Act. Under these sections an assignee of the tenant is not discharged from liability after he has assigned to someone else until he has given written notice to the landlord. If this notice is given between two gale days (days on which rent is due) it is effective only after the next gale day.

C. Covenants between Freeholders

11. Privity of contract

Covenants being contracts, even where there is no relationship of landlord and tenant between the parties, a covenant can be enforced where there is privity of contract. This flows simply from the ordinary rules relating to contracts. Thus a covenant made between freeholders, such as a covenant between neighbours, may be enforced between the original parties.

Similarly, again on ordinary contract principles, provided that a covenant is not purely personal in nature, the benefit may be expressly assigned as a chose in action under section 28 of the Judicature (Ireland) Act 1877, or in equity.

12. Running of benefit at common law

In some instances, the benefit of a covenant can pass at common law on a transfer of land to which it relates without any need for an express assignment. For this to happen, several conditions must be satisfied. First, the benefit of the covenant must touch and concern the land of the covenantee (*i.e.* the person in whose favour it was made). Secondly, the covenant must be intended to enure for the benefit of that land even after a change of ownership. Thirdly, the covenantee must have had a legal estate in the land, and his successor in title seeking to enforce the covenant must have the same legal estate: *Gaw* v. *C.I.E.* (1953); *Shayler* v. *Woolf* (1946); *Rogers* v. *Hosegood* (1900). Finally, the land benefited must be identified, but this may be done by means of extrinsic evidence: *Smith* v. *River Douglas Catchment Board* (1949).

Where these conditions are satisfied, the benefit of the covenant is said to be *annexed* to the land benefited, so as to pass automatically to a purchaser of the legal estate without express assignment. The "covenant" does not have to be made by deed, and the benefit may be annexed whether the covenant is positive or restrictive in nature.

13. Running of burden at common law

The ordinary rule at common law is that the burden of a covenant can be enforced only against the original covenantor. If he has sold the land intended to be affected, he may still be liable under the covenant, but the purchaser from him will not.

A number of devices may be used to circumvent the ordinary rule. One is to employ the principle of benefit and burden, as in the case of *Halsall* v. *Brizell* (1957) (see p. 179). A second is that an estate rentcharge may be used: see English Law Commission Report on Rentcharges 1975, Law Com. No. 68. Another is to use a lease or a leasehold fee farm grant instead of a sale, so that the leasehold rules, discussed above, apply. A variant on this is to grant a long lease with a term of at least 300 years and at a peppercorn rent. Such a lease is capable of enlargement into a fee simple by section 65 of the Conveyancing Act 1881, the covenants remaining enforceable as if there had been no enlargement. Yet another device is to employ a chain of indemnity covenants. Since the original covenantor remains liable after parting with the land, he will almost invariably require a purchaser from him to covenant to indemnify him against any future breaches. By means of the chain of covenants created on each successive transfer, the original covenant is indirectly enforceable against the land. This method, however, suffers from the drawback that it fails if the chain is broken in consequence of the death or disappearance of any of the parties in the chain.

D. Restrictive Covenants

14. The intervention of equity

None of the ways of avoiding the common law rule concerning the running of the burden of covenants is entirely satisfactory. Owing to the influence of equity, however, more liberal rules have been developed for covenants restrictive in nature. These rules permit both benefit and burden to run. Although not all the features of restrictive covenants enforceable in equity have been settled, they bear many similarities to true servitudes such as easements. As the rules of equity relating to restrictive covenants have developed, so have the similarities to servitudes become more prominent.

15. The case of Tulk v. Moxhay

There were some earlier decisions, but the case of *Tulk* v. *Moxhay* (1848) is generally taken as the historic starting-point of the development of the special rules of equity concerning restrictive covenants. The plaintiff owned several buildings in Leicester Square, London, and also the vacant land in the centre of the square. He sold this vacant land, the purchaser covenanting on behalf of himself, his heirs and assigns that they would keep and maintain the land "in an open state, uncovered with any buildings in neat and ornamental order." The defendant was a successor in title of the original covenantor, and had bought with notice of the covenant. Despite this, he proposed to erect buildings on the land. The court granted an injunction to prevent him. This and other early decisions rested upon the inequity of a purchaser with notice disregarding the covenant. Later decisions have seen this principle as too wide and have restricted the doctrine by analogy with easements.

16. Enforcing the benefit of restrictive covenants

Four conditions must be satisfied before a person can enlist the aid of equity to enforce a restrictive covenant. First, the covenant must have been intended to benefit nearby land and not to have been for the mere personal benefit of the covenantee: see *Roake* v. *Chadha* (1983). Secondly, the covenant must touch and concern the dominant land: *Rogers* v. *Hosegood* (1900). Thirdly, the person seeking to enforce the covenant must hold the dominant land: *Formby* v. *Barker* (1903);

London County Council v. *Allen* (1914). Even if the plaintiff is the original covenantee, he cannot enforce a restrictive covenant against someone other than the original covenantor if he has parted with the dominant land.

There is, in these first three conditions, a clear analogy with easements. The analogy continues, for even where the dominant land is not identified in the document containing the covenant, "it is sufficient if in the light of the attendant circumstances the identity of the dominant land is in some other way ascertainable with reasonable certainty": *Re Union of London and Smith's Bank Ltd.'s Conveyance, Miles* v. *Easter* (1933); *Newton Abbot Co-operative Society Ltd.* v. *Williamson and Treadgold Ltd.* (1952).

The fourth condition does not continue the analogy with easements. This is that the person seeking to enforce the covenant must show, if he is not the original covenantee, that the benefit has passed to him by assignment, by annexation, or by virtue of a local scheme.

17. Assignment of benefit of restrictive covenant

For the benefit of a restrictive covenant to pass by assignment, the assignment must be contemporaneous with a transfer of the dominant land: *Re Union of London and Smith's Bank Ltd.'s Conveyance, Miles* v. *Easter* (1933). Once again this rule derives from the analogy with servitudes. Where equity permits restrictive covenants to be enforced, it is because they are taken for the benefit of land, and once the link between the land and the covenant has been severed, the covenant is treated as spent.

The assignment itself may be made either expressly by means of words showing an intention that the benefit of the covenant is to pass; or the assignment may take place by operation of law such as by devolution to the personal representatives of the covenantee: *Newton Abbot Co-operative Society Ltd.* v. *Williams and Treadgold Ltd.* (1952). Where there are successive transfers of the dominant land it seems that it is necessary for there to be an assignment of the benefit of the covenant on each occasion: *Stilwell* v. *Blackman* (1968).

18. Annexation of benefit of restrictive covenant

The benefit of a restrictive covenant may become annexed to the dominant land so that it passes with any subsequent transfer of that land irrespective of any knowledge, notice or assignment. For annexation to take place expressly, the document containing the covenant must show an intention to annex. In *Drake* v. *Gray* (1936), Greene L.J. said that there were two familiar methods of showing this intention. "One is to describe the character in which the covenantee receives the covenant. That is the form which is adopted here, a covenant with so-and-so, owners or owner for the time being of whatever the land may be. Another method is to state by means of an appropriate declaration that the covenant is taken "for the benefit of" whatever the lands may be." It is important that the phrase used should refer to land or to the ownership of land (*Renals* v. *Cowlishaw*, 1878; 1879), but if this land is only vaguely described, extrinsic evidence may be admitted to identify it more clearly.

There is no Irish decision upon the point, but the English cases show that a difficulty can arise over whether the benefit of a restrictive covenant is annexed to the dominant land as an entire whole or whether it is annexed to all parts of the dominant land. If the court construes words of annexation as purporting to annex the benefit to the dominant land as an entirety, the annexation will fail unless substantially the whole of the land is capable of benefiting: *Re Ballard's Conveyance* (1937). A further difficulty surfaces if part only of the land is sold. If the covenant was annexed to the dominant land as a unity, the benefit does not pass on a sale of part only unless there is an express assignment: *Russell* v. *Archdale* (1964); *Stilwell* v. *Blackman* (1968). A successor in title must hold substantially the whole of the dominant land if he is to succeed in claiming the benefit of a covenant annexed to the land as a whole: *Wrotham Park Estate Co. Ltd.* v. *Parkside Homes Ltd.* (1974).

These difficulties are avoided if the covenant is expressed to be taken for "each and every part" or for "the whole or any part or parts" of the dominant land. The covenant will then be treated as annexed to such part or parts of the dominant land as are capable of benefiting: *Marquess of Zetland* v. *Driver* (1939); *Re Selwyn's Conveyance* (1967). The difficulties arising in this part of the law are somewhat artificial, and it may well be that they would not be followed in Ireland: see the criticisms of the English Court of Appeal in *Federated Homes Ltd.* v. *Mill Lodge Properties Ltd.* (1980).

19. Implied annexation

The English Court of Appeal in the *Federated Homes* case (above) has held that, even without express words of annexation, section 78 of the English Law of Property Act 1925 operates automatically to cause the benefit of a restrictive covenant to be annexed to the dominant land provided that the covenant "relates" to that land. Section 78 of the 1925 Act replaced section 58 of the Conveyancing Act 1881, the provision which remains in force in Ireland. This latter section contains significantly different wording, and it is most unlikely that it could be held to have the same effect in causing implied annexation.

It is possible, however, that annexation may be implied where there is clear evidence from the circumstances attending the creation of a covenant that it was intended to benefit certain land: *Marten* v. *Flight Refuelling Ltd.* (1962).

20. Local schemes

It is common for covenants to be reciprocal or mutual. That is, the owners of adjoining lands will agree with each other that neither will use their lands for certain purposes. Such reciprocal covenants are often found in housing developments. Where such mutual covenants are found, they may establish a "local scheme" in which both benefit and burden run with each plot within the scheme to create a kind of local law.

The conditions for the recognition of a local scheme were set out with some particularity in the leading case of *Elliston* v. *Reacher* (1908). These are: (i) the plaintiff and defendant must both derive title from a common vendor; (ii) the common vendor must have laid out the estate involved in defined plots subject to common restrictions consistent only with a general scheme of development; (iii) the common vendor must have intended the restrictions to be for the benefit of all plots within the scheme; (iv) the original purchasers must have acquired their plots on the understanding that the restrictions could be enforced by the owners of all the other plots; and (v) the area which the scheme covers must be clearly defined: *Reid* v. *Bickerstaff* (1909). See also *Fitzpatrick* v. *Clancy* (1964).

While it is prudent for any new scheme to comply with these conditions, more recent decisions have relaxed the requirements of a local scheme. Even if there is neither a common vendor nor a division into lots, a common scheme of mutually enforceable restrictions can be established where there is a clear intention to create such a scheme and the area affected is clearly defined: *Baxter* v. *Four Oaks Properties Ltd.* (1965); *Re Dolphin's Conveyance* (1970).

21. The running of the burden of restrictive covenants

Provided that the person seeking to enforce a restrictive covenant satisfies the conditions discussed above, there are but two conditions to be satisfied for the burden to bind successors in title to the servient land of the covenantor. These conditions are that the covenant must be restrictive in nature, and it must have been intended to bind the servient land. The usual way of establishing the latter is by expressing the covenant to be made by the covenantor for himself, his heirs and assigns.

It seems that the requirement that the covenant be restrictive, or negative in nature, flows from the analogy with easements: *London and South Western Railway Co.* v. *Gomm* (1882). Like easements, therefore, a restrictive covenant cannot involve the servient owner in expenditure. An obligation to build or repair cannot be enforced as a restrictive covenant: *Haywood* v. *Brunswick Permanent Benefit Building Society* (1881).

22. Persons who are bound by restrictive covenants

Restrictive covenants, again pursuing the analogy with easements, create a burden upon the servient land enforceable against all in possession or in occupation of it. This is subject only to the rules relating to registration (see below) and to the general qualification to all equitable rights that they cannot be enforced against a bona fide purchaser of a legal estate for value without notice. Thus a restrictive covenant imposed upon a tenant can be enforced against a sub-tenant by the landlord even though there is no privity of estate between the two. The landlord's reversion will in such a case suffice as the dominant land. He need not have any interest in neighbouring land: *Craig* v. *Greer* (1899). Restrictive covenants may also be enforced against a licensee with notice of the covenant (*Mander* v. *Falcke*, 1891) and against a person in adverse possession since even if he has no notice of the covenant he cannot claim to be a purchaser: *Re Nisbet and Potts' Contract* (1906). The question of notice will be irrelevant if the deed creating the covenant is registered in the Registry of Deeds. If not so registered, actual notice will be required to bind someone claiming under a registered deed.

23. Remedies for breach of restrictive covenants

The primary remedy for a breach or threatened breach of a restrictive covenant is the injunction, but like all equitable remedies it is discretionary. The court has a jurisdiction under the Chancery Amendment Act 1858 (in Northern Ireland, the Judicature (N.I.) Act 1978) to award damages in lieu of an injunction: *Wrotham Park Estate Co. Ltd.* v. *Parkside Homes Ltd.* (1974).

24. Discharge and modification of restrictive covenants

The owner of the dominant land may expressly waive the benefit of a restrictive covenant. He may also by his conduct be estopped from enforcing a covenant: *Chatsworth Estates Co.* v. *Fewell* (1931); *Hepworth* v. *Pickles* (1900). There is not, in the Republic, any statutory power to discharge or modify restrictive covenants without the consent of the dominant owner, but such a power is conferred on the Lands Tribunal of Northern Ireland by the Property (N.I.) Order 1978.

25. Registration of restrictive covenants

Restrictive covenants affecting unregistered land will normally be contained in deeds of conveyance, memorials of which are registered in the Registry of Deeds. Where a covenant is independently created by a separate deed, that deed will be registrable in the Registry of Deeds.

Restrictive covenants affecting registered land are registrable as burdens on the folio of the servient land and such registration is essential if they are to bind subsequent purchasers: Registration of Title Act 1964, s.69; Land Registration Act (N.I.) 1970, s.39, Sched. 6.

18 Security

A. Nature and Forms of Security

1. What is security?

A security right is a right of resort to ensure the payment of money due. One type of security is personal security. Here, in the event of default by the debtor, the creditor may resort to another person for payment. One way of achieving this is for a guarantee to be taken from a person other than the debtor that the debt will be paid. It is common, for instance, where a loan is made to a minor for repayment to be guaranteed by a parent. A similar result to a guarantee may be achieved by taking an indemnity against any loss arising from non-payment of a debt. Personal security is very important in commercial practice, but falls outside the law of property.

There are types of security, however, which give rights of recourse against property in the event of a debt not being paid. These are the concern of the law of property. They comprise possessory and proprietary rights, charges and liens. Rights of security against property are taken for two prime reasons: to guarantee payment against a reluctant debtor; and to guarantee payment in full in priority to other creditors in the event of the debtor becoming insolvent.

2. Possessory security

With possessory security the person lending money, or otherwise entitled to a payment, retains goods, or very exceptionally, land, until payment is made. For instance a car repairer may retain possession of a car he has repaired until he is paid for this work, and an unpaid solicitor may retain his client's papers. Possessory security over land is much less common than over goods since a landowning borrower will rarely wish to part with possession of the land. To do so would in many cases defeat the purpose of the loan. Nevertheless possessory security over land is conceptually possible and was at one time relatively common in Ireland. It occurred with what is known as a "welsh mortgage." The lender under such a mortgage was given the possession of land by way of security, and took the rents and profits from the land in lieu of interest until the capital was repaid, the income from the land sometimes also being taken over a period of years in lieu of repayment of the capital. The possessory nature of the security in a welsh mortgage is shown by the fact that if the borrower had an express power to sell the land, the transaction would not be construed as a welsh mortgage: *Re Cronin* (1914).

3. Proprietary security

The essence of proprietary security is that the lender takes an estate or interest in the property itself by way of security. In the event of a failure to repay the loan the lender would retain the estate or interest, but if the loan is repaid, the lender undertakes to retransfer the interest in the property to the borrower. With early forms of proprietary security the lender might well have taken possession in lieu of interest as well as acquiring a right in the land. Since the right in the property is sufficient security on its own, the modern practice is for the borrower to retain possession, and this kind of security arrangement is known as a mortgage.

4. The equity of redemption

The standard way in which a mortgage is created over unregistered land is that the borrower will transfer his fee simple (or fee farm or leasehold interest) to the lender with a provision for redemption (*i.e.* for a retransfer of ownership on repayment of the loan). At common law the right of the borrower to redeem could only be exercised in strict compliance with the terms of the mortgage. This usually provided for repayment on a fixed date, often only a few months from the loan having been made. The loan would rarely exceed more than a proportion of the value of the land, and it would also often be contemplated that the loan might remain outstanding after the legal date fixed for redemption. In these circumstances equity intervened to prevent the lender from taking unfair advantage of his legal rights, and would permit the borrower to redeem even after the legal date for redemption had passed. The result is that although the borrower has technically parted with ownership to the lender, he retains rights of considerable value. His rights are known collectively as the *equity of redemption*. For all practical purposes the borrower (the *mortgagor*) remains the owner of the property subject to the rights of the lender (the *mortgagee*). The equity of redemption is a valuable proprietary interest which can be bought and sold, mortgaged or given away. If Mr. and Mrs. Murphy buy No. 5 Personalty Place (see pp. 8–9) for £20,000 using £5,000 of their own accumulated savings, borrowing the remainder from a building society on the security of a mortgage, we would consider the Murphys to be owner occupiers. Their equity of redemption is worth £5,000 since they can recover full ownership at any time on repaying the building society loan, and if they sell the house, their net proceeds after discharging the loan will be that sum. Moreover, they might well, under the terms of the mortgage, have a right to possession and they certainly will in practice be permitted to remain in possession provided that they do not default in repaying the instalments of capital and interest due under the loan. In the event of an appreciation in property prices the Murphys will reap the whole of the increased value of their home (although they equally bear the risk of a depreciation in property values).

A mortgagor (such as the Murphys) may, even without the consent of the mortgagee (the building society in the Murphys' case), sell the mortgaged property subject to the mortgage or charge by means of a sale of the equity of redemption: *Maxwell* v. *Tipping* (1903). Such a conveyance may, however, be a breach of an express covenant by a mortgagor not to assign, let or part with possession of the mortgaged property without the written consent of the mortgagee.

A mortgagor in possession is entitled to the rents and profits of the land without being obliged to give an account to the mortgagee: *Campion* v. *Palmer* (1896). A mortgagor may also, at common law, grant leases of his equity of redemption, and while in possession, has a statutory power to grant leases binding the mortgagee under the Conveyancing Act 1881, s.18, although these powers are frequently excluded by the express terms of the mortgage. A mortgagee similarly may grant leases at common law which do not bind the mortgagor, and when in possession he has the same statutory powers under the Conveyancing Act 1881 as a mortgagor in possession.

5. Substance and form

The intervention of equity has meant that the form of a mortgage often does not agree with its substance. The mortgage deed conveys to the mortgagee the borrower's estate in the land, yet many (even most) of the incidents of ownership remain with the borrower: possession; the risk of profit or loss; the power to decide if and when to sell; the assurance that his rights are not precarious. The mortgage deed may specify a fixed date for redemption, but the mortgagor will be permitted in equity to redeem even when this date has passed. As will be seen later, equity goes further and will not permit a mortgagee to reserve rights which are inconsistent with the nature of a mortgage as a form of security. Moreover, in equity any conveyance of property which is intended simply for security will be treated as a mortgage even if it has not been made in the usual form, as for instance where a borrower "sells" land to the lender for the sum lent, but retains an "option" to repurchase at a sum representing repayment of capital and interest: *Re South City Market Co.* (1884).

It was Maitland who described the ordinary form of mortgage deed as "one long *suppressio veri* and *suggestio falsi*" (*Equity*, p. 182). To a large extent this remains true, although modern building society mortgage deeds concede reality more than those of the past. In relation to registered land the reality of the security is better recognised still, for here a mortgage is created by way of a registered charge which involves no transfer of the mortgagor's estate.

6. The importance of mortgages

Mortgages of land have a very important role in modern Ireland. In Great Britain about 55 per cent. of all households are owner-occupied, and over half of those are in the course of being bought out by means of a mortgage. Lord Diplock has spoken of "the emergence of a property-owning, particularly a real-property-mortgaged-to-a-building-society-owning-democracy": *Pettitt* v. *Pettitt* (1970). In the Republic of Ireland the proportion of owner-occupiers is much higher, at about 76 per cent. of all households. A lower proportion (under 45 per cent.) own subject to an existing mortgage liability, which is partly due to people moving house less often in Ireland than in Britain, although other factors too are involved. For most young people seeking to own a house of their own, however, a mortgage offers the only way of raising the necessary finance. It provides a way in which comparatively large sums may be raised for house purchase at a reasonable rate of interest over a very long period, often of 25 years, and with the house being used as security.

For farmers, too, the mortgage is a useful form of security. The majority of farmers in Ireland, owing to the policy of the Land Purchase Acts, own their own farmland. This farmland is a valuable asset which, by means of a mortgage, can be used as collateral for loans which may be used to finance improvements or to acquire stock.

The main lending agencies are no longer the wealthy individuals of the nineteenth century, but the banks and the building societies which act as conduits for investment by those who deposit with them. The banks and building societies also act as a buffer between the lender and the borrower, cushioning the effect of a borrower who seeks to repay before the expected date, or of a lender who suddenly needs his money back.

B. Creation of Mortgages and Charges

7. Legal mortgages of unregistered land

A mortgage will be legal or equitable according as the lender takes a legal or an equitable interest in the property mortgaged. A legal mortgage can of course be created only where the mortgagor (the borrower) has a legal estate to charge. If he owns only an equitable interest, then clearly no more than an equitable mortgage can be created, but even where he holds a legal estate the mortgage may be equitable only if the proper methods for creating a legal mortgage are not used.

There are two means of creating a legal mortgage in unregistered land. The first is by the mortgagor conveying or assigning to the mortgagee his whole legal estate or interest, but subject to a proviso for redemption. The second is by the mortgagor granting to the mortgagee some lesser legal estate or interest, here subject to a proviso for cesser on redemption.

In relation to a mortgage of a fee simple the first method would involve a conveyance of the fee simple to the mortgagee. The *proviso for redemption* would consist of a covenant by the mortgagee to reconvey the fee simple to the mortgagor upon repayment of the loan. The mortgage would normally need to be made by deed to operate to convey a legal fee simple estate, and the use of a deed confers upon the mortgagee certain statutory remedies. A conveyance of a leasehold fee farm grant need not be made by deed to convey a legal estate (see p. 121). Following the conveyance by way of mortgage of his fee simple, the mortgagor will retain only his equity of redemption.

The alternative form of mortgage for a fee simple consists of the grant of a long term of years to the mortgagee with a *proviso for cesser on redemption*, that is a provision that the lease will automatically come to an end upon redemption. Although the term of years is commonly so long (even for 10,000 years) that it scarcely differs in value from a fee simple, the mortgagor will often appoint the mortgagee his attorney to convey the fee simple reversion to any purchaser of the term of years, thus in effect enabling the freehold to be sold. Mortgages by demise are less common than mortgages by conveyance, but they have the advantage with a fee farm grant that the lender avoids liability for the fee farm rent and any other covenants or conditions annexed to the estate: *Re Sergie* (1954).

In relation to mortgages of a leasehold interest the two alternative forms are the same *mutatis mutandis* as for a fee simple. They are an assignment of the residue of the lease with a proviso for redemption; and a sublease for a term slightly shorter than that held by the mortgagor, with a proviso for cesser on redemption. The second method is the more commonly used because, like the mortgage by demise of a fee farm grant, it avoids the mortgagee incurring liability for rent and other obligations imposed by the lease on the tenant.

8. Equitable mortgages of unregistered land

Equitable mortgages may be created in three ways. The first method is by means of the assignment of an equitable interest subject to a provision for redemption. This method will, perforce, be the best available where the mortgagor has only an equitable interest, for instance, because he has only an equitable interest under a trust, or because he has already assigned or conveyed by way of a legal mortgage any legal interest he previously owned. A mortgage by assignment of an equitable interest should be made by deed, in writing, or by will: Statute of Frauds (Ireland) 1695, s.6.

The second way in which an equitable mortgage arises is where there is a specifically enforceable agreement to create a legal mortgage. Here the maxim "equity treats as done that which ought to be done" applies, and the contract is treated as an effective grant of an equitable mortgage: *Re Hurley's Estate* (1894). In order to be specifically enforceable the money must already have been advanced since equity will not normally enforce an unperformed contract to make a loan: *Sichel* v. *Mosenthal* (1862). The contract must also be evidenced in writing to comply with section 2 of the Statute of Frauds (Ireland) 1695, or be sufficiently supported by some act of part performance. A purported legal mortgage, for instance a mortgage made in writing where a deed is required, if supported by consideration by the loan having been advanced, will be treated in equity as if it were a contract to create a legal mortgage.

The third way of creating an equitable mortgage is by a deposit of title deeds. This is a very convenient and straightforward means of creating a mortgage. It has been accepted ever since *Russel* v. *Russel* (1783) that the deposit of title deeds by way of security operates both as a contract to create a mortgage, and also as part performance of that contract, so that no proof in writing is needed to make the contract enforceable on either side. There must be an intention to deposit the title deeds by way of security rather than for some other purpose, such as for safe-keeping: *National Bank Ltd.* v. *McGovern* (1931). The deposit, with an intention to give security, is sufficient in itself to create an equitable mortgage without the need for any writing or proof in writing. Where there is no written memorandum of the transaction, this form of mortgage has at least two attractions apart from its simplicity. No stamp duty is payable and the mortgage is not a matter of record on the title deeds. If there is a written memorandum, it is registrable under the Registration of Deeds Act (Ireland) 1707 and the Registration of Deeds Act (N.I.) 1970, and must therefore be registered to ensure priority. A written memorandum, on the other hand, can serve the purpose of avoiding disputes, and if made by deed, attracts the special statutory powers conferred on mortgagees by the Conveyancing Act 1881. The ordinary practice of the banks is to ask the borrower to read a printed statement declaring that the deeds are deposited by way of security, but to avoid stamp duty and registration in the Registry of Deeds no receipt is issued, and no document is signed by the borrower.

9. Charges of registered land

The appropriate way of using registered land (*i.e.* land title to which is registered under the Registration of Title Act 1964 or the Land Registration Act (N.I.), 1970) for security is not by way of mortgage, but by way of registered charge. Section 62 of the Registration of Title Act 1964 permits a registered owner by will or by an instrument of charge, to charge the land with the payment of money. When registered:

> "the instrument of charge shall operate as a mortgage by deed within the meaning of the Conveyancing Acts, and the registered owner of the charge shall, for the purpose of enforcing his charge, have all the rights and powers of a mortgagee under a mortgage by deed, including the power to sell the estate or interest which is subject to the charge."

Similar provisions are found in the Land Registration Act (N.I.), 1970, s.41, and Sched. 7. A registered charge, although not technically a mortgage since it involves no transfer of an estate with a proviso for redemption, nevertheless operates, with some minor exceptions, in the same way as a mortgage. The owner of a registered charge is entitled to delivery of a certificate of charge from the Registrar: 1964 Act ss.62(5) and 105; 1970 Act, s.79(1).

In addition to the creation of a registered charge, it is also possible to create an informal charge by a deposit of a land certificate or certificate of charge: Registration of Title Act 1964, s.105(5); Land Registration Act (N.I.), 1970, s.50. This has the same effect as a deposit of the title deeds of unregistered land.

10. Equitable charges

It is possible in equity to make the discharge of a debt or some other obligation a charge upon land or other property without changing the ownership of the property in law or in equity. An equitable chargee does not have the same rights as a mortgagee, but an equitable charge is an effective form of security. It arises where there is a clear intention to burden certain property with the discharge of an obligation, made or evidenced in writing or by will, and otherwise than by way of mortgage: *Matthews* v. *Goodday* (1861). No special form of words is necessary: *Coonan* v. *O'Connor* (1903).

11. Successive mortgages or charges

A landowner may, if he wishes, create a succession of mortgages or charges, although some lenders may be reluctant to lend on the security of a second mortgage or charge, and building societies are prohibited by statute from lending on anything but a first mortgage or charge. If the first mortgage has been created by an outright conveyance of the mortgagor's legal estate (if any), all subsequent mortgages or charges must be equitable. If the mortgagor uses a mortgage by demise or sub-lease, however, it is possible for there to be a series of legal mortgages. The question of the priority of successive mortgages is dealt with below. A mortgage which ranks below another is said to be a *puisne* mortgage or to be puisne to the prior mortgage (from the French *puis,* after, and *ne,* born).

C. Enforcement of Security

12. Enforcing a mortgage as security

The rights available to a mortgagee or chargee seeking to enforce a mortgage or charge as security may include the right to possession, to appoint a receiver, to foreclose or to sell. He will also have a personal action for debt against the borrower where a loan has been made, and if the security proves inadequate, he may have an action against a negligent valuer or surveyor who acted on his behalf: *London and South of England Building Society* v. *Stone* (1983). In practice a mortgagee will endeavour to persuade a mortgagor to repay before resorting to his other remedies, for as will be seen in many cases the exercise of these remedies is made contingent upon prior demand for payment having been made of the mortgagor. The mortgagor may also deprive a mortgagee of his rights under the mortgage by exercising his own right to redeem. The personal action for debt is important since it is not affected by the remedies of the mortgagee against the property. If for instance on a sale insufficient money is raised to discharge the loan, the mortgagor remains personally liable for the balance.

A mortgagee may also have various other rights, in addition to those already mentioned. Two relate to priority through the doctrine of consolidation and the right to tack. For these, see Part *E* of this Chapter. Where the mortgage is made by deed, the mortgagee has a statutory power to insure the mortgaged property against damage by fire and to add the premiums to the mortgage advance: Conveyancing Act 1881, s.19. The power also extends to registered charges: Registration of Title Act 1964, s.62(6); Land Registration Act (N.I.) 1970, Sched. 7, Pt. 1, para. 5. The amount of the insurance may not exceed the amount specified in the mortgage deed, or where no amount is specified, two thirds of the cost of reinstating the building in the event of total destruction. The implied statutory right may be excluded or varied by express agreement. It does not apply where the mortgagor maintains insurance in accordance with the mortgage, nor where the mortgage is silent, and the mortgagor maintains insurance for at least the statutory amount: Conveyancing Act 1881, s.23.

The mortgagee may also be entitled to the title deeds. He will clearly be entitled where a mortgage is created by the deposit of title deeds or of the land certificate. He will also be entitled to the title deeds on a mortgage created by conveyance, or to the lease on a mortgage created by assignment of a leasehold term, since the owner in each case is automatically entitled to these documents. On a mortgage by demise or sub-demise the mortgagee will be entitled to the mortgagor's documents of title only where this is expressly stipulated in the mortgage. In the case of a registered charge, a special charge certificate is issued to the chargee: Registration of Title Act, 1964, s.62(5); Land Registration Act (N.I.) 1970, s.79(2)(*a*). The chargee is not entitled to the land certificate: Registration of Title Act 1964, s.67; Land Registration Rules (N.I.) 1977, Rule 82.

A mortgagee holding title deeds must return them to the mortgagor on redemption, and he must also permit the mortgagor to inspect and copy the deeds at reasonable times and on payment of the mortgagee's costs: Conveyancing Act 1881, s.16. Where the mortgagee loses or damages the deeds he will be liable to compensate the mortgagor on redemption but it seems that there is no implied term or duty of care in negligence to take reasonable care of the title deeds, during the subsistence of the mortgages, even though such a duty would appear to be required on general principles of negligence: *Gilligan* v. *National Bank Ltd.* (1901); *Browning* v. *Handiland Group Ltd.* (1976).

13. The right to possession

Although in practice a mortgagor will be left in possession, provided that he is not in default, a legal mortgagee has, by virtue of his estate in the land, a right to possession. In a well-known passage, Harman J. has said,

> "The right of a mortgagee to possession in the absence of some contract has nothing to do with default on the part of the mortgagor. The mortgagee may go into possession before the ink is dry on the mortgage unless there is something in the contract, express or by implication, whereby he has contracted himself out of that right." (*Four-Maids Ltd.* v. *Dudley Marshall* (*Properties*) *Ltd.*, 1957).

The mortgagor will often have an express contractual right to possession in building society mortgages so long as he is not in default and a right to possession on the part of the mortgagor will be implied where the mortgage provides that the mortgagee is entitled to possession should the mortgagor default in repayments: *Birmingham Citizens Permanent Building Society* v. *Caunt* (1962).

An equitable chargee, having no estate in the land, is not entitled automatically to possession. Whether a charge of registered land or an equitable mortgage confers an automatic right to possession is unclear, but in both cases the court may make an order for possession, in the former case by virtue of the Registration of Title Act 1964, s.62(7) (but only where the principal money under the mortgage is due) and Land Registration Act (N.I.) 1970, Sched. 7, Part I, para. 5(2), and in the latter case, by inherent equitable jurisdiction: *Re O'Neill.* (1967). The only basis upon which it could be argued that the registered owner of a charge is automatically entitled to possession is by virtue of the statutory provision that he "shall, for the purpose of enforcing his charge, have all the rights and powers of a mortgagee under a mortgage by deed" (see above). Against this, it could be argued that the restrictions on recovery of possession in the 1964 and 1970 Acts would be meaningless if there were an automatic right to possession.

The usual reason why possession is sought is as a prelude to sale since a higher price is likely to be realised on a sale with vacant possession. There is little advantage in a mortgagee seeking possession for its own sake since when in possession a mortgagee is liable to account strictly to the mortgagor. He must account not only for any rents and profits actually made from the land, but also for any profits which he could have made: *O'Connell* v. *O'Callaghan* (1863); *White* v. *City of London Brewery Co.* (1889). Receivership is a more satisfactory option for a mortgagee seeking to attach the income from the land.

Where an application is made to court for an order for possession, the court has no discretion at common law to refuse an order to a legal mortgagee with a right to possession, although it may stay the order for a short period to enable the mortgagor to redeem the mortgage if there is a reasonable prospect that he might be able to do so: *Birmingham Citizens Permanent Building Society* v. *Caunt* (1962). There may also be a wider equitable jurisdiction to restrain a mortgagee from getting possession except when it is sought bona fide and reasonably for the purpose of enforcing the security: *Quennell* v. *Maltby* (1979). Even when a mortgagee's right to possession does not derive from a legal estate, but relies upon the discretionary jurisdiction of the court, an order for possession will normally be made to facilitate a sale with vacant possession: *Irish Permanent Building Society* v. *Ryan* (1950).

A statutory power to stay an order for possession in Northern Ireland is contained in section 36 of the Administration of Justice Act 1970 (United Kingdom) as amended by section 8 of the Administration of Justice Act 1973 (United Kingdom). The equitable jurisdiction is recognised by the Judicature (N.I.) Act 1978, s.86 which permits a stay to be made "on equitable grounds" subject to such conditions as the court thinks fit. In the Republic the Family Home Protection Act 1976, s.7 permits an action for possession to be adjourned to enable a spouse who is not a party to a mortgage to pay off any arrears.

14. The mortgagee's power of sale

The sale of property subject to a mortgage or charge is the most useful right of a mortgagee or chargee to enforce his security, and the most often used. Normally a mortgagee will seek possession before a sale, although if the property is let to a tenant, it might be sold subject to the tenancy. The power of sale exists in three cases: where it has been expressly reserved in the mortgage or charge; where the mortgage or charge is made by deed so that the provisions of section 19 of the Conveyancing Act 1881 apply; and failing these, pursuant to an order of the court.

Where there is an express power of sale, it will be exercisable according to its terms although equity will not permit a mortgagee to retain from the net proceeds of sale more than is required to repay the mortgage debt with interest thereon.

Mortgagees in many cases will rely upon the statutory power of sale available under the Conveyancing Act 1881, s.19 where the mortgage or charge is made by deed, or by way of registered charge (see p. 220). In considering the statutory power of sale a distinction has to be drawn between the power *arising* and the power becoming properly *exercisable*. The power arises when the "mortgage money has become due." With a mortgage providing for repayment on a fixed date, that will be the relevant date. With "instalments mortgages" of the kind normally used for house purchase, the capital is repaid in instalments over the whole period of the mortgage. Nevertheless, it is usually provided that if there is any default in paying instalments, the whole capital sum becomes due. It has also been held that even without such an express provision the statutory power of sale arises as soon as any instalment is in arrear: *Payne* v. *Cardiff Rural District Council* (1932).

Once the power of sale has arisen, the mortgagee can sell the property to a purchaser free from the mortgagor's equity of redemption and without need for application to court. He will, however, be liable to the mortgagor in damages should he exercise the power of sale before it becomes exercisable. The power is exercisable only when one of three events has occurred. These are that a written notice for repayment of the mortgage debt has been served, and there has been three months default; or some mortgage interest is two months or more in arrear; or the mortgagor is in breach of some provision in the mortgage deed or under the 1881 Act, other than a covenant to pay the mortgage money or interest: Conveyancing Act 1881, s.20. A purchaser will only be affected by the power of sale not being exercisable where he knows or has some substantial reason to believe that there is some impropriety or irregularity in the sale: Conveyancing Act 1881, s.21; Conveyancing Act 1911, s.5; *Bailey* v. *Barnes* (1894).

The statutory power of sale under the Conveyancing Acts is exercisable without any court order, and the sale may be by auction or by private treaty. While a mortgagee need not take every effort to obtain the highest price which could possibly be obtained on a sale, he must take reasonable care to ensure that he obtains the fair market price for the property. His duty is not that of a trustee, but he must still seek to get the best price which can reasonably be obtained: *Holohan* v. *Friends Provident and Century Life Office* (1966); *Cuckmere Brick Co. Ltd.* v. *Mutual Finance Ltd.* (1971); Building Societies Act (N.I.) 1967, s.36; Building Societies Act 1976, s.82. A sale by auction does not conclusively indicate that the best price was obtained: *Tse Kwong Lam* v. *Wong Chit Sen* (1983). The proceeds of the sale are to be applied in the order specified in section 21 of the Conveyancing Act 1881, namely discharge of prior incumbrances, payment of the costs of sale, discharge of the mortgage, and the balance is then to be transmitted to the person next entitled, *i.e.* the next mortgagee, or if there is none, the mortgagor.

A sale under the Conveyancing Act 1881 passes to the purchaser

> "such estate and interest therein as is the subject of the mortgage, freed from all estates, interests and rights to which the mortgage has priority, but subject to all estates, interests, and rights which have priority to the mortgage."

Although a different interpretation would be possible (*Re White Rose Cottage,* 1965), it has been held that under this provision a sale by a mortgagee transfers only the interest conveyed to the mortgagee by way of mortgage: *Re Hodson and Howe's Contract* (1887). Thus if a fee simple is mortgaged by the grant of a long lease, or a leasehold interest by a sub-demise, the mortgagee has only statutory power to sell the long lease or sub-lease respectively, and not the whole interest of the mortgagor. Similarly in equitable mortgages of a legal estate, the statutory power may extend only to the equitable interest. For this reason it is normal conveyancing practice for a mortgage by demise or sub-demise and for equitable mortgages by deed to contain some conveyancing device to extend the power of sale to the entire interest of the mortgagor. This may be by a power of attorney permitting the mortgagee, when exercising the power of sale, to convey the whole property in the name of the mortgagor: *Re White Rose Cottage* (1965). Alternatively the mortgagor may constitute himself a trustee of his reversionary interest for the mortgagee or his nominee: *London and County Banking Co.* v. *Goddard* (1897); *Re Sergie* (1954).

Where the provisions of the Conveyancing Act 1881 do not apply, for instance because there is no deed, and the mortgage has not conferred any express power of sale, a sale may still be made by order of the court. The form such an order takes is a declaration that the amount secured is well and truly charged on the land, and an order for sale if the mortgagor does not pay the amount due under the mortgage within three months. An order for possession may be made at the same time. The sale takes place under the supervision of the court, which will ensure the utmost "fair play": *Bank of Ireland* v. *Smith* (1966). The mortgagee is the vendor, and it is his task to seek a court order for possession should this be necessary: *Bank of Ireland* v. *Waldrow* (1944).

Although not a power of sale belonging to the mortgagee another way in which a sale can take place is where the mortgagor voluntarily sells, redeeming the mortgage out of the proceeds of sale.

15. Appointment of receiver

The strict supervision which the court exercises over a mortgagee in possession makes the taking of possession a poor remedy. A far more desirable remedy for a mortgagee is the appointment of a receiver. As with the power of sale the power to appoint a receiver may be conferred expressly in the mortgage or be implied under the Conveyancing Act 1881, and the court also has inherent and statutory powers to appoint a receiver: Judicature (Ireland) Act 1877, s.28; Judicature (N.I.) Act 1978, s.93. The power to appoint a receiver under the Conveyancing Act 1881, ss.19 and 24 arises and is exercisable on the same events as the power of sale. The appointment must be made in writing, as must any removal of a receiver: Conveyancing Act 1881, s.24.

The function of a receiver is to manage the mortgaged property, receiving any rents or profits and applying these in the order specified in the Conveyancing Act or mortgage deed. In so doing he is deemed to be the agent of the mortgagor, if appointed under the 1881 Act. This means that the mortgagee is not liable for the acts and defaults of the receiver: *Chatsworth Properties Ltd.* v. *Effiom* (1971). At least in Northern Ireland, however, most receivers insist upon an idemnity from the mortgagee. The order of payment specified by the 1881 Act requires the receiver to pay the rents, rates, taxes and other outgoings on the mortgaged property; then to meet any payments due under prior incumbrances; then to pay his own commission, insurance premiums and cost of repairs; then to meet the interest due under the mortgage; and then to pay the balance to the person next entitled.

16. Foreclosure

Foreclosure has no more than a theoretical existence in Ireland. A foreclosure order is an order in which the court extinguishes the mortgagor's equity of redemption and vests in the mortgagee the mortgagor's estate or interest in the property. In exceptional circumstances a mortgagor may have the foreclosure re-opened: *Campbell* v. *Holyland* (1877).

The courts in Ireland have always claimed an inherent jurisdiction to order a sale in lieu of foreclosure, and the settled practice for centuries has been to exercise this jurisdiction by decreeing a sale: *Bruce* v. *Brophy* (1906). There is nevertheless a remote possibility that in most exceptional circumstances (and it is difficult to envisage what these could be), a court might order foreclosure: *Waters* v. *Lloyd* (1911).

D. Redemption

17. Right to redeem

As has already been observed (see Sections 4 and 5, above) the essential characteristic of a mortgage is that it is a conveyance of property as security with a right to recover the property on the discharge of the obligation it secures. Similarly with property subject to a charge, the charge is dissolved once the obligation it secures has been performed.

The right of a mortgagor or chargor to redeem and so recover his property free from incumbrance is a right which cannot be excluded. An attempt to exclude the mortgagor's right to redeem will be void as inconsistent with the nature of a mortgage or charge, which is simply to provide security, normally for a loan of money. A provision in the mortgage enabling the mortgagee to acquire the property himself would, if exercised, operate to exclude redemption and so is void. Thus in *Samuel* v. *Jarrah Timber and Wood Paving Corporation Ltd.* (1904) an option in a mortgage deed under which the lender was given the right to purchase mortgaged debenture stock was held void. Had this option been given independently of the mortgage it would have been valid. In *Reeve* v. *Lisle* (1902) an option granted ten days after a mortgage was upheld. What is important is not that the mortgagee has a right to purchase, but that the exercise of an option in the mortgage could leave no property for the mortgagor to redeem. So, in *Browne* v. *Ryan* (1901) the court held invalid a condition of a mortgage obliging the mortgagor to sell the land mortgaged within a year using the services of the mortgagee, an auctioneer, or paying his usual commission if not using his services.

18. Right to redeem illusory

Even if the right to redeem is not entirely excluded, the courts are unlikely to accept a provision in a mortgage which deprives the right to redeem of any real value. In *Fairclough* v. *Swan Brewery Co. Ltd.* (1912) the tenant of a brewery with only seventeen and a half years of the lease unexpired entered into a mortgage. The mortgage contained a provision preventing redemption until only six weeks of the lease would remain unexpired. The Privy Council held that this provision made the right to redeem illusory. The Judicial Committee therefore ruled that redemption could take place before the date fixed in the mortgage deed.

Merely postponing the right to redeem, though, is not normally objectionable. In *Knightsbridge Estates Trust Ltd.* v. *Byrne* (1939) the Court of Appeal upheld a mortgage term postponing for 40 years the right to redeem a mortgage for a substantial sum on the best market terms available at the date on which it was taken out. The mortgage was repayable by instalments over the 40 year period, an arrangement which had been requested by the mortgagors. Unlike building society instalment mortgages, however, there was no provision permitting early redemption. The reason why the mortgagors sought to redeem early was that interest rates had fallen and they hoped to negotiate a new loan at a lower interest charge. In rejecting the mortgagor's claim to be entitled to early redemption the Court of Appeal pointed out that the mortgage had been freely negotiated between powerful commercial enterprises and there was nothing oppressive or unreasonable in the mortgage.

19. Unconscionable bargains

Courts administering the rules and principles of equity have an over-riding jurisdiction to set aside unconscionable bargains, a jurisdiction which can be invoked to set aside an unconscionable term in a mortgage. An unconscionable bargain is one which is unreasonable, unfair and oppressive. Unreasonableness in itself is not sufficient for a bargain to be set aside, and in making a decision all the circumstances of the case, including the relative bargaining strength of the parties, will be taken into account. So in the *Knightsbridge Estates Trust* case (above) a commercial bargain was upheld, although a different decision might have been reached had the mortgagor been an ordinary purchaser of domestic residential property. Another case in which a hard bargain was upheld was *Multiservice Bookbinding Ltd.* v. *Marden* (1979). A mortgage of commercial premises made in 1966 provided for a high rate of interest, and also for repayments to be index-linked to the Swiss franc. By 1976, when repayment was due, the rate of exchange had fallen from just over Sf. 12 to the £ to just over Sf. 4 to the £. The value of the mortgaged property had more than doubled. Browne-Wilkinson J. considered that the terms of the mortgage were unreasonable. The mortgage was not, however, unconscionable. It was a hard bargain made by businessmen with their eyes open, with independent advice, with no sharp practice, and not constrained by necessity.

Two other cases may be contrasted. In *Cityland and Property (Holdings) Ltd.* v. *Dabrah* (1968) the defendant, who had been the tenant of a house for 11 years, bought the freehold from his landlords for £3,500. He paid £600 in cash and borrowed the remainder from the landlords on mortgage. No interest was payable as such, but the defendant agreed to repay £4,553 by way of monthly instalments. In the event, he defaulted in repayments after only one year and the plaintiffs, the former landlords, claimed the full sum of £4,553 less the value of payments already made. Goff J. held that the premium, which amounted to 57 per cent. of the capital sum, was unconscionable. He substituted a reasonable rate of interest. Similarly in *Wells* v. *Joyce* (1905) the court was prepared to reopen a loan on unfavourable terms pressed upon a Connemarra farmer in financial difficulties. See also *Kevans* v. *Joyce* (1896).

In Northern Ireland, further protection is given to individual (but not corporate) mortgagors by the Consumer Credit Act 1974 (United Kingdom). This Act gives the court power to rewrite extortionate credit bargains, including mortgages. A credit bargain may be extortionate because it requires payments to be made which are grossly exorbitant or because it otherwise grossly contravenes ordinary principles of fair dealing. Loans made by building societies are exempted from the Act.

20. Restrictions on right to redeem and collateral advantages

Judicial attitudes have changed in the last century and a half in relation to provisions associated with mortgages which entitle the mortgagee to something more than the repayment of the money lent, with interest. The traditional analysis divides these "collateral" advantages into three groups. First, if the provision conferring a collateral advantage makes it last only for the duration of the mortgage, then it will be valid unless it is otherwise unconscionable. In *Biggs* v. *Hoddinott* (1898), the owner of a public house mortgaged it to a brewer. The mortgage provided for the mortgagor to take his supplies of liquor only from the mortgagee during the continuance of the mortgage. This was upheld. It was not unconscionable and it did not "clog or fetter" the equity of redemption once the mortgage had been redeemed.

Secondly, on the other hand, advantages which extend beyond the date of redemption have been struck down as "fettering" the equity of redemption. In *Noakes and Co. Ltd.* v. *Rice* (1902) the mortgage of a public house included a tie agreement which was to continue after redemption for the entire duration of the lease. This was held void so far as it applied after redemption.

The third group comprises cases where an advantage, although associated with a mortgage, is independent of it. Here the advantage will be valid, unless unconscionable, even if it may continue after redemption. An example is *Kreglinger* v. *New Patagonia Meat and Cold Storage Co. Ltd.* (1914). A firm of woolbrokers lent a firm of meat packers the sum of £10,000. The woolbrokers agreed not to call in the principal for five years, but earlier repayment by the meat packers was permitted. A clause in the agreement gave the lenders for five years a right of pre-emption for all the meat packers' sheepskins, and a commission of 1 per cent. on all sheepskins sold to persons other than the lenders. The House of Lords held that the right of pre-emption and right to a commission constituted a collateral advantage independent of the mortgage, and so were valid. See also *Browne* v. *Ryan* (1901); *Maxwell* v. *Tipping* (1903).

Although the three categories can be reconciled with each other so that the categorisation of something as a "collateral" advantage is a question of fact, nevertheless the decision in the *Kreglinger* case reflects a willingness to uphold commercial transactions freely entered into. According to Cheshire and Burn's *Modern Law of Real Property* (13th. ed., 1982), p. 639:

> "The *Kreglinger* case . . . reveals a judicial appreciation of a mortgage as a transaction freely concluded by business men without colour of oppression, which should therefore form no exception to the maxim *pacta sunt servanda.*"

This attitude is far removed from that of judges even up to the middle of the nineteenth century who viewed all collateral advantages as invalid (see *Jennings* v. *Ward,* 1705; *Re Edwards Estate,* 1861), a view derived from the fact that collateral advantages could be used to circumvent the usury laws, restricting the amount of interest which could be charged, and that mortgagors were characteristically impecunious and unequal in bargaining power to the mortgagee. Much of this was changed by the industrial revolution.

21. Restraint of trade

Mortgages are subject to the common law doctrine invalidating contracts which are in restraint of trade. In *Esso Petroleum Co. Ltd.* v. *Harpers Garage (Stourport) Ltd.* (1968) a mortgage of a petrol filling station, which contained a solus agreement obliging the garage proprietor to acquire all his supplies of petroleum products from the plaintiffs, was irredeemable for 21 years. It was held that the exclusive purchasing agreement was void as being in restraint of trade, since the tie was for too long a period, and the mortgage could accordingly be redeemed before the 21 years had expired. See also *Irish Shell and B.P. Ltd.* v. *Ryan* (1966).

22. Mode of redemption

The mortgagor or any other person with an interest in the equity of redemption may redeem at any time on or after the legal date for redemption, except that where a party seeks to exercise the equitable right to redeem after the date fixed by the mortgage, reasonable notice must be given to the mortgagee. This is usually taken to be six months notice. Alternatively, the mortgagor may pay six months interest in lieu of notice. The mortgage itself may of course provide for the conditions regarding notice upon which redemption may be made.

The person seeking to redeem must pay the principal owing to the mortgagee, together with interest and the proper costs of the mortgagee. The proviso for redemption or for cesser on redemption will then operate. Where the mortgage was created by conveyance of a fee simple or by assignment of a lease, a reconveyance or reassignment will be required in the Republic of Ireland. Where a mortgage of a fee simple is created by demise, the lease ends automatically and merges with the mortgagor's reversion under the Satisfied Terms Act 1845, but that Act does not apply to subleases so that the discharge of a mortgage by sub-demise in the Republic of Ireland requires a surrender of the lease by deed or in writing under section 7 of Deasy's Act 1860. In the case of a mortgage to a building society discharge by the appropriate method just described may be used but an alternative is available by means of a simple form of special statutory receipt: Building Societies Act (N.I.) 1967, s.37 and Sched. 6; Building Societies Act, 1976, s.84. The same method has been extended to all mortgages in Northern Ireland by the Property (Discharge of Mortgage by Receipt) (N.I.) Order 1983. A registered charge is discharged by the registration of a note of satisfaction on the register: Registration of Title Act 1964, s.65; Land Registration Act (N.I.) 1970, s.49(1).

A mortgage by deposit of title deeds or other documents is discharged simply by the return of those deeds or documents while an indorsed receipt is probably sufficient for a mortgage by assignment of an equitable interest: *Firth & Sons Ltd.* v. *I.R.C.* (1904).

E. Priority Between Mortgages

23. The rules governing priorities

Since the same land may be mortgaged several times in succession, it is sometimes necessary to determine their respective priorities, for instance, where on a sale, the proceeds are insufficient to satisfy all the mortgagees. The borrower in some cases may have acted fraudulently, concealing the existence of prior mortgages on the land. The rules concerning priorities are not specially applicable to mortgages. They are the ordinary rules described in Chapter 3, subject to the special rules applicable to registered land.

24. Priorities in registered land

The basic principle in registered land is that entry on the register, rather than the date of creation, governs priorities between registered charges: Registration of Title Act 1964, s.68; Land Registration Act (N.I.) 1970, s.32. A charge before registration takes effect only in equity and is liable to be defeated by any other disposition or charge which is registered before it is registered itself. It will, nevertheless, have priority to any subsequent unregistered disposition or charge.

A mortgage created by a deposit of the land certificate also takes effect in equity only, but cannot be protected by registration. It will be subject to any existing registered or equitable interests (*e.g.* an unregistered transfer): *Tench* v. *Molyneux* (1914), but it will have priority to any subsequent equitable interests: *Re White Rose Cottage* (1965); *Barclays Bank Ltd.* v. *Taylor* (1974). Registration of a matter subsequent to the creation of a mortgage made by deposit, if under an instrument given for valuable consideration, would have the effect of defeating or postponing the equitable mortgage. A mortgagee by deposit, however, is protected by having possession of the land certificate, for most matters cannot be registered without production of the land certificate, and the depositee cannot be compelled to produce it for the purpose of effecting a registration which would have priority to his equitable charge or lien: Registration of Title Act 1964, s.105; Land Registration Act (N.I.) 1970, s.50; Land Registration Rules (N.I.) 1977, R. 125.

25. Priorities in unregistered land

Priorities of mortgages in unregistered land are determined by a combination of the rules relating to registration of deeds and the equitable doctrine of notice. If the priority of a mortgage made by deed or other instrument *inter vivos* in writing (*Murphy* v. *Leader,* 1841) is to be ensured against any subsequent charge or disposition, the mortgage must be registered in the Registry of Deeds. It will then take priority over any subsequent registrable charge or other disposition, either registered or unregistered and for this purpose it makes no difference whether the first mortgage is legal or equitable: Registration of Deeds Act (Ireland) 1707, s.4; Registration of Deeds Act (N.I.) 1970, s.4(1). The registration of a mortgage does not, in itself, give it priority over a subsequent unregistrable disposition such as a mortgage by deposit of title deeds: *Re Greer* (1907).

Where a mortgage could be registered, but is not, then it is liable to be defeated or postponed by the registration of a subsequent disposition or charge for value. Under the Registration of Deeds legislation, an unregistered deed is void as against any registered deed, even though the registered deed may have been executed second in point of time: Registration of Deeds Act (Ireland) 1707, s.5; Registration of Deeds Act (N.I.) 1970, s.4(2): *Re Flood's Estate* (1862).

By way of exception to this, however, if at the time when the second transaction was made, (or possibly at the time it was registered) the second grantee or mortgagee had actual notice (personally or through his agent) of the prior mortgage, then he would not be able to claim statutory priority. This is because of the principle that a statute may not be used as an instrument of fraud (*Re Rorke's Estate,* 1863), a principle which has been recognised by the Registration of Deeds Act (N.I.) 1970, s.4(3) and (4).

Where the issue of priority arises between a registrable, but unregistered, mortgage, and another subsequent unregistered transaction, the issue will be governed by the common law rules. If the first mortgage is a legal mortgage, then, in the absence of some special consideration such as fraud or gross negligence on the part of the mortgagee, or an estoppel operating against him, this mortgage will take priority over any subsequent unregistered dealing with the land. If the first mortgage is an equitable mortgage, it will be similarly enforceable against all subsequent purchasers of an interest in the land unless they can prove they are bona fide purchasers of a legal estate for value without notice (see below). Whether the first mortgage is legal or equitable, of course, it is, if capable of registration in the Registry of Deeds, liable to lose any priority it may have where a subsequent transaction is registered by a purchaser for value without actual notice.

Mortgages by deposit of title deeds, unaccompanied by any memorandum of deposit, are incapable of registration in the Registry of Deeds, and their priority is governed by the equitable doctrine of notice. Being equitable only, they will take subject to any existing charges or interests, but will have priority to any subsequently created charges or other transactions, except where the purchaser can claim to be "equity's darling," being the bona fide purchaser of a legal estate for value without notice (as to which see pp. 13 *et seq.*). Registration of a subsequent transaction will not, in itself, confer priority over a previous unregistrable disposition such as an equitable mortgage by deposit of title deeds. Most purchasers will in any event have notice of a prior equitable mortgage through the mortgagee's possession of the title deeds. The fact that the vendor or mortgagor does not have these deeds will call for an explanation.

26. Tacking further advances

It is common for a mortgage to provide that it is security not only for the sum originally advanced, but also for any sums subsequently advanced. In some cases, particularly where a bank is lending to a commercial client, the mortgagee any undertake to make further advances, subject, perhaps, to an overall limit. These further advances may be "tacked" onto the original security. A problem of priorities can arise, however, where a second mortgage intervenes between the first mortgage and a further advance. The first mortgagee would have priority in relation to further advances if the intervening incumbrancer agrees. Otherwise, further advances can only be tacked on to the mortgage of a mortgagee with a legal estate, or where the terms of the mortgage cover any subsequent advances. Even in these cases, however, the further advances will only have priority if at the time of making them the mortgagee has no notice of the intervening mortgage. This is so even although the first mortgage might have obliged the mortgagee to make further advances, but in such a case the mortgagee is discharged from his obligation when the mortgagor deprives him of his right to priority by the creation of the subsequent charge. Registration of a subsequent mortgage in the Registry of Deeds does not amount to notice for the purpose of tacking: *Re O'Byrne's Estate* (1885).

Tacking of further advances is possible in the case of registered land by virtue of Registration of Title Act 1964, s.75 and Land Registration Act (N.I.) 1970, s.43. Under these provisions, where a registered charge is expressed to be created for the purpose of securing future advances, it confers priority for such advances over any subsequent charge, except where the chargee has express notice in writing of the subsequent charge when he makes a further advance.

27. Consolidation

In very limited circumstances, a mortgagee can insist on the simultaneous redemption of mortgages of two or more different properties. He might wish to do so where the value of one property, perhaps owing to developments in the neighbourhood, has very seriously declined in value so that it is no longer sufficient security for the advance. The right to consolidate can only be exercised where the right to do so is reserved in one of the mortgages concerned (Conveyancing Act 1881, s.17); the legal dates fixed for redemption have passed; all the mortgages concerned were made by the same mortgagor; and there was a stage where the mortgages were vested in a single mortgagee and the equities of redemption were all simultaneously vested in one person, who need not be the original mortgagees and mortgagor. The right to consolidate can be exercised by a mortgagee where the above conditions are satisfied even though the equities of redemption may have become vested in different persons when redemption is sought.

F. Non-proprietary Charges

28. Charges

As has already been pointed out (see Section 5, above), the intervention of equity has meant that a mortgage, although in form a transfer of a proprietary interest, operates in substance only as a means of securing the discharge of a money obligation. It is not essential to have a conveyance of a proprietary interest to achieve this, as can be seen from registered land where a registered charge confers exactly the same rights as a mortgage (except perhaps the automatic right to possession) although it is not in form a transfer of a proprietary right in the land (see Section 9, above). The creation of equitable charges (see Section 10, above), particularly where made by deed, further shows that it is possible to divorce the powers and remedies a lender needs by way of security from the conveyance of an estate in the land. Given especially the absence of foreclosure as a practical remedy in Ireland there is nothing which would prevent the abolition of mortgages and their replacement with a statutory charge upon land conferring identical powers and remedies. This has been recommended by the Land Law Working Group in Northern Ireland.

29. Equitable liens

Equity has, in two special cases, recognised a non-possessory and non-proprietary right of security. These are the vendor's lien and the purchaser's lien. A vendor of land who has not been paid in full retains a lien over the land for the amount unpaid. This can be enforced in the same ways as an equitable charge against the original purchaser and against his successors in title, unless they are purchasers of a legal estate for value without notice. The right is not lost where the purchaser takes possession, or even where a receipt for the purchase price has been given (although a subsequent purchaser would be entitled to rely upon the receipt as proof that the whole price had been paid). The lien arises independently of any agreement by the parties. See generally *Munster & Leinster Bank Ltd.* v. *McGlashan* (1937). A similar lien arises in favour of a purchaser who has paid money by deposit or part payment of the purchase price to a vendor of land, and who, without fault on his part, has obtained no conveyance: *Rose* v. *Watson* (1864); *Woods* v. *Martin* (1860); *Tempany* v. *Hynes* [1976] I.R. 101.

G. Judgment Mortgages

30. Judgment mortgages in the Republic

A judgment mortgage is a mortgage created under the Judgment Mortgage (Ireland) Act 1850 by the registration in the Registry of Deeds or the Land Registry of an affidavit recording an order of the court that a debt be paid and containing also certain particulars of the debtor's land. Registration of such an affidavit operates "to transfer to and vest in the creditor . . . all the lands, tenements and hereditaments mentioned therein, for all the estate or interest of which the debtor mentioned in such affidavit shall at the time of such registration be seised or possessed or have disposing power at law or in equity," subject to redemption on payment of the debt: Judgment Mortgage (Ireland) Act 1850, s.7. Registration in the Land Registry in the case of registered land creates a statutory registered charge: Registration of Title Act 1964, s.71. A judgment mortgage will usually be enforced by way of a court order for sale.

31. Charging orders in Northern Ireland

Judgment mortgages cannot be created in Northern Ireland since 1970. Instead, an order charging land may be made by the Enforcement of Judgments Office under the Judgments (Enforcement) Act (N.I.) 1969. When registered in the Registry of Deeds or the Land Registry, such a charge may be enforced by a sale out of court under the powers conferred on mortgagees by deed by the Conveyancing Acts 1881–1911.

Index